Studio Visual Steps

Textbook MOS Excel 2016 and 2013 + Extra Exercises

Visual Steps™

www.visualsteps.com

This book has been written using the Visual Steps™ method.
Cover design by Studio Willemien Haagsma bNO

© 2018 Visual Steps BV
Author: Studio Visual Steps
Translation: Bart Roelands, BeeCommunication and Chis Hollingsworth, 1st Resources.

First printing: January 2018
ISBN 978 90 5905 754 8

Resources used: Some of the computer terms and definitions seen here in this book have been taken from descriptions found online at the Windows Help and Support, Microsoft Office Help and the Microsoft website.

Do you have any questions or suggestions?
Email: info@visualsteps.com

Website for this book:
www.visualstepsmosbooks.com/excel2016.php

Sign up for the free Visual Steps Newsletter and stay informed of new books and updates:
www.visualsteps.com/newsletter.php

Would you like more information?
www.visualsteps.com

Access code for access to the MOS exam exercises:
24552

Table of Contents

Table of Contents Workbook

Foreword

Excel is a calculation program, also called a 'spreadsheet program'. Working in *Excel* is actually like working on a large sheet of graph paper. You can type something in each square (cell). This can be a number, text or date, but also an underlying formula which allows you to perform calculations automatically.

Not only can you calculate figures with *Excel*, you can also select, sort and arrange them. It is therefore an ideal program to create summaries with calculations or to organize lists with data.

Once you have gone through this book, you will have the opportunity to take a Microsoft Office Specialist® (MOS) examination. After successfully passing the examination, you will receive an official certificate. This is a document that is very important in the workplace and an asset on your curriculum vitae.
For optimum preparation for the examination, this book also comes with supplementary materials such as practice files.

This book is your best possible preparation for the examination!

We wish you a lot of success with this book,

Studio Visual Steps

P.S. We welcome all your comments and suggestions regarding this book. Our email address is: mail@visualsteps.com

Stay Informed

On our website www.visualstepsmosbooks.com you can subscribe to our **free Visual Steps Newsletter**. In the Newsletter you will receive periodic information by email regarding new books about other programs, updates or supplementary materials when they become available.

Introduction to Visual Steps™

This Visual Steps handbook is the best instructional material available for learning how to work with *Excel*. Nowhere else will you find better support for getting started with *Excel*.

Properties of the Visual Steps books:
- **Comprehensible contents**
  Addresses the needs of beginner or intermediate user for a manual written in simple, straight-forward English.
- **Clear structure**
  Precise, easy to follow instructions. The material is broken down into small enough segments to allow for easy absorption.
- **Screenshots of every step**
  Quickly compare what you see on your screen with the screenshots in the book. Pointers and tips guide you when new windows or alert boxes are opened so you always know what to do next.
- **Get started right away**
  All you have to do is turn on your computer or laptop and have your book at hand. Perform each operation as indicated on your own device.
- **Layout**
  The text is printed in a large size font and is clearly legible.

In short, I believe these instructions will be excellent guides for you.

Dr. H. van der Meij
Faculty of Applied Education, Department of Instructional Technology, University of Twente, the Netherlands

What You Will Need

To be able to work through this book, you will need a number of things:

The primary requirement for working with this book is having the English version of **Microsoft Excel 2016** or **Microsoft Excel 2013** installed on your computer.
It does not matter whether this is the stand-alone version of *Excel*, *Excel* as part of the *Office* suite or as part of the *Office 365* suite.
The screenshots in this book were created using *Excel 2016*. If you use *Excel 2013*, the screenshots may vary slightly. This does not make a difference for the working method.

The English version of **Windows 10**, **8.1** or **7** needs to be installed on your computer. You can check this yourself by turning your computer on and looking at the start-up screen.

You will need an active Internet connection, for example to download the practice material from the website that accompanies this book.

Some of the exercises require the use of a printer. If no printer is available, then you can skip the printing exercises.

Basic Knowledge

In order to work with this book, you will need to have some experience with *Windows* and simple word processing. Knowledge of *Excel* is not necessary.

How to Use This Book

This book has been written using the Visual Steps™ method. The method is simple: just place the book next to the computer and perform each task step by step directly on your computer. With the clear instructions and the multitude of screenshots, you will always know exactly what to do next. By performing the tasks directly, you will quickly and smoothly learn how to work with *Excel 2016* or *Excel 2013*.

In this Visual Steps™ book you will see various icons. Their meaning is as follows:

Actions
These icons indicate an action to be carried out:

   The mouse icon means you need to do something with the mouse.

   The keyboard icon means you should type something on your keyboard.

   The hand icon means you should do something else, for example, turn on the computer or carry out a task previously learned.

In addition to these icons, in some areas of this book extra assistance is provided to help you successfully work through each chapter.

Help
These icons indicate that extra help is available:

   The arrow icon warns you about something.

   The bandage icon will help you in case something went wrong.

   The hand icon is also used in the exercises. These exercises help you to repeat the actions independently.

Have you forgotten how to do something? The number next to the footsteps tells you where to look it up at the end of the book in the appendix *How Do I Do That Again?*

In separate boxes you will find tips or additional background information about *Excel 2016* and *Excel 2013*.

Extra information

Information boxes are denoted by the following icons:

The book icon gives you extra background information that you can read at your convenience. This extra information is not necessary for working through the book and is also not important for the examination.

The light bulb icon indicates an extra tip on how to use *Excel*. The tips in the last paragraph of each chapter are not important for the examination.

The Screenshots

The screenshots used in this book are intended to indicate exactly which button, folder, file or hyperlink you should click on your screen. In the instruction text (in **bold** letters) you will see a small image of the item you need to click. The line will point you to the right place on your screen.

The small screenshots that are printed in this book are not meant to be completely legible all the time. This is not necessary, as you will see these images on your own computer screen in real size and fully legible.

Here you see an example of an instruction text and a screenshot. The line indicates where to find this item on your own computer screen:

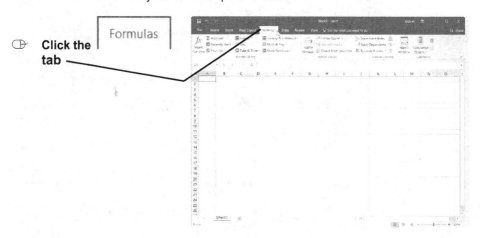

☞ **Click the tab**

Sometimes the screenshot shows only a portion of a window. Here is an example:

In the top right of the window:

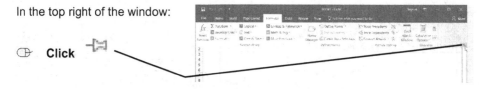

☞ **Click**

It really will **not be necessary** for you to read all the information in the screenshots in this book. Always use the screenshots in combination with the image you see on your own computer screen.

The Website and Supplementary Materials

This book is accompanied by the website
www.visualstepsmosbooks.com/excel2016.php. The website features practice files
and supplementary materials that you can download. Check the website often to see if
there are any additions or errata published for this book.

Practice files
The practice files used in this book can be downloaded from
www.visualstepsmosbooks.com/excel2016-practicefiles.php. If these practice
files are not yet on your computer, you will need to copy them first to your *(My)
Documents* folder. A PDF file on the website describes how to do this. Carefully follow
the instructions from the PDF file! If you do not do this, the practice files may end up
in the wrong folder.
If you are working through this book at a school or other educational facility, then
kindly ask your instructor where the practice files are located on the computer you are
working on.

Extra Practice

Once you have gone through this book, you will know how to perform important tasks
in *Excel*. This however does not mean that you have mastered everything. In order to
prepare yourself properly for the Microsoft Office Specialist® (MOS) examination, the
extra exercises are essential. The many exercises in this book, which you can find
from page 259, offer various types of assignments that provide extra practice. This
extra practice will help to ensure that you pass the examination.

For Teachers

The Visual Steps books are written as self-study materials for individual use. These
books are also perfectly suited as teaching materials for use in a group or a classroom
setting.
A free teacher's guide is available as a service from Visual Steps for books about
MOS. You can find the available teacher's guides and supplementary materials on the
website for this book: **www.visualstepsmosbooks.com/excel2016.php**

More Books about MOS

There are more books about other programs in the *Microsoft Office* suite, such as
Word. For more information visit **www.visualstepsmosbooks.com**

1. Setting Up Excel and Basic Functions

You can adjust the screen layout in *Excel* to suit your own preferences. If you use specific commands regularly, you can place their buttons in the *Quick Access* toolbar. Then you can access these commands quickly and easily with just a single click. You can also add commands to tabs that are hidden by default. If you use *Excel* often, this can save you time and it enables you to work more efficiently. It can help to make working with *Excel* a much more pleasant experience.

Using *Excel* is different than using a word processing program, database or drawing program. *Microsoft Excel* is a calculation program, also called a 'spreadsheet program'. Working in *Excel* is actually like working on a large sheet of graph paper. You can type something in each square (cell). This can be a number, text or date, but also an underlying formula which allows you to perform calculations automatically.

But it is not just the calculation of numbers that can be done with *Excel*, you can select and sort a wide range of data types. *Excel* is therefore an ideal program for creating summaries of calculated figures or sorting and arranging large lists of data.

This chapter will show you how to set up *Excel* and use basic functions to enter data, adjust the layout and create simple formulas.

In this chapter you will learn how to:

- use the *Quick Access* toolbar;
- use the tabs and the ribbon;
- add or remove commands to the *Quick Access* toolbar;
- add commands to a tab;
- restore the default layout;
- add worksheets;
- name worksheets;
- change the tab color;
- move and delete worksheets;
- navigate the worksheet;
- enter text and numbers;
- adjust column width and row height;
- enter simple formulas and to copy formulas;
- copy using the fill handle;
- save the workbook;
- add numbers using the *Sum* function;
- select multiple cells, rows and columns;
- adjust the layout of selected cells;
- set the number of decimals;
- add a currency symbol;
- merge cells;
- insert rows and columns;
- save a worksheet under a different name.

Please note:

In order to perform all the exercises in this book, you will need to download the corresponding practice files from the website accompanying this book (**www.visualstepsmosbooks.com/excel2016-practicefiles.php**) and save them to your *(My) Documents* folder. You will find instructions on how to do this on the web page.

It is possible that your teacher has already downloaded the practice files on the computer you are using. They may have been saved in another folder. If you cannot locate the files, then kindly ask your teacher where the practice files have been saved.

1.1 Opening Excel

This is how you open *Microsoft Excel* in *Windows 10*. At the bottom of the screen:

Click  or

In the search box:

Type: excel

Click

In *Windows 8.1* in the lower left corner of the desktop:

Click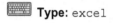

Type: excel

Click

In *Windows 7*:

Click , ▶ All Programs, Microsoft Office,
 Microsoft Excel

When you open *Excel*, you will see this window:

Open a blank workbook:

⊕ **Click**

The *Excel* window is opened.

The title bar displays the name of the workbook:

Furthermore, you will see:
- the *Quick Access* toolbar
- the ribbon
- the tabs

You will also see a blank worksheet:

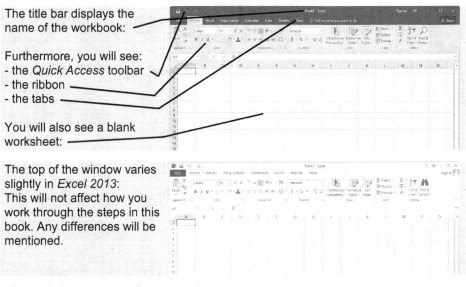

The top of the window varies slightly in *Excel 2013*:
This will not affect how you work through the steps in this book. Any differences will be mentioned.

 HELP! I see different windows.

When you open an *Office* suite program for the first time, you will see a number of different windows. For example, you may need to decide whether information is sent:

⊕ **If necessary, click the radio button ⦿ by** No thanks

⊕ **Click** Accept

Choose the default file type:

⊕ **Click the radio button ⦿ by** Office Open XML formats

⊕ **Click** OK

If necessary, close the Welcome window that appears:

⊕ **If necessary, click** ✕

1.2 The Ribbon

The ribbon has been designed to help you quickly find the commands you need while working on your documents. Have a look at the ribbon on your computer screen.

The ribbon consists of several tabs:

Each tab is divided into logical groups. A group contains corresponding commands:

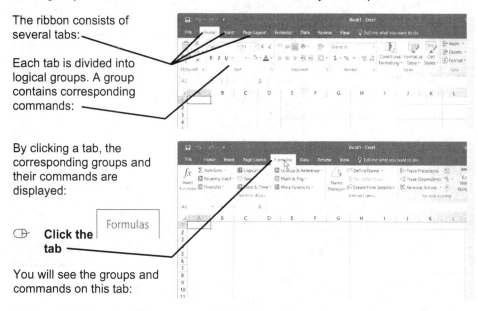

By clicking a tab, the corresponding groups and their commands are displayed:

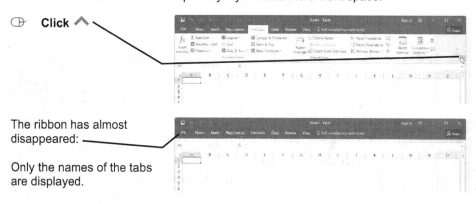

☞ **Click the** Formulas **tab**

You will see the groups and commands on this tab:

You can minimize the ribbon temporarily if you need more work space:

☞ **Click** ⌃

The ribbon has almost disappeared:

Only the names of the tabs are displayed.

You can easily restore and pin the ribbon again:

☞ **Click the** Home **tab**

☞ **Click** 📌

HELP! The ribbon looks different on my screen.

The display of the commands in the ribbon is automatically adjusted to the size of your screen, the current resolution and the size of the *Excel* window. The larger your screen and the higher the resolution, the more information the ribbon can display.

On a high resolution monitor – from 1600 pixels wide – the ribbon is fully displayed:

With a low resolution – 1024 pixels wide – the ribbon looks slightly different:

You will see that all groups are maintained, but the view and displayed information changes. The screenshots in this book are made with a resolution of 1280 pixels wide. If you use a different resolution, the ribbon on your screen may look different. In some cases, this means you will have to click a few more times to show all of the commands in a particular group.

1.3 Adjusting the Quick Access toolbar

If you want to use a command via the ribbon, you usually have to click twice. You need to click the tab and then the command. This quickly becomes inconvenient if you use a particular command quite often. Luckily, *Excel* provides a special toolbar called *Quick Access* . You can use this toolbar to access frequently used commands with just a single click.

You can see the *Quick Access* toolbar at the top of the *Excel* window:

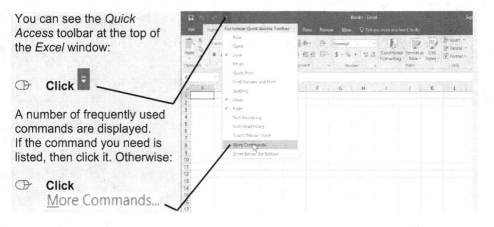

☞ **Click**

A number of frequently used commands are displayed. If the command you need is listed, then click it. Otherwise:

☞ **Click** More Commands...

⊕ **If necessary, drag the scroll bar downwards**

⊕ **Click the desired command, for example** 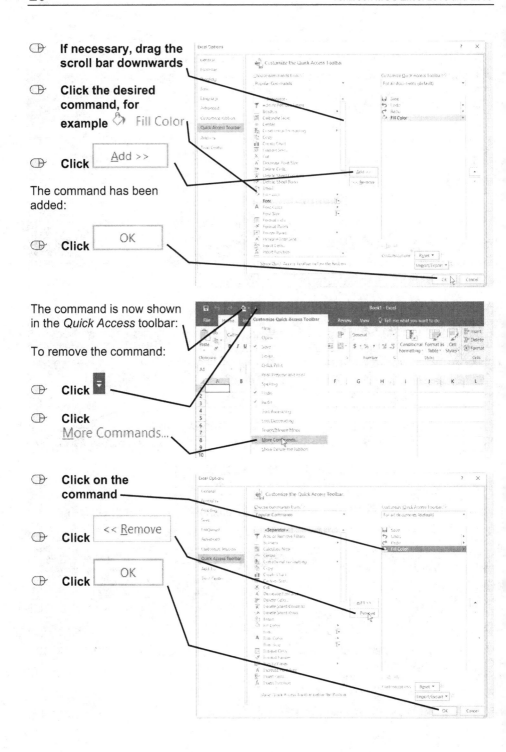 Fill Color

⊕ **Click** | Add >> |

The command has been added:

⊕ **Click** | OK |

The command is now shown in the *Quick Access* toolbar:

To remove the command:

⊕ **Click** ⏷

⊕ **Click** More Commands...

⊕ **Click on the command**

⊕ **Click** | << Remove |

⊕ **Click** | OK |

💡 Tip

Back to default layout

If you have applied several changes and are not happy with them, you can always restore the default setting of the toolbar or tabs:

⊕ **Click** [Reset ▼]

⊕ **Click the desired option**

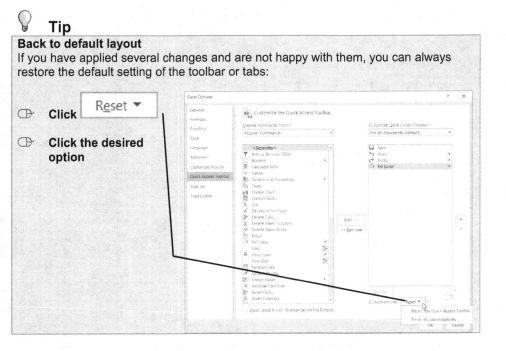

1.4 Adjusting the Ribbon

You can adjust the tabs in the ribbon yourself, for example to add commands you frequently use or even place them on another tab. Here is how you do that:

In the ribbon:

⊕ **Click** File

⊕ **Click** Options

First create a new group on a tab, for example on the *Formulas* tab:

☞ **Click** Customize Ribbon

Choose a tab where you want to add the group:

☞ **Double-click** Formulas

☞ **Click** New Group

The tab is opened and you will see the new group underneath the other groups:

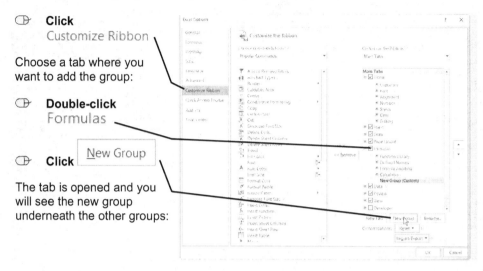

💡 Tip

New tab
You can also create a separate tab for your commands. For this, you need to go to New Tab.

You can change the name of the group with Rename... . This is not necessary now.

☞ **Click the desired command, for example** Calculate Now

☞ **Click** Add >>

The command is added to the group:

☞ **Click** OK

HELP! I cannot see the command.

By default, only the popular commands are displayed. In order to see other commands:

☞ **By**
   Choose commands from:

   click ▾

☞ **Click the category**

If you do not know the category in which the command is located, click All Commands .

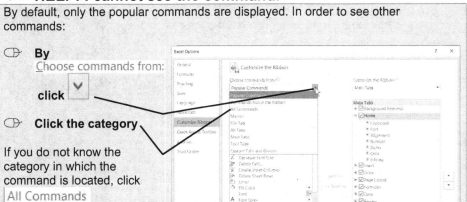

☞ **Click the** Formulas **tab**

The new command is displayed on the right side in the new group:

To reset the tab to default settings:

☞ **Click** File , Options , Customize Ribbon

☞ **Click** Reset ▾

☞ **Click**
   Reset only selected Rib

☞ **Click** OK

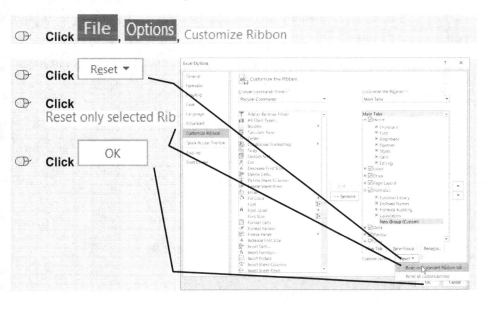

Tip

Remove a single command or group
You can also remove a single group or tab. To do this, click the group or the command and then click ⌊ << Remove ⌋.

The new group has disappeared:

☞ **Click the** ⌊ Home ⌋ **tab**

1.5 Managing Worksheets

A single *Excel* file is called a workbook. This workbook can contain multiple worksheets, for example to split costs and revenues or summaries of different branches.

By default, there is a single worksheet. You can see this in the tab at the bottom of the window:

This is how to add a new worksheet:

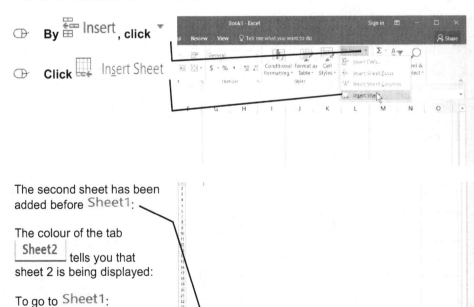

☞ **By** 🔲 Insert **, click** ▾

☞ **Click** 🔲 Insert Sheet

The second sheet has been added before Sheet1:

The colour of the tab ⌊ Sheet2 ⌋ tells you that sheet 2 is being displayed:

To go to Sheet1:

☞ **Click** Sheet1

💡 Tip

Adding worksheets
You can also add a new worksheet by clicking the ⊕ icon that is shown after the tabs.
The new worksheet is then placed after the previous sheet.

Click ⊕

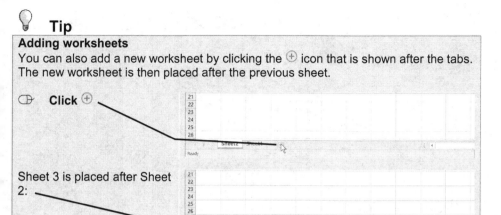

Sheet 3 is placed after Sheet 2:

You see Sheet1:

You can rename sheets:

Click 📋 Format ▾

Click Rename Sheet

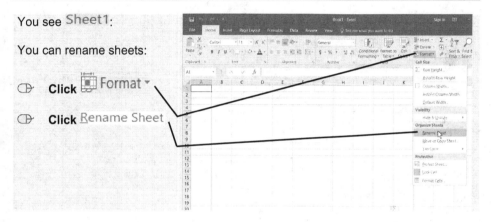

🐾 Please note:

Make sure the sheet you wish to rename is currently open.

⌨ **Type the name of the sheet:** Costs

Enter

⌨ **Press**

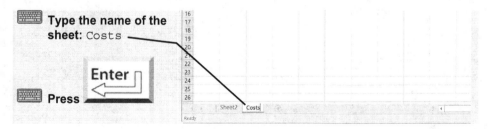

Sheet1 is now renamed to *Costs*:

You can also adjust the color of the tab:

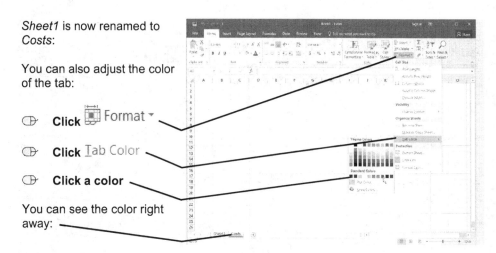

👉 **Click** 🖫 Format ▾

👉 **Click** Tab Color

👉 **Click a color**

You can see the color right away:

You can change the order of the worksheets by dragging the tabs:

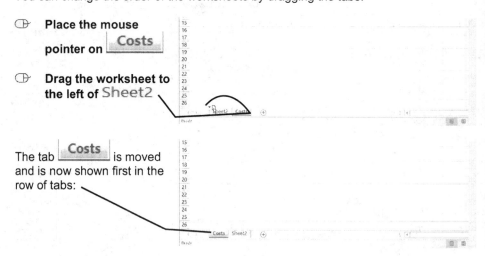

👉 **Place the mouse pointer on** Costs

👉 **Drag the worksheet to the left of** Sheet2

The tab Costs is moved and is now shown first in the row of tabs:

Worksheets that are unnecessary can also be removed. To remove Sheet2 :

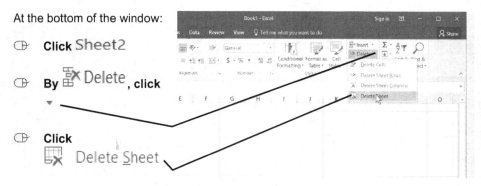

At the bottom of the window:

👉 **Click** Sheet2

👉 **By** 🖳 Delete **, click**
   ▾

👉 **Click**
   🖳 Delete Sheet

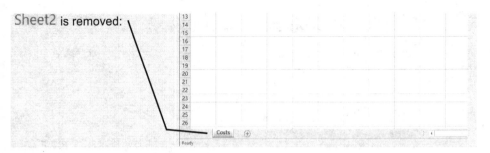

Sheet2 is removed:

🩹 HELP! I see different windows.

If the sheet contains data, you will need to confirm the deletion. This helps to prevent the accidental deletion of a sheet:

You will see this window:

To permanently delete the sheet:

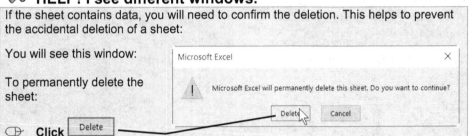

⏵ **Click** Delete

Now close *Excel.* In the next section you will open a new worksheet:

⏵ **Click** ✕

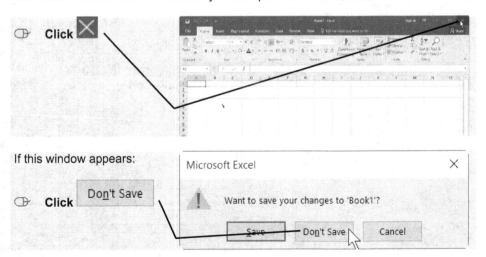

If this window appears:

⏵ **Click** Don't Save

Excel is closed.

1.6 Moving the Pointer

A worksheet has a completely different layout and working method than for example a word processing document. In this section you will learn how to move the pointer around the worksheet.

☞ **Open *Excel* ❧¹ and open a blank workbook ❧²**

A workbook consists of one or more worksheets with columns and rows:

A worksheet is divided into squares. These are called cells. The first cell has a thick outline. This means the cell is currently selected.

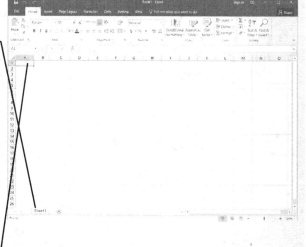

Above the selected cell, you see the letter **A**. On the left side of the cell you see the number **1**. The letter and number indicate the column and row you are working in. The selected cell is therefore A1:

The box displayed on the left above the columns and rows of the worksheet is the *name box*. This also shows the currently selected cell:

Here you can see that cell A1 is selected:

There are several ways to select another cell:

With the arrow keys:

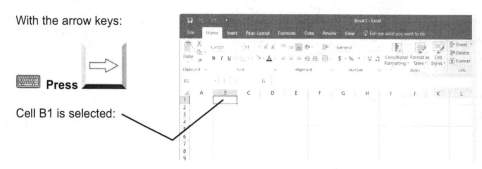

⌨ **Press** ➡

Cell B1 is selected:

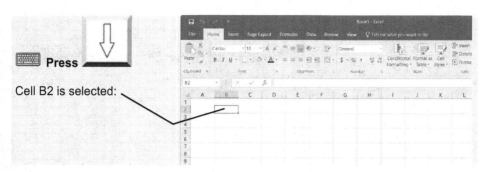

Press

Cell B2 is selected:

💡 Tip

Using other keys

You can also go to the next column by using **Tab** .

You can also go to the next row by using **Enter** .

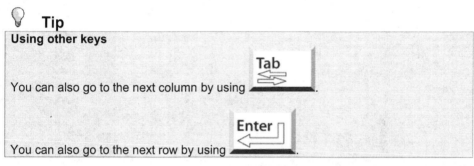

Using the mouse:

☞ **Click in cell C4**

🖐 Please note:

Do not forget to click in the cell. If you only position the pointer on the cell, it is not yet selected. Once you click a cell, it will have a thick outline. This means it is selected.

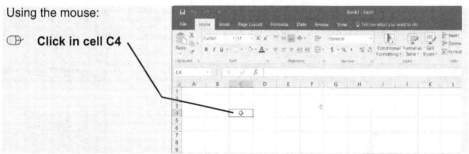

Using the name box:

☞ **Click the name box**

⌨ **Type:** g10

⌨ **Press** **Enter**

Cell G10 is selected:

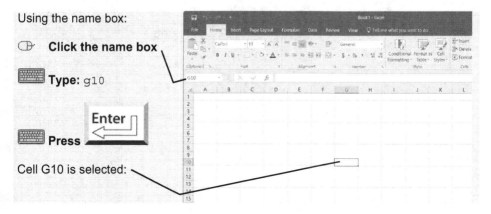

To go back to cell A1 right away:

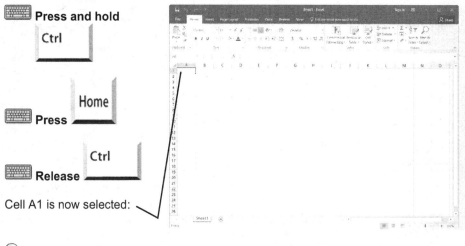

Press and hold **Ctrl**

Press **Home**

Release **Ctrl**

Cell A1 is now selected:

💡 **Tip**

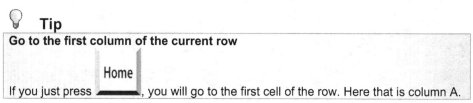

1.7 Entering Data

You can enter various types of data, such as:

* numbers
* text
* formulas and functions
* dates

Excel automatically adjusts the layout of the cell to the type of data that you enter:

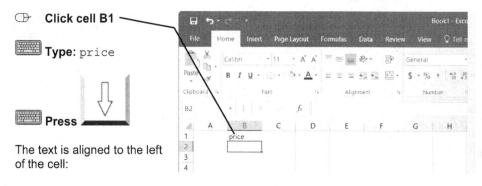

👆 **Click cell B1**

Type: price

Press ⬇

The text is aligned to the left of the cell:

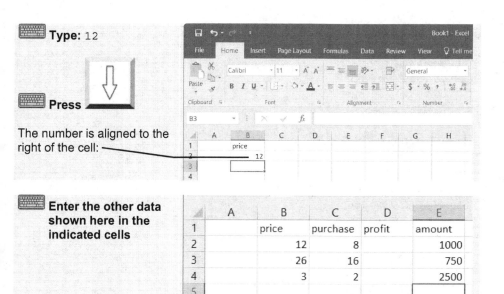

⌨ **Type:** 12

⌨ **Press** ⬇

The number is aligned to the right of the cell: ——

⌨ **Enter the other data shown here in the indicated cells**

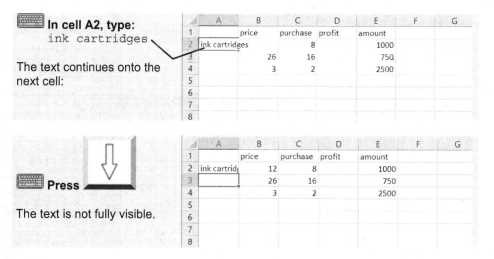

	A	B	C	D	E
1		price	purchase	profit	amount
2		12	8		1000
3		26	16		750
4		3	2		2500
5					
6					

1.8 Adjusting Column Width and Row Height

If a text is too long to fit in a cell, you can adjust the width of the column:

⌨ **In cell A2, type:** ink cartridges

The text continues onto the next cell:

	A	B	C	D	E	F	G
1		price	purchase	profit	amount		
2	ink cartridges		8		1000		
3		26	16		750		
4		3	2		2500		
5							
6							
7							
8							

⌨ **Press** ⬇

The text is not fully visible.

	A	B	C	D	E	F	G
1		price	purchase	profit	amount		
2	ink cartrid	12	8		1000		
3		26	16		750		
4		3	2		2500		
5							
6							
7							
8							

🩹 HELP! I typed something wrong.

While typing in a cell you can correct typing mistakes as usual.
If you have already selected another cell, then first click the cell containing the mistake and then type the correct text or the correct number.

Delete

In order to empty a cell, you need to click it first and then press .

In order to see the entire text, you can expand the column:

👉 **Place the pointer ✛ between the column headers**

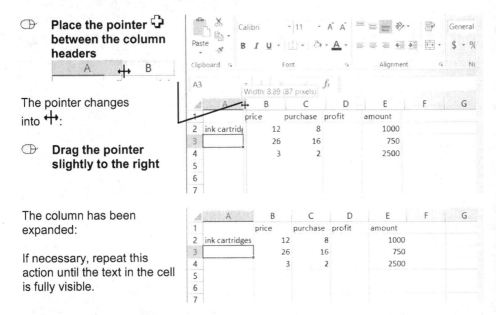

The pointer changes into ✛:

👉 **Drag the pointer slightly to the right**

The column has been expanded:

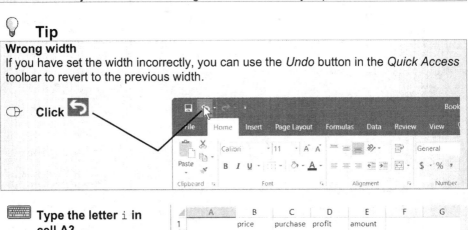

If necessary, repeat this action until the text in the cell is fully visible.

👈 Please note:

You cannot adjust the width of a single cell. You can only expand the whole column.

💡 Tip

Wrong width
If you have set the width incorrectly, you can use the *Undo* button in the *Quick Access* toolbar to revert to the previous width.

👉 **Click** ↩

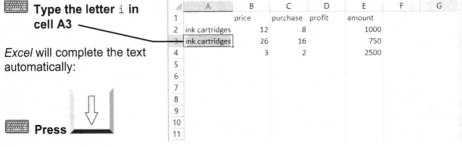

⌨ **Type the letter** i **in cell A3**

Excel will complete the text automatically:

⌨ **Press** ⬇

This is how you change the content of a cell:

⊕ **Click cell A3**

The text is also shown in the *formula bar:*

⊕ **Click the formula bar after the text**

Now you can change the text:

⌨ **Press the space bar**

⌨ **Type:** color

⌨ **Press** Enter

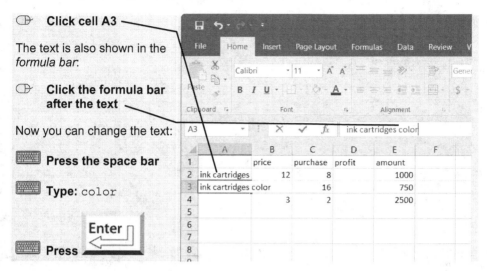

🔖 **Please note:**

You can exit the formula bar by pressing Enter, but not by pressing the arrow keys.

The column is too narrow again. You can allow the column to be adjusted automatically to the proper width by doing the following:

⊕ **Double click between the column headers**

The column will automatically be adjusted to the width of the longest text:

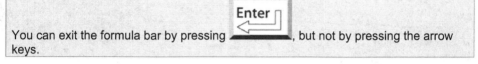

⌨ **In cell A4, type:** paper

⌨ **Press** ⬇

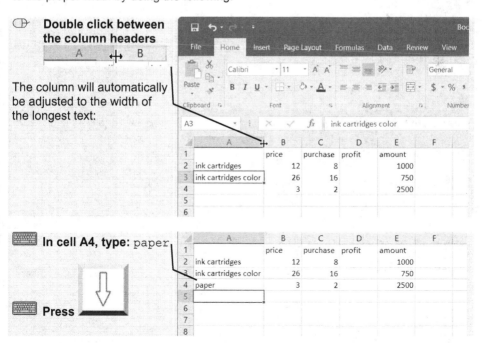

Tip

Adjusting row height
You can adjust the row height in the same way:

 Place the pointer between the row numbers

The pointer changes into ‡:

 Drag the pointer up or down

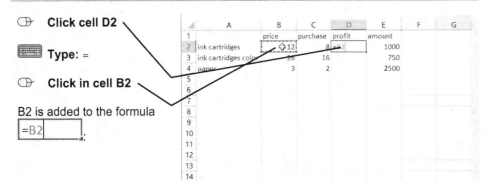

1.9 Entering Simple Formulas

You can enter formulas in *Excel* to perform calculations. For normal mathematical calculations you can use:

- + for adding
- - for subtracting
- * for multiplying
- / for dividing

Tip

Numeric part of the keyboard
These keys are conveniently grouped together on the numeric part of the keyboard.

Profit equals price minus purchase. To calculate this, enter the following formula.

➡ Please note:

A formula must be entered in the cell where the answer is supposed to be shown.

 Click cell D2

Type: =

 Click in cell B2

B2 is added to the formula
`=B2`

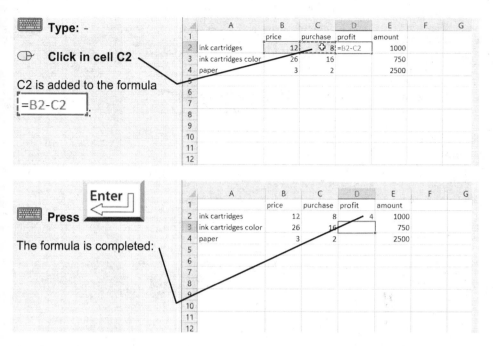

Type: -

Click in cell C2

C2 is added to the formula

=B2-C2

Press Enter

The formula is completed:

The formula is not visible anymore now. In order to see the formula:

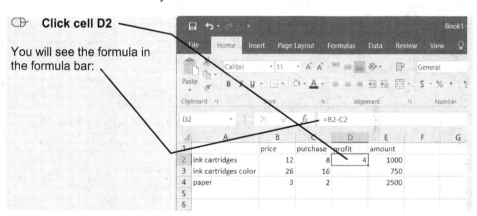

Click cell D2

You will see the formula in the formula bar:

Column E shows the amount sold. The total profit for this product can now be calculated in column F by multiplying the profit with the amount sold:

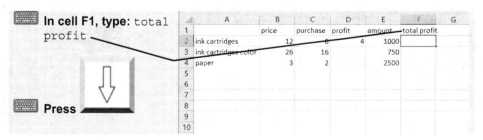

In cell F1, type: total profit

Press

The text is too wide for the column. Instead of increasing the width of the column, you can also divide the text into two lines. This is called *text wrapping*. Text wrapping is often used when the text in a column header is wider than the contents of the cells below. If you do not use text wrapping, the column will be unnecessarily wide.

⊕ **Click cell F1**

⊕ **Click**

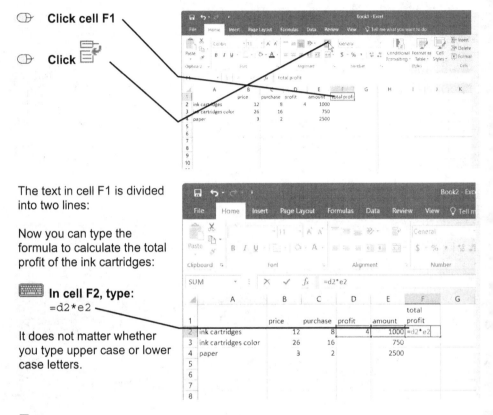

The text in cell F1 is divided into two lines:

Now you can type the formula to calculate the total profit of the ink cartridges:

⌨ **In cell F2, type:**
=d2*e2

It does not matter whether you type upper case or lower case letters.

Please note:
A formula always starts with the equal sign character =.

 Tip

Clicking or typing
It does not make a difference for the formula whether you type it or click the cells.

Enter

⌨ **Press**

The formula has been calculated:

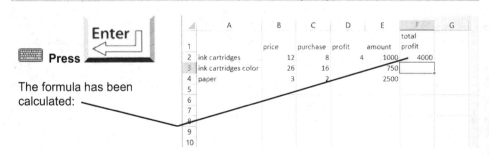

1.10 Copying Formulas

The formulas have to be entered in row 3 as well. Instead of typing them yourself, you can also copy them from row 2:

☞ **Click cell D2**

Copy this
formula to cell D3:

☞ **Click**

You will see a dotted line
around cell D2: [___4___].
This indicates that the
contents of this cell have
been copied to the clipboard.

☞ **Click in cell D3**

Paste the formula into the
cell:

☞ **Click**

The formula is copied and
calculated right away:

The formula bar shows you
that the formula has been
changed automatically from
$=B2-C2$ to $=B3-C3$:

You can ignore 📋 (Ctrl) ▾ for
now.

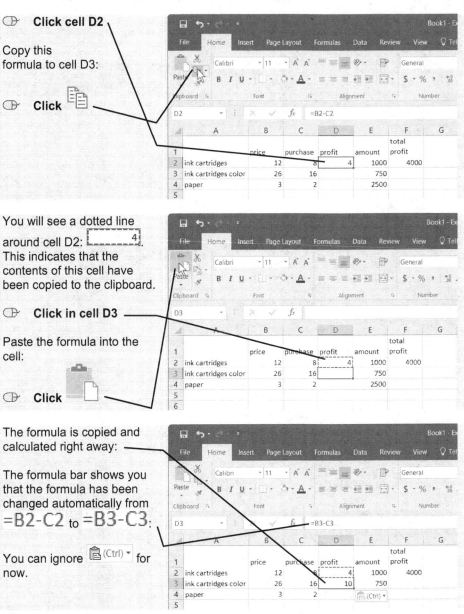

 Tip

Use simple numbers
When you are creating a worksheet yourself, first use simple numbers. This allows
you to quickly spot whether the answer of a formula is true or whether there may be
an error in the formula.

The dotted line around cell D2 is still there. This indicates that the contents of this cell is still on the clipboard. Paste the formula once more.

 HELP! The dotted line is gone.

If you have carried out another action, then the selection may have been removed from the clipboard and you cannot see the dotted line any more. You can copy the cell to the clipboard again:

⊕ **Click cell D2**

⊕ **Click**

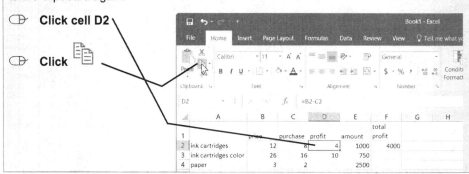

⊕ **Click cell D4**

⊕ **Click**

To cancel the selection:

⊞ **Press** **Esc**

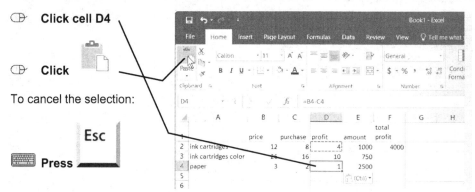

If there are many rows with items, there is an easier way to copy the formula. You can do this with the *fill handle*. This is a small square at the bottom-right corner of a selected cell:

⊕ **Click cell F2**

This cell contains the formula that needs to be copied.

⊕ **Place the pointer on the fill handle in the bottom-right corner of cell F2**

The pointer changes into ✛:

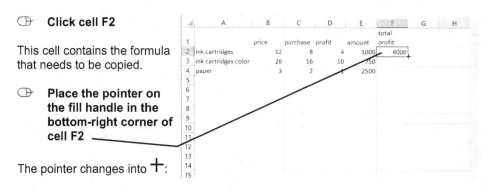

☞ **Drag the pointer to cell F4**

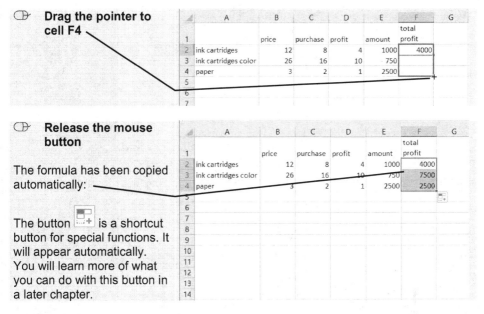

☞ **Release the mouse button**

The formula has been copied automatically:

The button ⊞ is a shortcut button for special functions. It will appear automatically. You will learn more of what you can do with this button in a later chapter.

Depending on the layout of the worksheet, you can use this same method to copy formulas up, left or right. The cell references in the formula are automatically adjusted.

If you change a value in the worksheet, the formulas are recalculated automatically:

⌨ **In cell B3, type:** 30

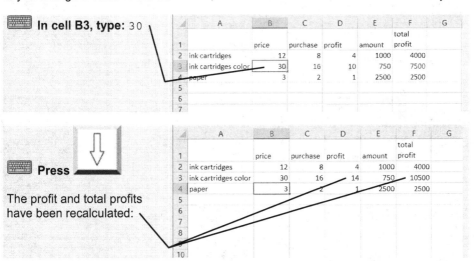

⌨ **Press**

The profit and total profits have been recalculated:

1.11 Saving the Workbook

Once you have finished part of your worksheet, it makes sense to save it before you continue. In case you make a mistake later on, or if there is some kind of other failure, then you can reopen your saved workbook. This prevents you from having to start everything all over again.

This is how to save a workbook:

In the *Quick Access* toolbar:

⊕ **Click**

The first time, the location and the name of the workbook have to be specified:

If the folder already exists, you can directly click it. In this example you will need to browse to a different folder:

⊕ **Click** 📁 Browse

First select the *(My) Documents* folder:

⊕ **Click** 🗎 Documents

⊕ **Click on the right side of the file name shown**

⌨ **Press** `⟵ Backspace` **until the name is deleted**

⌨ **Type:** Profit report

⊕ **Click** Save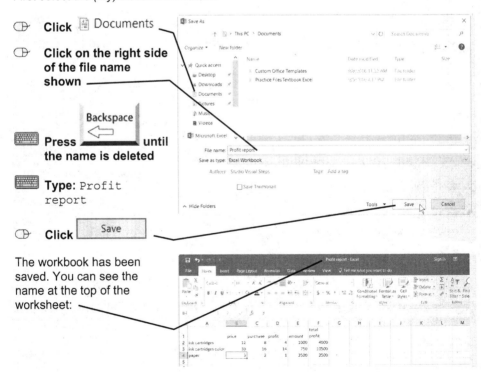

The workbook has been saved. You can see the name at the top of the worksheet:

1.12 Sum Function

In *section 1.9 Entering Simple Formulas* you have learned how to enter a simple formula to add up a few numbers. If you need to add up a whole column or row of numbers, then this can be quite tedious. Instead, you can use the *SUM* function. You can practice using this now to add up the total profits:

☞ **Click cell F5**

This is the cell where the total should be displayed.

☞ **Click** Σ

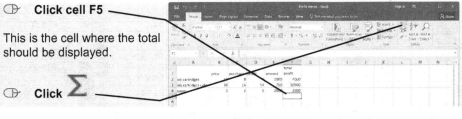

The dotted line indicates the area that will be added up automatically:

Press **Enter**

The numbers are calculated.

	A	B	C	D	E	F	G	H
1		price	purchase	profit	amount	total profit		
2	ink cartridges	12	8	4	1000	4000		
3	ink cartridges color	30	16	14	750	10500		
4	paper	3	2	1	2500	2500		
5						17000		
6								

 Please note:

If you see ####### in the cell containing the answer, then the column is too narrow. The number is too large for the cell and you need to widen the column to see the full number. $\mathcal{Q}\mathcal{Q}$18

The *Sum* function also allows you to calculate an average of a number of values. This is how to calculate the average profit per product:

☞ **Click cell D5**

This is the cell where the average profit should be displayed.

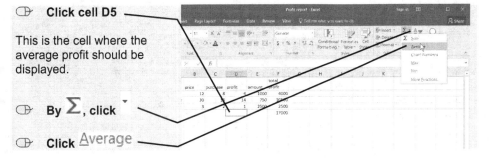

☞ **By** Σ**, click** ▾

☞ **Click** Average

The dotted line indicates the
amounts on which the
average will be calculated:

Press **Enter**

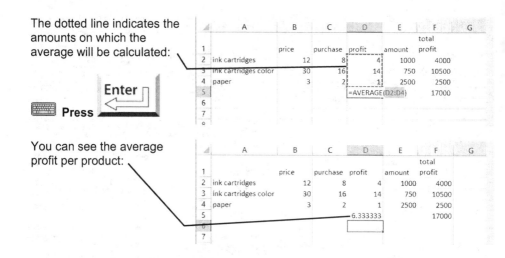

You can see the average
profit per product:

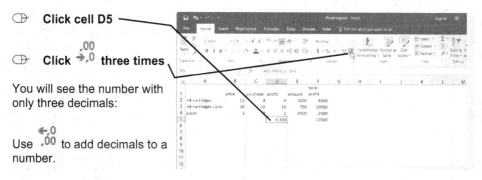

1.13 Selecting and Formatting Multiple Cells

Numbers and text in *Excel* are formatted with a default layout. To adjust this layout, you
can change the formatting of one or more cells. For example, if you want to show the
average profit with three decimals, this is what you do:

☞ **Click cell D5**

☞ **Click `.00` three times**

You will see the number with
only three decimals:

Use `.00` to add decimals to a
number.

👉 Please note:

Excel uses the numbers that are no longer visible in calculations. This can sometimes
lead to apparent differences in the calculation results that are shown on your screen. In
this example the two numbers 6.333 have been added up. Using 3 decimals, the
answer is correct, but without the visible decimals, it seems wrong:

6.333	6
6.333	6
12.666	13

If you increase the number of decimals once more using `.00`,
the correct answer is shown again. In order to prevent these
differences, *Excel* has a few special features that will be
discussed later on in this book.

To change the formatting of multiple cells, first select the cells:

☞ **Drag the cells D2 to D4**

Please note: from now on, an area you need to select will be indicated with a colon between the cells, for example D2:D4.

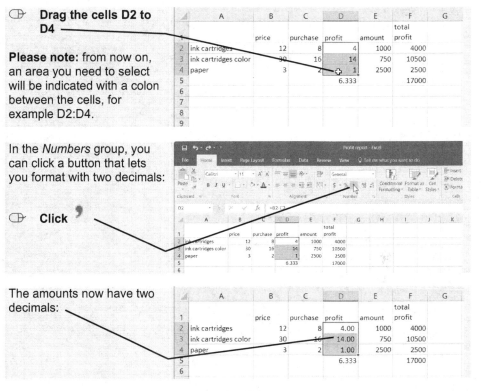

In the *Numbers* group, you can click a button that lets you format with two decimals:

☞ **Click**

The amounts now have two decimals:

By selecting a column, you can adjust its formatting all at once:

☞ **Click** F

There is also a separate button to place a $ sign before the amount:

☞ **Click** $

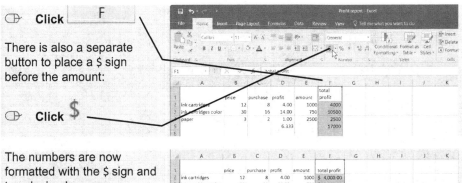

The numbers are now formatted with the $ sign and two decimals:

A comma is automatically inserted for thousands.

The column is widened automatically to fit the $ sign. This means the header text now also fits the column.

💡 Tip

Other currencies
If you do not need the $ sign, but instead the British Pound symbol:

👉 **By $, click** ▾

👉 **Click a currency symbol or**
More Accounting Forma

👉 **By Symbol:, click** ▾

👉 **Click the symbol**

At the bottom of the window:

👉 **Click** | OK |

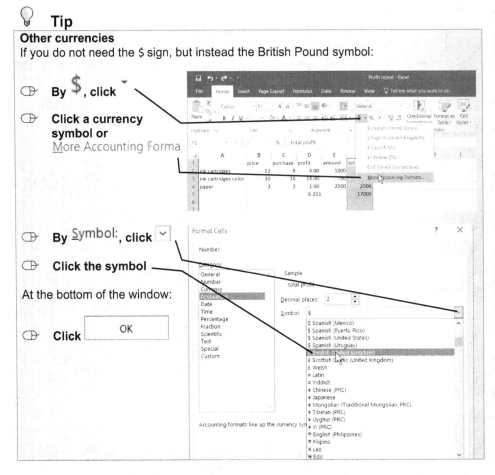

Instead of a single cell or column, you can select several columns at once:

👉 **Select the cells B2:C4**

👉 **Click** 🔸

Notice that all numbers in the selected cells have two decimals:

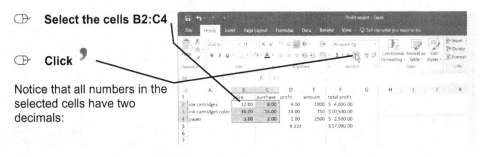

💡 Tip

Currency symbol, yes or no?
When numbers are displayed with a currency symbol, the column has to be wider than without that symbol. If it is already clear from the header of the column that the amounts are in $ for example, then the $ symbol for each amount may not be necessary.

You can also select several rows at once:

⊕ **Click** `1`

The formatting of the entire row can now be changed, for example centered:

⊕ **Click** ≡

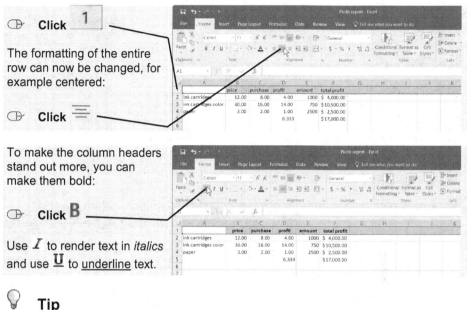

To make the column headers stand out more, you can make them bold:

⊕ **Click** B

Use *I* to render text in *italics* and use U̲ to underline text.

💡 **Tip**

Selecting the entire worksheet
To select the entire worksheet, use a special button at the top left of the worksheet:

⊕ **Click** ◢

The entire worksheet is now selected:

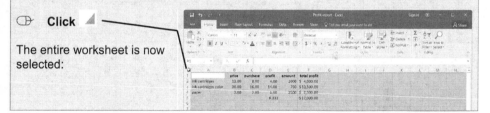

1.14 Inserting Rows and Columns

You can still adjust the layout of your worksheet even after making a lot of changes. Perhaps you would like to insert or delete some rows or columns. For example, you can add a new blank line above your data in order to add a title to this worksheet:

⊕ **Click a cell in row 1**

Since you are inserting a full new row, it does not matter which column you select.

⊕ **By** 🔲 Insert **click** ▼

⊕ **Click**
   ⬚ Insert Sheet Rows

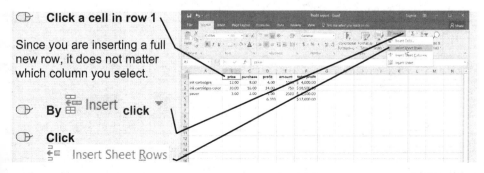

There is now a blank line
above the data:

🖐 Please note:

By default, a row or column is inserted before the current row or column.

If you want to add a title that is centered above the columns you have used, you will
need to merge cells A1 to F1 into a single cell:

☞ **Select the cells A1:F1**

☞ **Click**

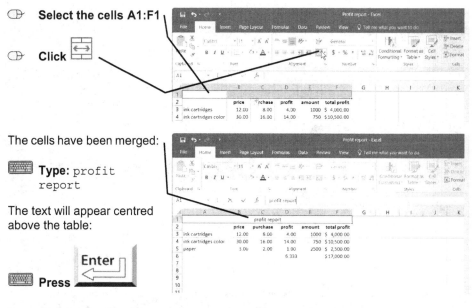

The cells have been merged:

⌨ **Type:** profit
report

The text will appear centred
above the table:

⌨ **Press** Enter

To emphasize the title, you can choose a larger font:

☞ **Click** profit report

☞ **By** `11` **click** ▾

☞ **Click** 16

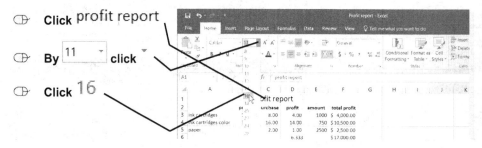

💡 Tip

Increasing or decreasing step by step

You can increase the text in the selected cell(s) by one step using the button A˄
and decrease it by one step using the A˅ button.

A new column can be inserted in the same way as you inserted a new row. In order to insert a column before column B:

☞ **Click a cell in column B**

Please note: do not click in the merged cell on row 1.

☞ **By 📑 Insert, click ▾**

☞ **Click**
ᵁ⬆ᵁ Insert Sheet Columns

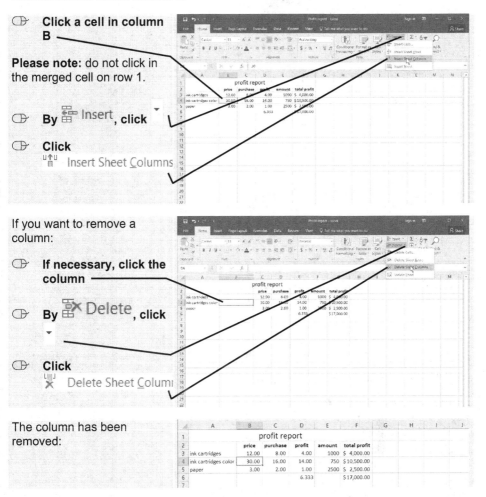

If you want to remove a column:

☞ **If necessary, click the column**

☞ **By 📑 Delete, click**
▾

☞ **Click**
✖ Delete Sheet Columns

The column has been removed:

	A	B	C	D	E	F	G	H	I	J
1			profit report							
2		price	purchase	profit	amount	total profit				
3	ink cartridges	12.00	8.00	4.00	1000	$ 4,000.00				
4	ink cartridges color	30.00	16.00	14.00	750	$ 10,500.00				
5	paper	3.00	2.00	1.00	2500	$ 2,500.00				
6				6.333		$ 17,000.00				
7										

1.15 Save As

Earlier in this chapter, you saved the file with the name *Profit report*. Then later you made some additional changes. In this example we will save the file with a different name. This way, the old file *Profit report* will still be kept. To save the file with another name, use the option Save As.

☞ **Click** File

⊕ **Click** Save As

Choose the *(My) Documents*
folder:

⊕ **Click** 📁 Browse

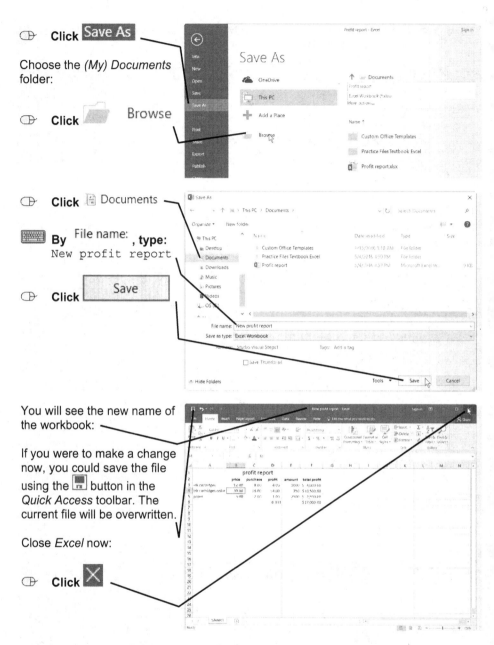

⊕ **Click** 📄 Documents

⌨ **By** File name: **, type:**
New profit report

⊕ **Click** Save

You will see the new name of
the workbook:

If you were to make a change
now, you could save the file
using the 🖫 button in the
Quick Access toolbar. The
current file will be overwritten.

Close *Excel* now:

⊕ **Click** ✕

In this chapter you have gotten acquainted with some of the basic concepts and
commands needed for working with *Excel*. With what you have learned so far, you can
already create simple worksheets with calculations. The next chapters will show you
how to use more complicated formulas and introduce you to some of the more
extensive *Excel* features.

1.16 Exercise

To help you retain what you have just learned, you can do the following exercises. Have you forgotten how to do something? Use the number beside the footsteps to look it up in the appendix *How Do I Do That Again?* at the end of the book.

Exercise: Adjusting the Quick Access toolbar and Ribbon and Filling a Worksheet

In this exercise you practice using the toolbar and the ribbon and fill a worksheet.

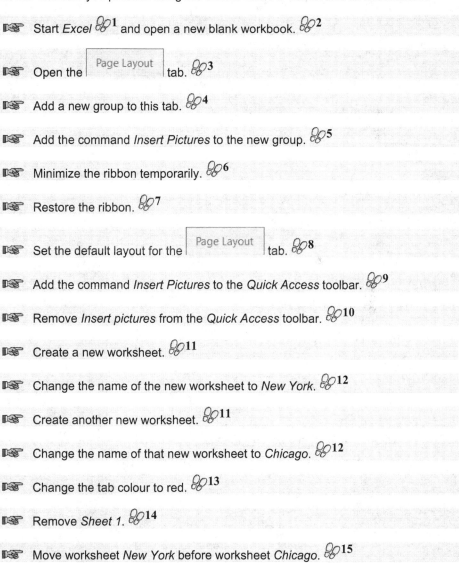

☞ Start *Excel* ⚘[1] and open a new blank workbook. ⚘[2]

☞ Open the Page Layout tab. ⚘[3]

☞ Add a new group to this tab. ⚘[4]

☞ Add the command *Insert Pictures* to the new group. ⚘[5]

☞ Minimize the ribbon temporarily. ⚘[6]

☞ Restore the ribbon. ⚘[7]

☞ Set the default layout for the Page Layout tab. ⚘[8]

☞ Add the command *Insert Pictures* to the *Quick Access* toolbar. ⚘[9]

☞ Remove *Insert pictures* from the *Quick Access* toolbar. ⚘[10]

☞ Create a new worksheet. ⚘[11]

☞ Change the name of the new worksheet to *New York*. ⚘[12]

☞ Create another new worksheet. ⚘[11]

☞ Change the name of that new worksheet to *Chicago*. ⚘[12]

☞ Change the tab colour to red. ⚘[13]

☞ Remove *Sheet 1*. ⚘[14]

☞ Move worksheet *New York* before worksheet *Chicago*. ⚘[15]

☞ Add a new worksheet. ⚘[11]

☞ Remove the worksheets *New York* and *Chicago*. 🐾14

☞ Fill in the following data 🐾17:

	A	B	C	D	E
1		Male	Female	total	
2	New York				
3	Los Angeles				
4	Chicago				
5					

☞ Widen column A until the text fits exactly. 🐾18

☞ Fill in the following data 🐾17:

	A	B	C	D	E
1		Male	Female	total	
2	New York	3794204	4214074		
3	Los Angeles	1841805	1853015		
4	Chicago	1405107	1490909		
5					

☞ Select the cells B2:C4. 🐾19

☞ Change the formatting of the numbers so that there is a comma between the thousands. 🐾20

☞ Remove the decimals. 🐾21

The summary will now look like this:

	A	B	C	D	E
1		Male	Female	total	
2	New York	3,794,204	4,214,074		
3	Los Angeles	1,841,805	1,853,015		
4	Chicago	1,405,107	1,490,909		
5					

☞ In cell D2, add up the New York males and females. 🐾22

☞ In cell B5, use the *Sum* function to add up all males. 🐾23

☞ Copy the formula from cell B5 to cell C5 to add up all females. 🐾24

☞ Use the fill handle to copy the formula from cell D2 to cells D3:D5. 🐾25

☞ Widen column D until the numbers are all visible. 🐾18

☞ Save the workbook in the folder (*My*) *Documents* with the name *Exercise 1.1.* 🐾26

☞ Select row 1. 🐾27

☞ Centre the cells in row 1. 🐾28

☞ In cell D1, type Total population 🐾17

☞ Set up text wrapping for cell D1. 🐾29

The model will now look like this:

	A	B	C	D	E
1		Male	Female	total population	
2	New York	3,794,204	4,214,074	8,008,278	
3	Los Angeles	1,841,805	1,853,015	3,694,820	
4	Chicago	1,405,107	1,490,909	2,896,016	
5		7,041,116	7,557,998	14,599,114	
6					

☞ Insert a blank row above row 1. 🐾30

☞ In cell A1, type Largest cities 🐾17

☞ Merge cells A1:D1. 🐾31

☞ Change the font size to 20. 🐾32

☞ Save the workbook in the folder (*My*) *Documents* with the name *Exercise 1.2.* 🐾33

☞ Close *Excel.* 🐾16

1.17 Tips

 Tip

Quick Access toolbar below the ribbon

If you use the *Quick Access* toolbar often, you may want to place it below the ribbon. In this way, it is shown directly above the worksheet and is easier to reach with the mouse:

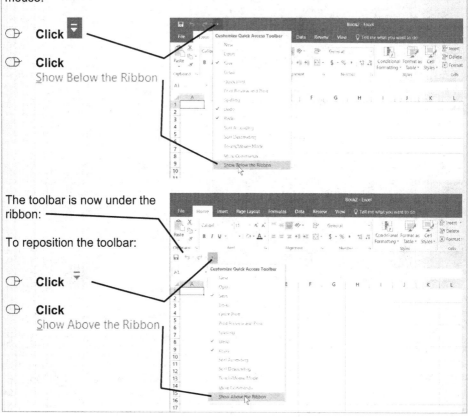

☞ **Click** ▼

☞ **Click**
  Show Below the Ribbon

The toolbar is now under the ribbon:

To reposition the toolbar:

☞ **Click** ▼

☞ **Click**
  Show Above the Ribbon

 Tip

Using the Quick Menu

Several actions in this chapter can also be performed using the Quick Menu:

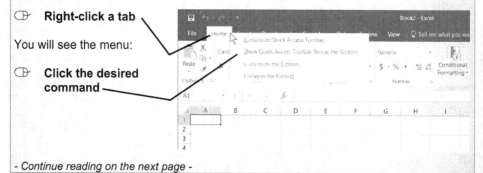

☞ **Right-click a tab**

You will see the menu:

☞ **Click the desired command**

- Continue reading on the next page -

Other shortcuts to commands can be reached by using a right-click on the tab at the bottom of the window or a right-click on a cell. In the menu that is shown, you will see several of the same options that can also be found on the ribbon.

 Tip

Adding up a column

In many cases the sum of a column needs to be displayed directly below that column. You can do this in the following way using the *Sum* function:

⬚ **Select the column that you want to add up**

⬚ **Click** Σ

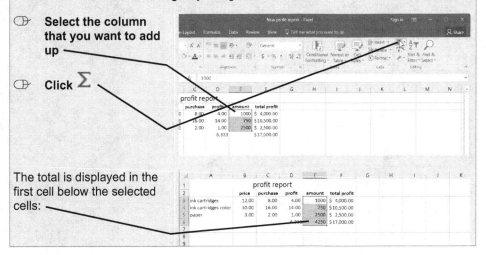

The total is displayed in the first cell below the selected cells:

 Tip

Showing sum, average and amount

If you want to know the sum, average or amount from just a group of cells, then you only need to select them. You can see the answer at the bottom of the window:

⬚ **Select the cells**

At the bottom of the window you see

Average: 1416.666667

Count: 3   Sum: 4250

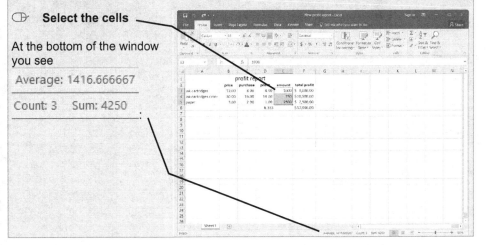

💡 Tip

Cell properties

You can also adjust the layout of a specific cell by changing the cell properties.

👉 **Right-click a cell with an amount**

👉 **Click**
📋 **Format Cells...**

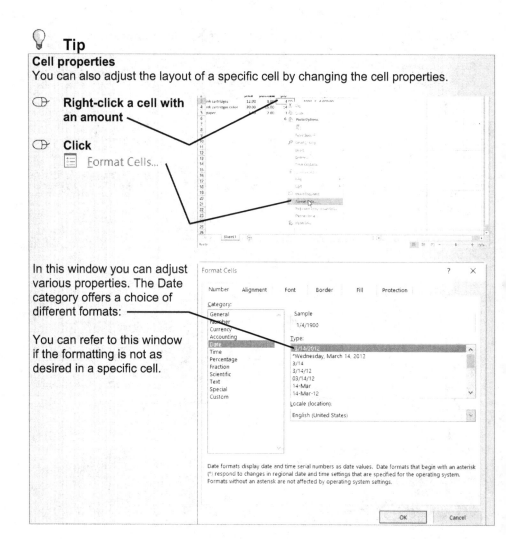

In this window you can adjust various properties. The Date category offers a choice of different formats: ─────

You can refer to this window if the formatting is not as desired in a specific cell.

2. Formulas and Series

In this chapter you will learn how to automatically complete a series of numbers, dates, or other items and work with more complex formulas in *Excel*. You will notice that creating an *Excel* data model is sometimes quite a considerable task. Therefore, these models are best used for regularly recurring calculations, such as monthly summaries or cost breakdowns.

The big advantage of a calculation model in *Excel* is that you can immediately see what the consequences are if the values change. For instance, you can view what happens if you implement a price increase or a cost savings without having to re-calculate the figures all over again.

In this chapter you will learn:

- how to copy a worksheet;
- how to automatically complete a sequence of months;
- what an absolute reference is;
- how *Excel* calculates;
- how to change the order of operation in a calculation;
- how to link cells to other worksheets;
- how to calculate a percentage;
- how to change cells into hyperlinks;
- how to protect worksheets;
- how to create unprotected cells;
- how to change the default settings of a workbook;
- how to set the number of worksheets;
- how to create a date series;
- how to create a series of weekdays;
- how to add your own series.

2.1 Copying a Worksheet

In the following exercise, you will need to open the practice file called *Telephone costs*:

☞ **Open** *Excel* &&^{1}

⊕ **Click**
   📁 **Open Other Workbc**

⊕ **Click** 📁 Browse

⊕ **Click** 🗒 Documents

⊕ **Double-click**
   📋 Practice Files Textb

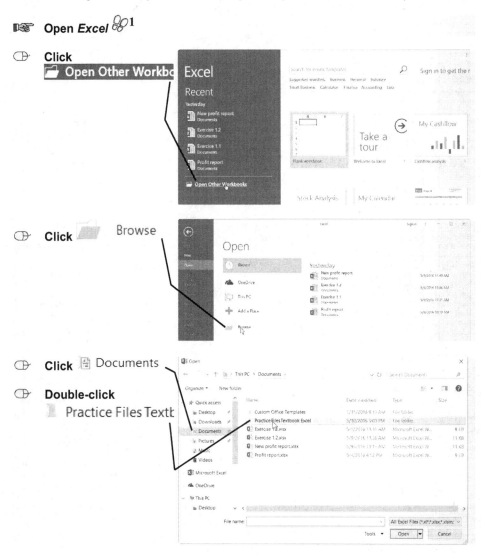

⊕ **Click**
    Cell phone expenses

⊕ **Click** | Open |

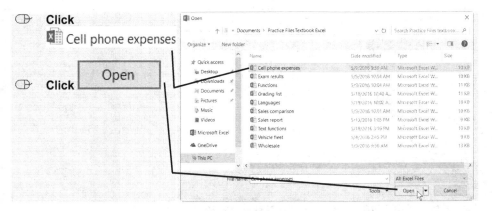

You will see the following
worksheet about a fictitious
cell phone plan:

First save this worksheet with
a different name:

  **Save the worksheet in
    the folder (*My*)
    Documents as** My
    cell phone
    expenses 👣33

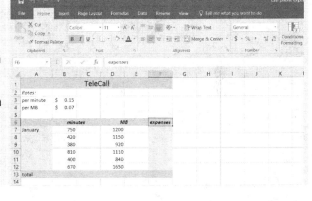

💡 **Tip**

Save it first
Try to make a habit of first saving original workbooks with a different name before you
change them. In case anything goes wrong while working on the workbook, you can
always revert to the original. This also prevents you from overwrite the original if you
accidentally use *Save* instead of *Save As*.

First copy this worksheet to two new worksheets so that you can calculate the data of
two other providers in those sheets:

⊕ **Click** Format ▾

⊕ **Click**
    Move or Copy Sheet...

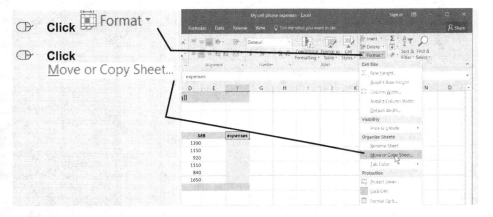

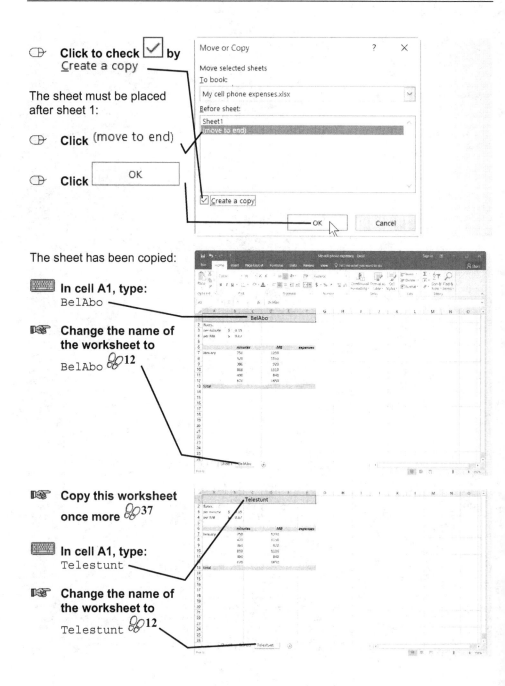

☞ **Click to check** ☑ **by**
Ϲreate a copy

The sheet must be placed
after sheet 1:

☞ **Click** (move to end)

☞ **Click** OK

The sheet has been copied:

⌨ **In cell A1, type:**
BelAbo

🖐 **Change the name of
the worksheet to**
BelAbo ✂12

🖐 **Copy this worksheet
once more** ✂37

⌨ **In cell A1, type:**
Telestunt

🖐 **Change the name of
the worksheet to**
Telestunt ✂12

☞ **Go to the** Sheet1
worksheet 👣41

☞ **Change the name of
the worksheet to**
TeleCall 👣12

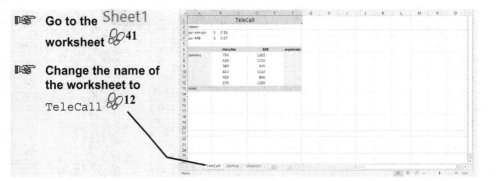

2.2 AutoFill

Excel can automatically complete several common sequences of data such as days
and months. By typing a single day or month, *Excel* can fill in the subsequent days or
months by itself. In this overview you will calculate the costs of a cell phone plan for the
first half year. To do this, you can use the *AutoFill* function. This will automatically place
the months February through June below January:

⬚ **Click cell A7**

⬚ **Point to the fill handle
in the right-corner of
cell A7**

⬚ **Drag the pointer to
cell A12**

You can see the month of
June shown at the last cell:

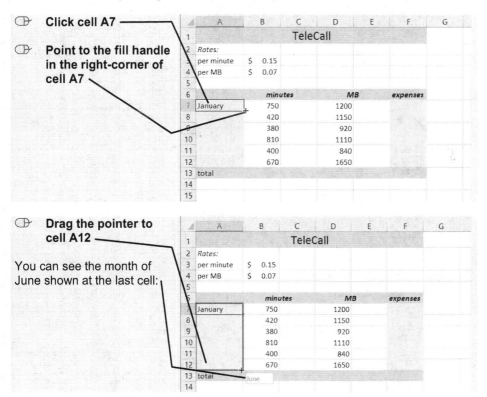

⊕ **Release the mouse button**

The months have now been completed:

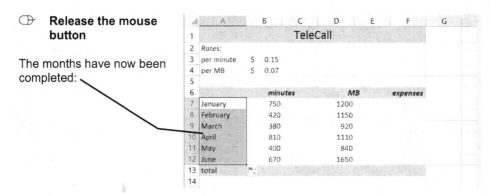

You can also do the same thing by using the ribbon. To do that:

☞ **Go to the** BelAbo **worksheet** ✂️**41**

☞ **Select cells A7:A12** ✂️**19**

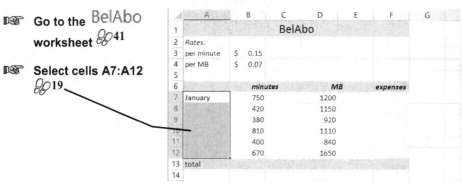

In the **Editing** group of the **Home** tab:

⊕ **Click** [↓] ▾

⊕ **Click** Series...

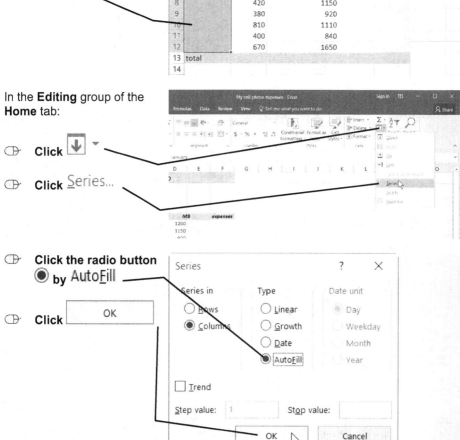

⊕ **Click the radio button** ⦿ **by** AutoFill

⊕ **Click** OK

The months have now been completed:

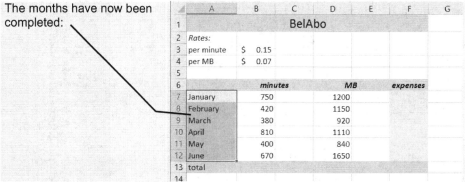

💡 Tip

The same contents for all cells
You can add the same contents to all cells:

☞ **Select the source cell and the target cells for the contents** 🔖19

☞ **Click** ⬇ ▾

☞ **Click** ⬇ Down

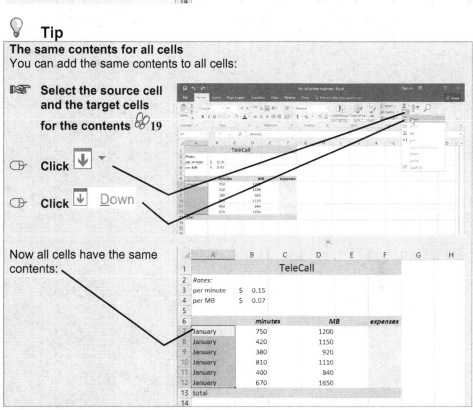

Now all cells have the same contents:

If a series has a regularity, you can use the *AutoFill* function to complete it automatically. The *Telestunt* bills are sent quarterly. In order to use *AutoFill*, you must enter at least the first two cells of the series. In this case: January and April:

☞ **Go to worksheet *Telestunt*** 🔖41

⌨ **In cell A8, type:** April

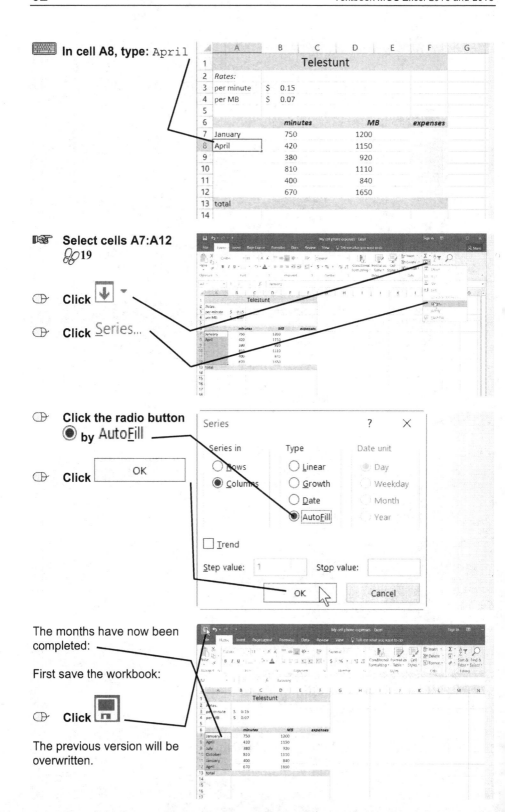

☞ **Select cells A7:A12**
✂19

☞ **Click** ⬇ ▾

☞ **Click** Series...

☞ **Click the radio button**
● **by** AutoFill

☞ **Click** OK

Series ? ✕

Series in   Type   Date unit
○ Rows   ○ Linear   ○ Day
● Columns   ○ Growth   ○ Weekday
                  ○ Date   ○ Month
                  ● AutoFill   ○ Year

☐ Trend

Step value: 1   Stop value:

OK   Cancel

The months have now been completed:

First save the workbook:

☞ **Click** 💾

The previous version will be overwritten.

2.3 Absolute References

In *Section 1.9 Entering Simple Formulas* you learned to create simple formulas and in *section 1.10 Copying Formulas* you learned how to copy them. You will now calculate the call costs for the month of January by multiplying the number of minutes by the costs per minute:

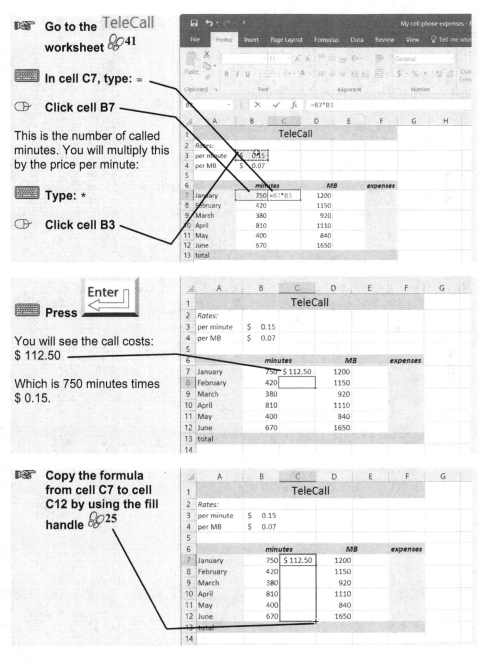

☞ **Go to the** TeleCall **worksheet** ✐41

⌨ **In cell C7, type:** =

☞ **Click cell B7**

This is the number of called minutes. You will multiply this by the price per minute:

⌨ **Type:** *

☞ **Click cell B3**

⌨ **Press** **Enter**

You will see the call costs:
$ 112.50

Which is 750 minutes times $ 0.15.

☞ **Copy the formula from cell C7 to cell C12 by using the fill handle** ✐25

Notice that the results are incorrect:

☞   **Click cell C11**

In the formula bar you will see that the formula has been changed to $=B11*B7$:

The reference to cell B11 is correct, but the reference to B7 is not. This should still have read B3.

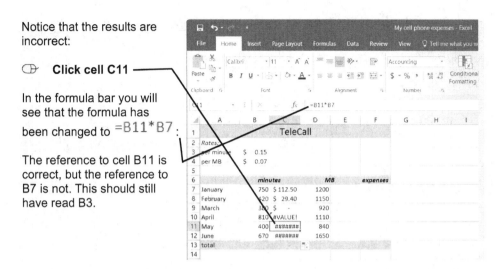

When copying formulas, they are automatically adjusted. As a result, they are no longer referring here to the price per minute, but to the cells below. These are called *relative references*. Relative references follow the movement on the worksheet. If you copy a formula two rows down, then all row references in that formula will be increased by two. This is also true for columns when you copy to the left or to the right.

You can correct the values by using an *absolute reference* for the price per minute:

First you have to undo the last action:

☞   **Click** ↶

The cells are empty again:

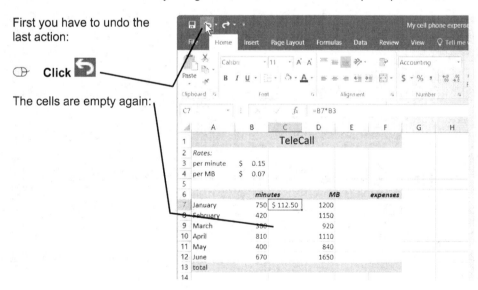

You can recognize an absolute reference in a formula by the dollar sign $ character before the column or row indication. You can use the following possibilities:

$A$1   Both the column and the row do not change during copying.

$A1   The column does not change, but the row does change during copying.

A$1   The column changes during copying, but the row does not change.

You can type the $ characters yourself in the formula or have it done automatically with

| F4 |

.

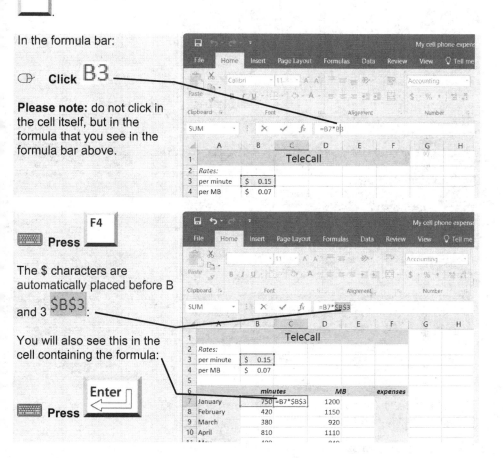

In the formula bar:

⊕ **Click** B3

Please note: do not click in the cell itself, but in the formula that you see in the formula bar above.

| F4 |

Press

The $ characters are automatically placed before B and 3 $B$3:

You will also see this in the cell containing the formula:

| Enter |

Press

👉 **Copy the formula from cell C7 to cell C12 by using the fill handle** ✂25

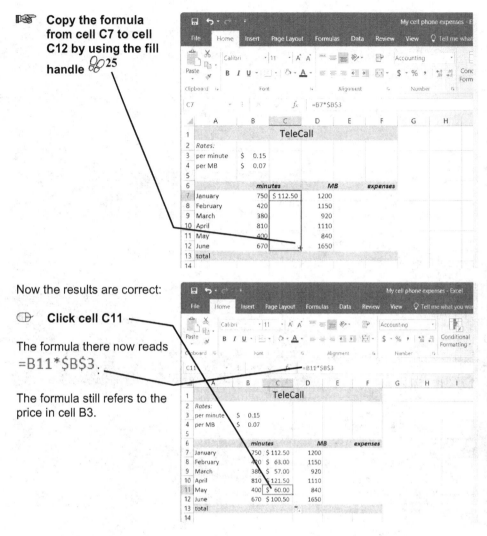

Now the results are correct:

👉 **Click cell C11**

The formula there now reads
=B11*$B$3.

The formula still refers to the price in cell B3.

This is called a *mixed reference* because it includes both a relative reference to B11 and an absolute reference to $B$3.

The costs per MB are calculated the same way with the following formula:

👉 **Type in cell E7 the formula =D7*B4** ✂22

Check the result:
1200*0.07=84

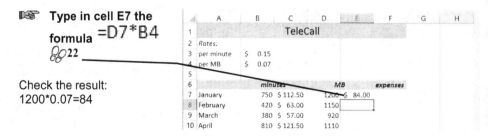

The price per MB in cell B4 is a fixed value valid for all months:

☞ **Change the reference to cell B4 to an absolute one** ✍38

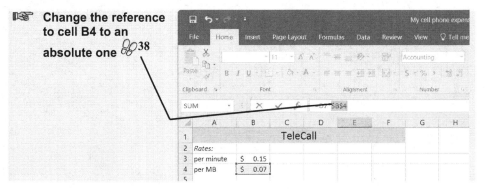

💡 **Tip**

Locking rows or columns
You can lock just the row or column. To do this, put a $ character before the row or column indicator. So for example $A3 to lock column A or A$3 to lock row 3. If you press F4 multiple times in a formula, you will also see these options..

☞ **Copy the formula from E7 to E8:E12** ✍25

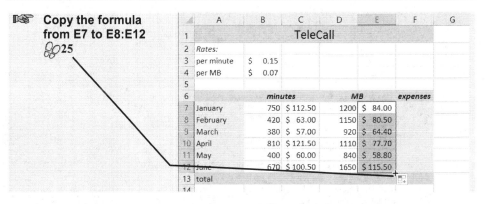

The total costs per month equal the costs of the call plus the costs of using the internet:

☞ **Type the formula to add up the amounts in C7 and E7 in cell F7** ✍22

☞ **Copy the formula from F7 to F8:F12** ✍25

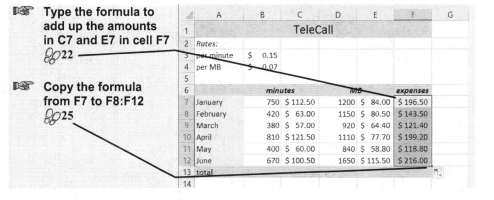

☞ **Have the costs added up using the *Sum* function** 𝒬𝒬23

The total costs equal $995.40:

	A	B	C	D	E	F	G
1			TeleCall				
2	Rates:						
3	per minute	$ 0.15					
4	per MB	$ 0.07					
5							
6			minutes		MB	expenses	
7	January		750 $ 112.50	1200	$ 84.00	$ 196.50	
8	February		420 $ 63.00	1150	$ 80.50	$ 143.50	
9	March		380 $ 57.00	920	$ 64.40	$ 121.40	
10	April		810 $ 121.50	1110	$ 77.70	$ 199.20	
11	May		400 $ 60.00	840	$ 58.80	$ 118.80	
12	June		670 $ 100.50	1650	$ 115.50	$ 216.00	
13	total					$ 995.40	
14							

2.4 Nested Formulas

So far you have been using formulas with only two references. Often you will need to create more complex formulas and then it is important to know what the order of processing is. *Excel* uses the same operator precedence as in mathematics. If there are multiple mathematical symbols in a single formula, *Excel* will perform the operations in the following order:

First: Raise to a power
Then: Multiply
             Divide
             Extraction of roots
             Add and subtract

In case of similar commands, they are processed from left to right.

Some examples:
5*10-20   The result is 30, because 5*10=50-20=30
20-5*10   The result is -30, because first 5*10 is calculated = 50, which then is subtracted from 20
5*10-20/2   The result = 40
               First, 5*10 is calculated = 50
               Then, 20/2 is calculated = 10
               Finally, 10 is subtracted from 50

The order of the calculation also determines the outcome. To deviate from this default order, you have to place the parts of the formula between parentheses. Terms inside parentheses are always calculated first, for example:

5*2+8   The result is 18, because 5*2=10+8=18
5*(2+8)   The result is 50, because first 2+8 is calculated =10, which then is multiplied by 5

Formulas with parentheses are called *nested formulas*. To gain even more control over your formulas, you can place parentheses inside one another; this is called *nesting parentheses*. *Excel* always evaluates the innermost set of parentheses first. These will be calculated from left to right.

You will now use this information to create a formula for the provider *BelAbo*. Let's say, you subscribed to a fixed plan of $25.00 with this provider that gives you 250 minutes and 500 MB per month. Excess use is charged at $0.20 per minute and $0.10 per MB.

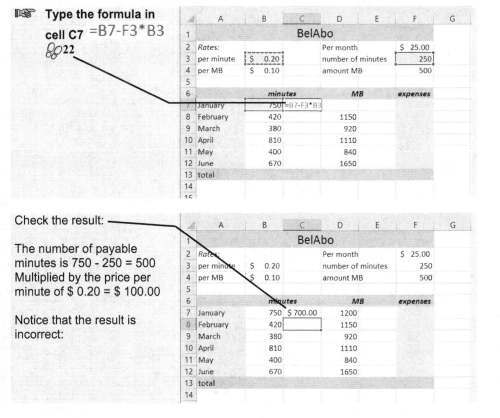

☞ Go to the BelAbo worksheet ✂41

⌨ In cell B3, type: 0.20

⌨ In cell B4, type: 0.10

☞ Type the data from this example in cells D2 to F4 ✂17

	A	B	C	D	E	F	G
1				BelAbo			
2	Rates:			Per month		$ 25.00	
3	per minute	$ 0.20		number of minutes		250	
4	per MB	$ 0.10		amount MB		500	
5							
6			minutes		MB		expenses
7	January	750		1200			
8	February	420		1150			
9	March	380		920			
10	April	810		1110			
11	May	400		840			
12	June	670		1650			
13	total						
14							

In order to calculate the costs of calling, you need to take into account the first 250 minutes that are free each month. In the formula, you will need to subtract them from the number of minutes called:

☞ Type the formula in cell C7 =B7-F3*B3 ✂22

	A	B	C	D	E	F	G
1				BelAbo			
2	Rates:			Per month		$ 25.00	
3	per minute	$ 0.20		number of minutes		250	
4	per MB	$ 0.10		amount MB		500	
5							
6			minutes		MB		expenses
7	January		750 =B7-F3*B3				
8	February	420		1150			
9	March	380		920			
10	April	810		1110			
11	May	400		840			
12	June	670		1650			
13	total						
14							
15							

Check the result:

The number of payable minutes is 750 - 250 = 500 Multiplied by the price per minute of $ 0.20 = $ 100.00

Notice that the result is incorrect:

	A	B	C	D	E	F	G
1				BelAbo			
2	Rates:			Per month		$ 25.00	
3	per minute	$ 0.20		number of minutes		250	
4	per MB	$ 0.10		amount MB		500	
5							
6			minutes		MB		expenses
7	January		750 $ 700.00	1200			
8	February	420		1150			
9	March	380		920			
10	April	810		1110			
11	May	400		840			
12	June	670		1650			
13	total						
14							

The result is incorrect, because *Excel* first calculates the multiplication F3*B3=50 and subtracts that from B7. This results in 700. To have the number of payable minutes calculated first, place B7-F3 between parentheses:

☞ **Click cell C7**

In the formula bar:

⌨ **Type a left parenthesis character before B7:** (

⌨ **Type a right parenthesis character after F3:**)

You will see: $=(B7-F3)*B3$

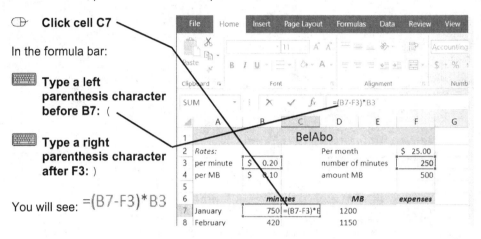

💡 **Tip**

Colors in formulas

In the formula you will see different colors $=(B7-F3)*B3$ for the cell references. You will also see these colors in the worksheet.

This way, you can see which cell is referred to in the formula:

The result is displayed in the green outlined cell:

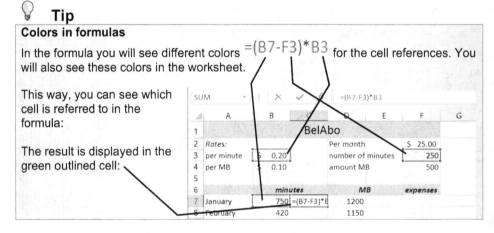

Enter

⌨ **Press**

Notice that the result is now correct: $ 100.00

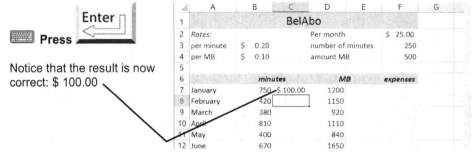

To copy the formula to the following months, you should now make two references absolute: not only the price per minute, but also the number of free minutes per month. These are after all valid each month. You do this in the same way as shown before:

⊕ **Click cell C7**

In the formula bar:

☞ **Change the reference to cell F3 to an absolute one** 𝒮𝒮38

☞ **Change the reference to cell B3 to an absolute one** 𝒮𝒮38

The formula is now:
=(B7-$F$3)*$B$3:

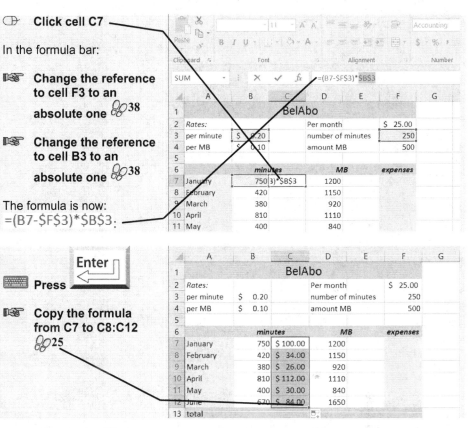

Enter

■ **Press**

☞ **Copy the formula from C7 to C8:C12** 𝒮𝒮25

💡 **Tip**

Enter nested formulas step by step
Creating nested formulas can be tricky, especially when it contains references to absolute cells. That is why it is best not to enter the formula all at once, but do it a step at a time as you learned to do in the above examples. Especially when using complex formulas, it is almost impossible to enter them at once without errors.

The costs per MB are calculated in the same manner using the following formula:

☞ **Type the formula in cell E7** =D7-F4*B4 𝒮𝒮22

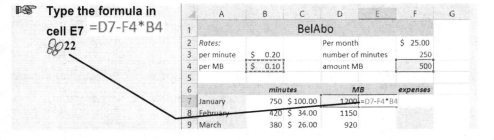

Place the parentheses in the formula to first calculate the amount of payable MB and then make the reference absolute:

In the formula bar:

☞ **Place** =D7-F4
between parentheses
𝒪𝒪39

☞ **Change the**
references to cells F4
and B4 to absolute
𝒪𝒪38

The formula is now:
=(D7-$F$4)*$B$4

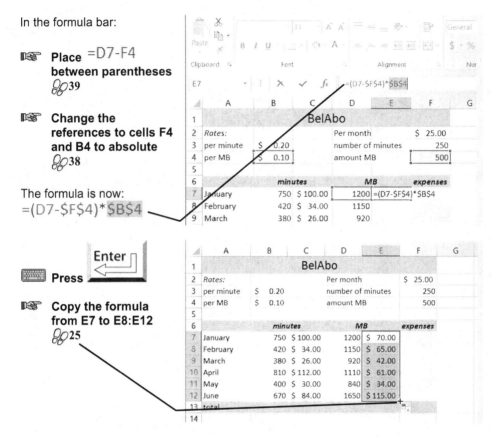

☞ **Press** Enter

☞ **Copy the formula**
from E7 to E8:E12
𝒪𝒪25

The total costs per month equal the costs of the cell phone plan plus the costs of calling and using the Internet:

☞ **In cell F7 type the**
formula: =C7+E7+F2
𝒪𝒪22

The cell phone plan has a
fixed monthly fee of $25.00:

☞ **In the formula bar,**
change the references
to F2 to absolute
𝒪𝒪38

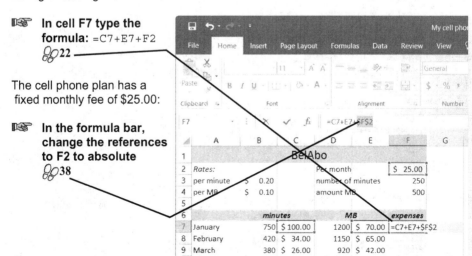

☞ **Copy the formula from F7 to F8:F12** $\%25$

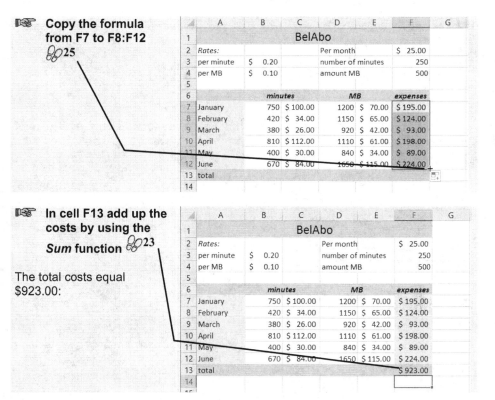

☞ **In cell F13 add up the costs by using the**

Sum function $\%23$

The total costs equal $923.00:

Before you continue, it is a good idea to save the workbook.

☞ **Save the workbook** $\%40$

2.5 References to other Worksheets

To be able to quickly and easily compare providers, you can create a new worksheet which only shows the names of providers and the total costs.

☞ **Add a new worksheet** $\%11$

☞ **Place the worksheet, if necessary, after the last sheet** $\%15$

☞ **Rename that sheet to** Recap $\%12$

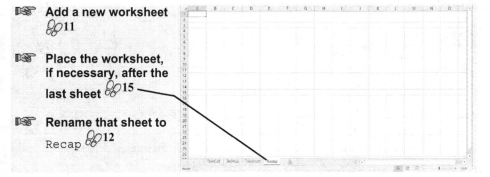

⌨️ **In cell A1, type:**
`Provider`

⌨️ **In cell B1, type:** `Costs`

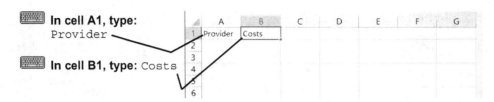

You do not have to type the name of the provider again. You can use a formula to refer to the name on the worksheet:

⌨️ **In cell A2, type:** =

☞ **Go to the** TeleCall **worksheet** ✂41

The name of the provider is in cell A1:

👆 **Click in cell A1**

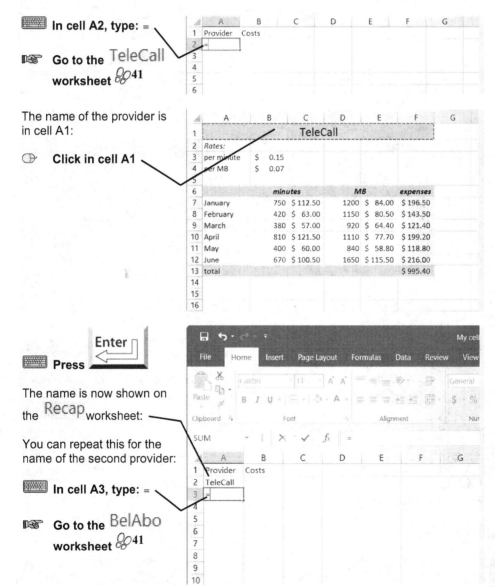

⌨️ **Press** Enter

The name is now shown on the Recap worksheet:

You can repeat this for the name of the second provider:

⌨️ **In cell A3, type:** =

☞ **Go to the** BelAbo **worksheet** ✂41

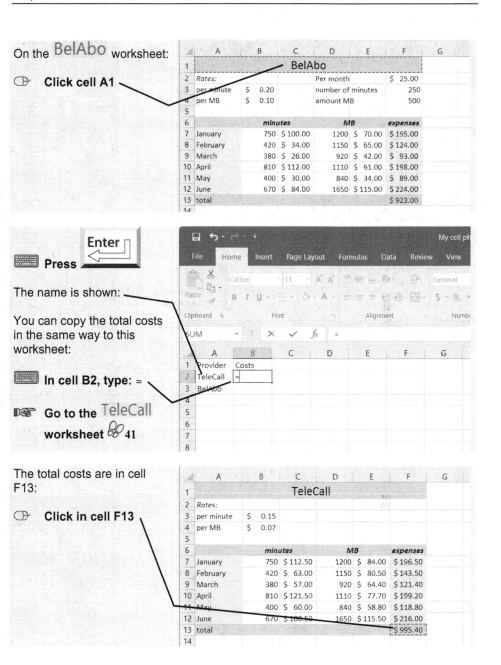

On the BelAbo worksheet:

☞ **Click cell A1**

	A	B	C	D	E	F	G
1				BelAbo			
2	Rates:			Per month		$ 25.00	
3	per minute	$ 0.20		number of minutes		250	
4	per MB	$ 0.10		amount MB		500	
5							
6			minutes		MB	expenses	
7	January		750 $ 100.00	1200	$ 70.00	$ 195.00	
8	February		420 $ 34.00	1150	$ 65.00	$ 124.00	
9	March		380 $ 26.00	920	$ 42.00	$ 93.00	
10	April		810 $ 112.00	1110	$ 61.00	$ 198.00	
11	May		400 $ 30.00	840	$ 34.00	$ 89.00	
12	June		670 $ 84.00	1650	$ 115.00	$ 224.00	
13	total					$ 923.00	
14							

Press Enter ⏎

The name is shown:

You can copy the total costs in the same way to this worksheet:

⌨ **In cell B2, type:** =

☞ **Go to the** TeleCall **worksheet** ✂41

	A	B	C	D	E	F	G
1	Provider	Costs					
2	TeleCall	=					
3	BelAbo						
4							
5							
6							
7							
8							

The total costs are in cell F13:

☞ **Click in cell F13**

	A	B	C	D	E	F	G
1				TeleCall			
2	Rates:						
3	per minute	$ 0.15					
4	per MB	$ 0.07					
5							
6			minutes		MB	expenses	
7	January		750 $ 112.50	1200	$ 84.00	$ 196.50	
8	February		420 $ 63.00	1150	$ 80.50	$ 143.50	
9	March		380 $ 57.00	920	$ 64.40	$ 121.40	
10	April		810 $ 121.50	1110	$ 77.70	$ 199.20	
11	May		400 $ 60.00	840	$ 58.80	$ 118.80	
12	June		670 $ 100.50	1650	$ 115.50	$ 216.00	
13	total					$ 995.40	
14							

Press Enter

You will see the costs:

Do the same for the costs by *BelAbo*:

In cell B3, type: =

⊕ **Click** BelAbo

⊕ **Click cell F13**

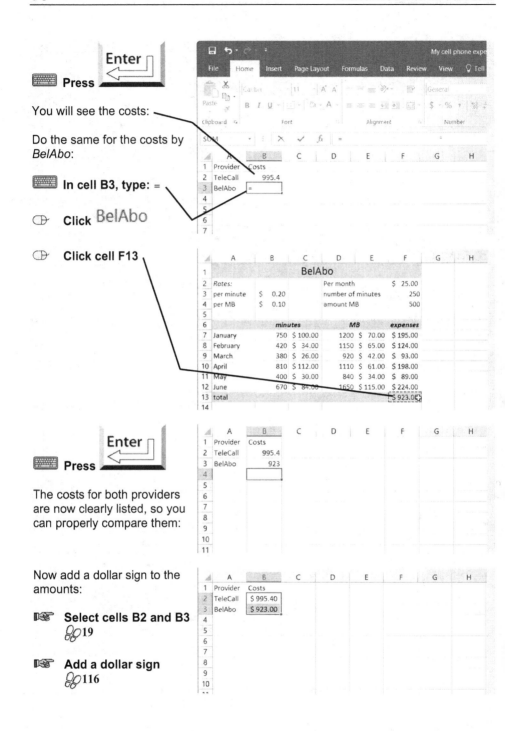

Press Enter

The costs for both providers are now clearly listed, so you can properly compare them:

Now add a dollar sign to the amounts:

☞ **Select cells B2 and B3**
🦶19

☞ **Add a dollar sign**
🦶116

Tip

Sheet and folder references in formulas

If you select a cell with a formula, you can also see the reference to the worksheet in the formula:

In cell B2 you see

=TeleCall!F13

This refers to cell F13 on the *TeleCall* worksheet. The exclamation mark is the separator. You do not have to fill this in yourself.

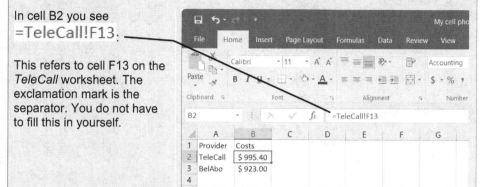

In the same way, you can create references to other workbooks. The reference may look like this, for example: ='[Profit report.xlsx]Sheet1'!$B$3 . This is a reference to:

- the *Profit report* workbook
- sheet1
- cell B3

It is preferable to create the formula by clicking the cells. You can type these references yourself, but this greatly increases the chance of errors.

The cells in the *Recap* worksheet are linked to the other sheets. If *TeleCall* reduces the price per minute to $0.12, you can see right away whether this provider is cheaper or not:

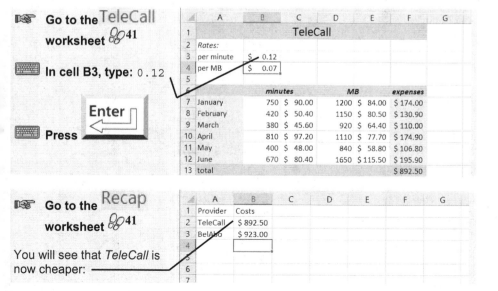

☞ **Go to the** TeleCall **worksheet** ✍41

▨ **In cell B3, type:** 0.12

Enter

▨ **Press**

☞ **Go to the** Recap **worksheet** ✍41

You will see that *TeleCall* is now cheaper:

2.6 Percentages

If you want to know how much more expensive *BelAbo* is compared to *TeleCall*, you can calculate the price difference. This can be expressed as a percentage:

☞ **In cell B4, deduct the costs of *TeleCall* from those of *BelAbo*** ✂22

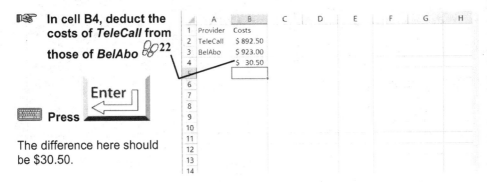

Press Enter

The difference here should be $30.50.

In cell C4, express this as a percentage of the costs of *TeleCall*:

☞ **In cell C4, divide the difference by the costs of *TeleCall*** ✂22

The formula should be:

$$=B4/B2$$

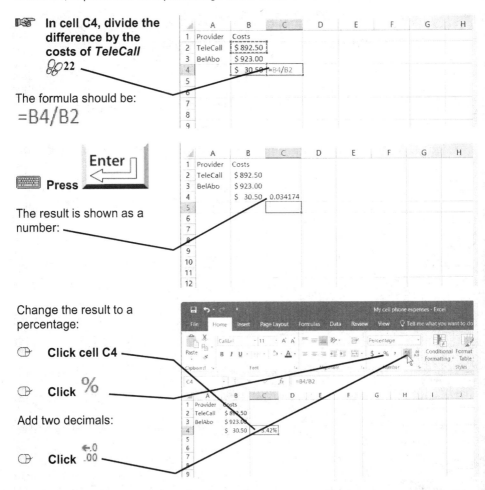

Press Enter

The result is shown as a number:

Change the result to a percentage:

☞ **Click cell C4**

☞ **Click %**

Add two decimals:

☞ **Click .00**

2.7 Adding Hyperlinks

Just as on the Internet, you can use hyperlinks in *Excel* to quickly navigate to another sheet, another book or a web page. Here is how to turn cell A2 into a hyperlink to go directly to the *TeleCall* sheet:

☞ **Click cell A2**

☞ **Click tab** Insert

☞ **Click** Hyperlink

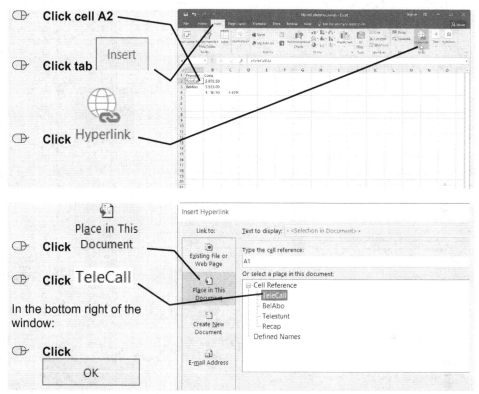

☞ **Click** Place in This Document

☞ **Click** TeleCall

In the bottom right of the window:

☞ **Click** OK

Tip

Another location on the worksheet
By default, the hyperlink will refer to cell A1 on the chosen worksheet. But you can easily change the cell reference:

By Type the cell reference **type the cell the hyperlink should refer to**

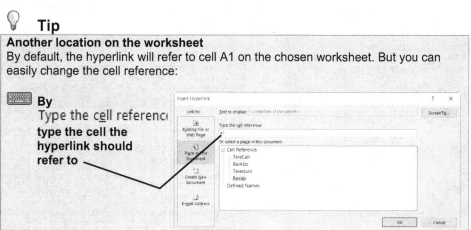

The text in the cell has now become a hyperlink:

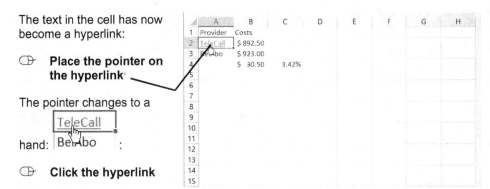

☞ **Place the pointer on the hyperlink**

The pointer changes to a hand:

☞ **Click the hyperlink**

The *TeleCall* worksheet will be opened:

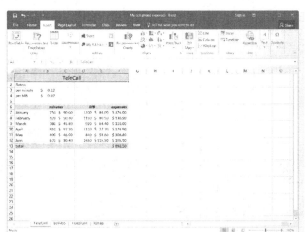

☞ **Go to the** Recap **worksheet** ⚓41

This is how to remove a hyperlink:

☞ **If necessary, click the cell with the hyperlink**

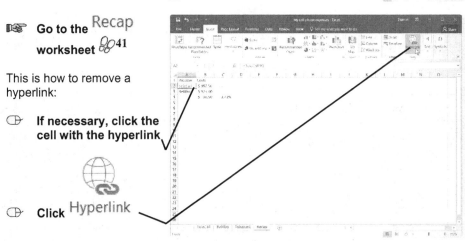

☞ **Click** Hyperlink

➥ Please note:

You must first select the cell that contains the hyperlink before you can remove it.

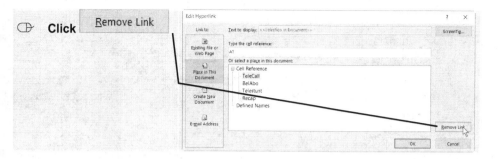

Click   Remove Link

2.8 Protecting a Worksheet

Once a worksheet is ready, you can protect it to prevent someone from accidentally changing the formulas or otherwise tampering with the data. This is how to protect a worksheet:

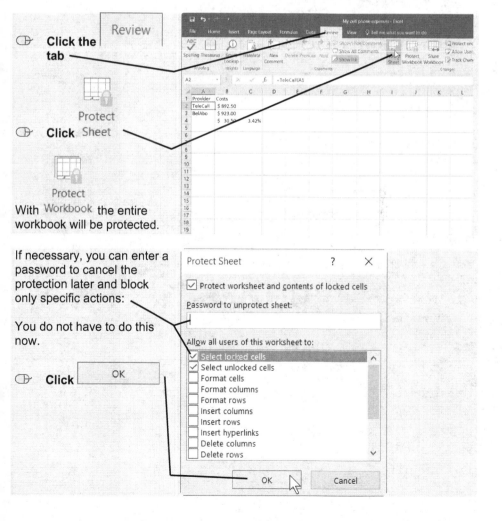

Click the tab   Review

Click   Protect Sheet

With Protect Workbook the entire workbook will be protected.

If necessary, you can enter a password to cancel the protection later and block only specific actions:

You do not have to do this now.

Click   OK

⤷ Please note:

Be careful with assigning passwords. If you enter a password and you cannot remember it later on, you will not be able to change anything!

The button Protect Sheet is

replaced by Unprotect Sheet :

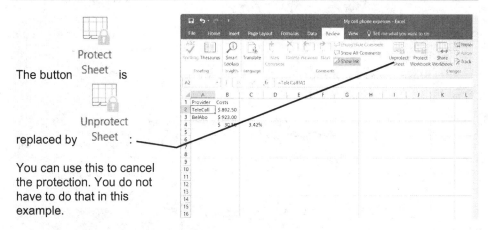

You can use this to cancel the protection. You do not have to do that in this example.

Try to see if you can change anything:

☞ **Click a cell**

⌨ **Type a letter or number**

An error message will pop up right away:

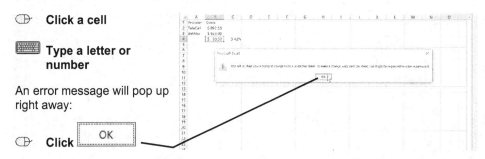

☞ **Click** OK

Nothing in this sheet can be changed any more. This protection is not needed for the moment as the data on this sheet is automatically updated from the other worksheets.

You can turn off the protection for certain areas of the worksheet:

☞ **Go to the** TeleCall **worksheet** ♻41

☞ **Select cells B3:B4** ♻19

☞ **Click** Allow Users to Edit Rar

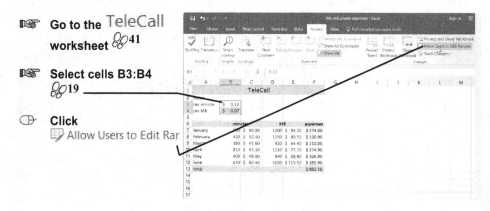

Now indicate the areas that do not need to be protected:

☞ **Click** New...

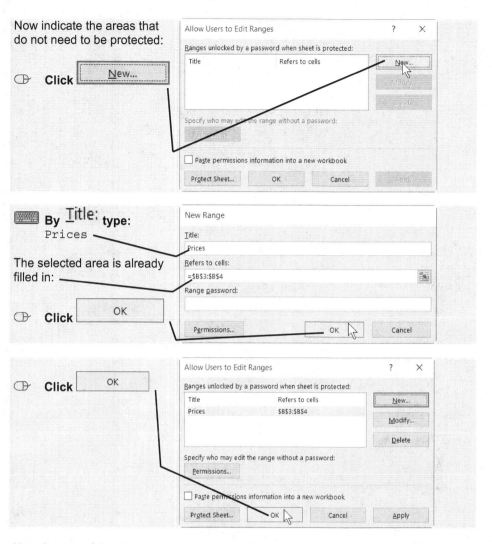

⌨ **By** Title: **type:**
Prices

The selected area is already filled in:

☞ **Click** OK

☞ **Click** OK

Now the rest of the sheet can be protected:

☞ **Click** Protect Sheet

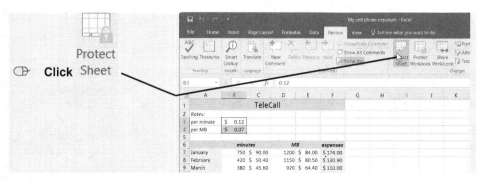

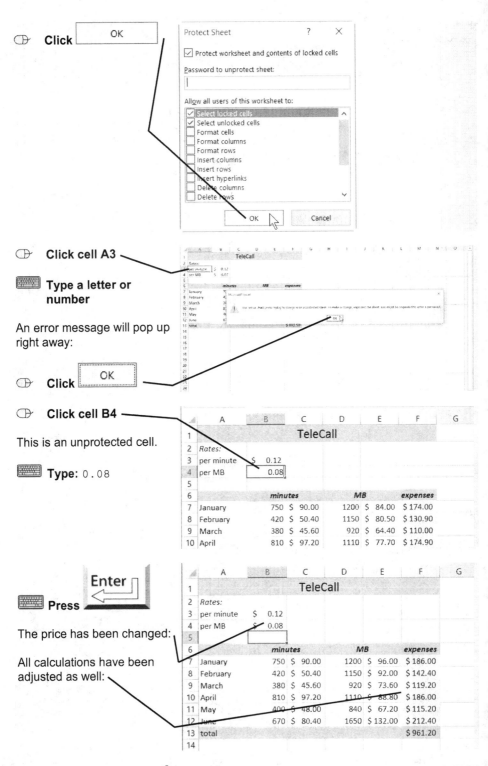

👆 **Click** [OK]

👆 **Click cell A3**

⌨ **Type a letter or number**

An error message will pop up right away:

👆 **Click** [OK]

👆 **Click cell B4**

This is an unprotected cell.

⌨ **Type:** 0.08

⌨ **Press** [Enter]

The price has been changed:

All calculations have been adjusted as well:

👉 **Save the workbook** ⌨⌨40

2.9 Changing Options

When opening a new workbook, several options are shown by default. These options allow you to change many settings yourself:

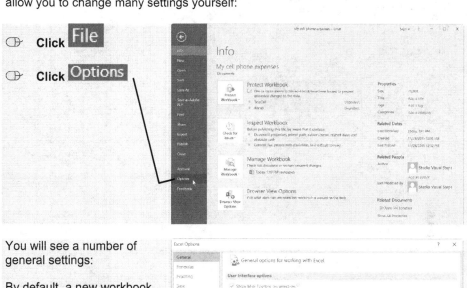

☞ Click **File**

☞ Click **Options**

You will see a number of general settings:

By default, a new workbook has a single worksheet. Change this to two sheets:

☞ **By**
Include this many sheets:

   click ▲

Now it reads 2. A new workbook will now contain two worksheets.

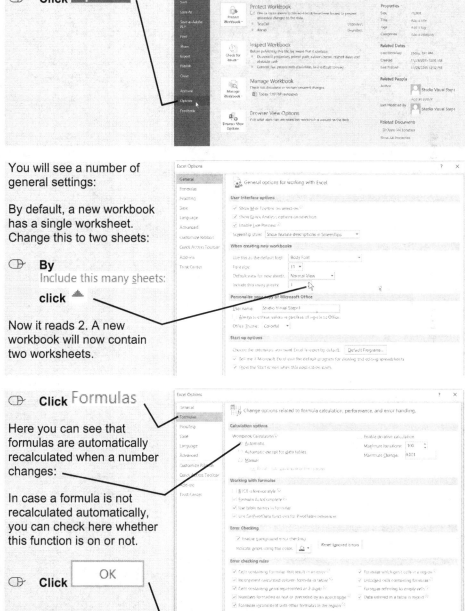

☞ Click **Formulas**

Here you can see that formulas are automatically recalculated when a number changes:

In case a formula is not recalculated automatically, you can check here whether this function is on or not.

☞ Click **OK**

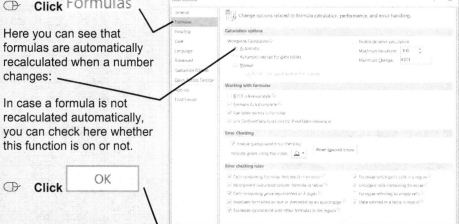

Tip

View the settings
Do you want to know more about the available default settings? Then check out some of the other options listed on the left.

Open a new workbook:

☞ **Click** File

☞ **Click** New

☞ **Click**

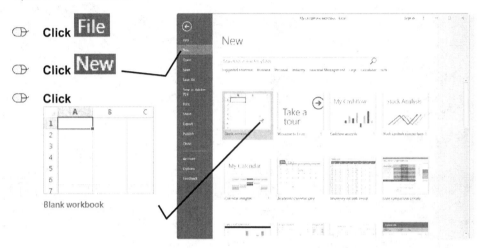

Blank workbook

The new workbook has two worksheets:

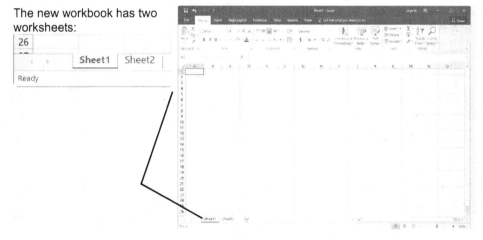

Change the default number of worksheets back to one again:

☞ **Click** File

☞ **Click** Options

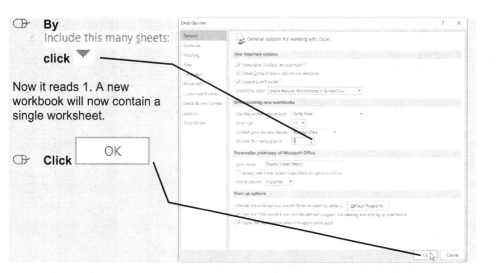

By
Include this many sheets:

click ▼

Now it reads 1. A new workbook will now contain a single worksheet.

Click | OK

2.10 Special Series

In *Section 2.2 AutoFill* you learned how to automatically fill a column with a series of subsequent items. That was done on the basis of one or two typed values. *Excel* understands many other series of numbers or text-and-number combinations that can save you a lot of typing with the built-in *AutoFill* function. Not just days or months, but other numbers, dates or even your own lists. In this section you will learn more about these options.

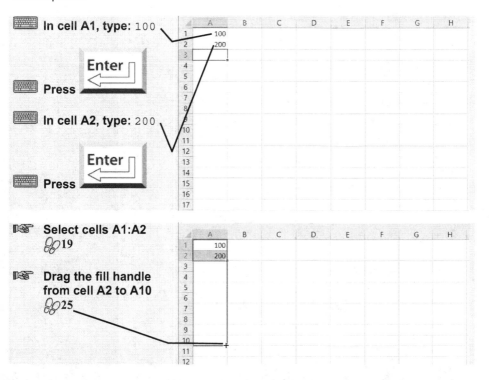

In cell A1, type: 100

Press **Enter**

In cell A2, type: 200

Press **Enter**

Select cells A1:A2
℧℧19

Drag the fill handle from cell A2 to A10
℧℧25

The series is appended
automatically: ────────

☞ **Click in cell C1**

⌨ **Type:** 2/10/2016

Enter

⌨ **Press**

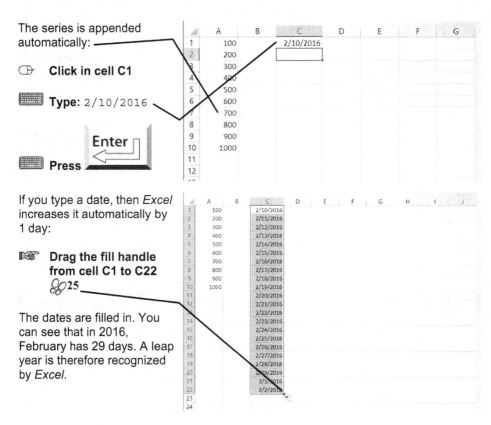

If you type a date, then *Excel*
increases it automatically by
1 day:

☞ **Drag the fill handle
   from cell C1 to C22**
   🖉**25**

The dates are filled in. You
can see that in 2016,
February has 29 days. A leap
year is therefore recognized
by *Excel*.

If you want to create a list of working days, you may want to eliminate the dates that fall
in the weekend right from the start. *Excel* can do that automatically as well:

⌨ **In cell E1, type:**
   2/10/2016

Enter

⌨ **Press**

☞ **Select cells E1:E22**
   🖉**19**

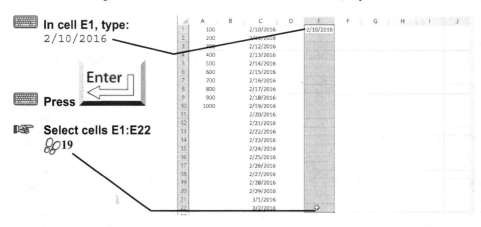

🢑 **Please note:**

This time, do not use the fill handle to select cells.

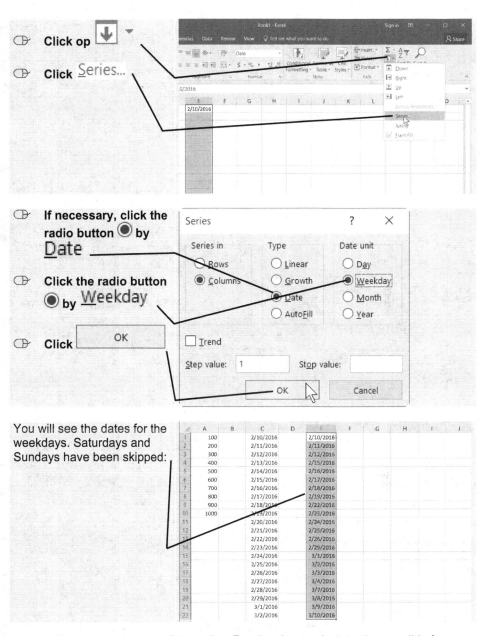

☞ **Click op** ⬇ ▾

☞ **Click** _Series..._

☞ **If necessary, click the radio button ◉ by**
Date

☞ **Click the radio button**
◉ by _Weekday_

☞ **Click** OK

You will see the dates for the weekdays. Saturdays and Sundays have been skipped:

Beyond the standard series of items that *Excel* understands, it is also possible for you to enter your own series. For example, you can create a series with colors:

☞ **Click** File

☞ **Click** Options

⊕ **Click** Advanced

⊕ **Drag the scroll bar
downwards**

⊕ **Click**

Edit Cus̲t̲om Lists...

You will see the existing
series:

⊕ **Click the box under
List e̲ntries:**

⌨ **Type:** red, white,
blue

⊕ **Click** Add

The series has been added:

⊕ **Click**

OK

⊕ **In the next window, click** OK

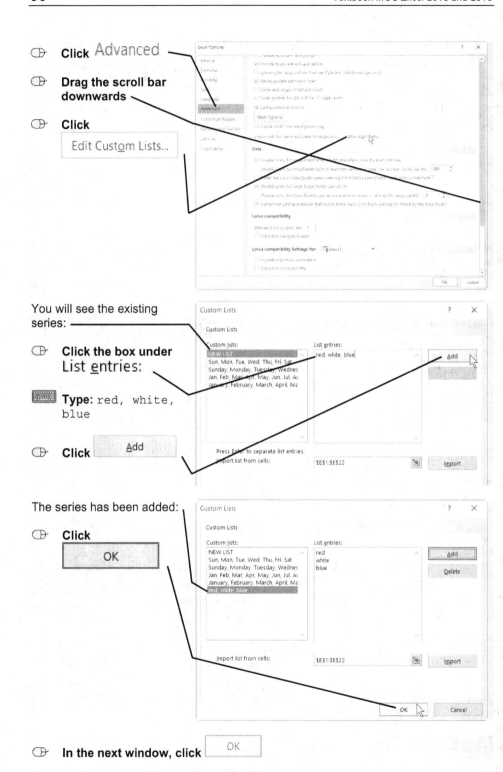

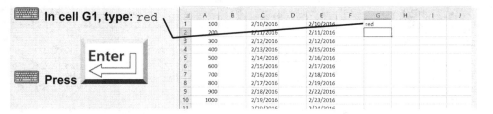

In cell G1, type: red

Enter

Press

You can create series both vertically and horizontally. To create a horizontal series:

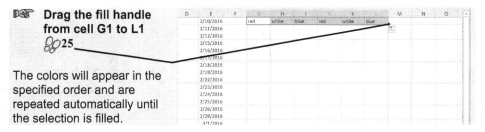

☞ **Drag the fill handle from cell G1 to L1** ✂25

The colors will appear in the specified order and are repeated automatically until the selection is filled.

This chapter has shown you how to create more complex formulas and how to automatically fill a series with subsequent items. In the following chapter you will get acquainted with data tables and other standard functions in *Excel*.

You can close *Excel* for now. You have already saved the changes to the My cell phone costs workbook. You do not need to save the exercises in this last worksheet.

☞ **Close *Excel* without saving the changes to the workbooks** ✂16

2.11 Exercise

To learn how to quickly apply what you have just learned, you can do the following review exercises. Use the number beside the footsteps to look it up in the appendix *How Do I Do That Again?* at the end of the book.

Exercise: Formulas and series

In this exercise you can practice using formulas and series a bit more.

☞ Start *Excel* 🐾¹ and open a new blank workbook. 🐾²

☞ Enter the following data. 🐾¹⁷

	A	B	C	D	E
1	price gasoline	$ 1.60			
2	number of miles per year	15000			
3					
4		Car 1	Car 2	Car 3	
5	insurance and tax	480	620	600	
6					
7	number of miles per gallon	14	12	15	
8	amount of gallons of gasoline				
9	costs gasoline				
10					
11	costs per mile				
12					

First calculate the amount of gallons of gasoline for car 1:

☞ In B8, divide the *number of miles per year* by the *number of miles per gallon*. 🐾²²

☞ Copy the formula from B8 to C8:D8. 🐾²⁵

Notice that the results are incorrect.

☞ Change the reference to cell B2 to an absolute one in the formula in B8. 🐾³⁸

☞ Copy the formula from B8 once more to C8:D8. 🐾²⁵

The results are now correct.

☞ In cell B9, calculate the total gasoline costs by multiplying the *number of gallons of gasoline* by the *gasoline price*. 🐾²²

☞ Change the reference to the *gasoline* price to an absolute one. 🐾³⁸

☞ Copy the formula from B9 to C9:D9. 🐾²⁵

☞ If necessary: widen the columns where it reads ########. 🐾¹⁸

☞ The summary should look like this then:

	A	B	C	D	E
1	price gasoline	$ 1.60			
2	number of miles per year	15000			
3					
4		Car 1	Car 2	Car 3	
5	insurance and tax	480	620	600	
6					
7	number of miles per gallon	14	12	15	
8	amount of gallons of gasoline	1071.4286	1250	1000	
9	costs gasoline	$1,714.29	$2,000.00	$1,600.00	
10					
11	costs per mile				
12					

In order to calculate the total costs per mile, you have to add up the *costs for insurance and tax* to the *gasoline costs* and divide that by the number of miles per year:

☞ In cell B11, enter the formula =B5+B9/B2 . 🐾22

Notice that the result, $480.11 cannot be the price per mile. Because *Excel* performs the division in the formula first, the result is incorrect. The addition should be performed first, thus you need to place it between parentheses.

☞ Change the formula to =(B5+B9)/B2 . 🐾39

Furthermore, the reference to the number of miles per year has to become an absolute one in order to be able to copy the formula to the other cars.

☞ Change the reference to B2 to an absolute one in the formula in cell B11. 🐾38

☞ Copy the formula from B11 to C11:D11. 🐾25

In order to see an accurate price, have *Excel* show an extra decimal.

☞ Select B11:D11. 🐾19

☞ Show an extra decimal. 🐾21

☞ Car 1 is the cheapest per mile:

	A	B	C	D	E
1	price gasoline	$ 1.60			
2	number of miles per year	15000			
3					
4		Car 1	Car 2	Car 3	
5	insurance and tax	480	620	600	
6					
7	number of miles per gallon	14	12	15	
8	amount of gallons of gasoline	1071.4286	1250	1000	
9	costs gasoline	$1,714.29	$2,000.00	$1,600.00	
10					
11	costs per mile	$ 0.146	$ 0.175	$ 0.147	

☞ Copy *Sheet 1* to a new worksheet. 🐾37

☞ In the new worksheet, change the gasoline price to $ 2.00. ✂️**17**

☞ Car 3 is now the cheapest:

	A	B	C	D	E
1	price gasoline	$ 2.00			
2	number of miles per year	15000			
3					
4		Car 1	Car 2	Car 3	
5	insurance and tax	480	620	600	
6					
7	number of miles per gallon	14	12	15	
8	amount of gallons of gasoline	1071.4286	1250	1000	
9	costs gasoline	$ 2,142.86	$ 2,500.00	$ 2,000.00	
10					
11	costs per mile	$ 0.175	$ 0.208	$ 0.173	

☞ Save the workbook with the name *Car costs*. ✂️**33**

☞ Add a new worksheet. ✂️**11**

☞ In cell A1, type red ✂️**17**

☞ Drag the fill handle to A3. ✂️**42**

You will now see the colors of the Dutch flag. Even if you do not begin with the first item of the series, you can still use the fill handle.

☞ In cell C1, type white ✂️**17**

☞ Drag the fill handle to C3. ✂️**42**

The colors start with white and now you will see the colors of the Russian flag: white, blue and red.

☞ Close *Excel* without saving the changes. ✂️**16**

2.12 Tips

 Tip

Create series by using the right mouse button
A faster way to create a series of subsequent items is by dragging with the right
mouse button. This is how to create a list with only the weekdays:

⌨ **Type the first day**

☞ **With the right mouse
button, drag the fill
handle through the
cells where the list
should be**

You will see a drop down
menu appear:

☞ **Click** Fill Weekdays

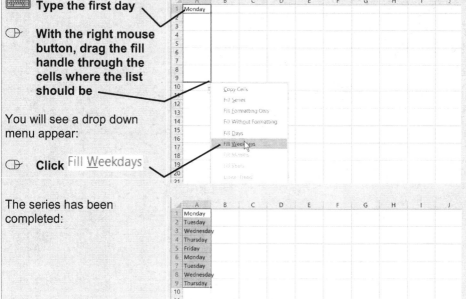

The series has been
completed:

 Tip

Automatic backup
Excel regularly creates a backup while you are working. You can adjust the time and
location of this backup:

☞ **Click** File

☞ **Click** Options

☞ **Click** Save

Set the time here:
Save AutoRecover informati

Set the location here:
AutoRecover file location:

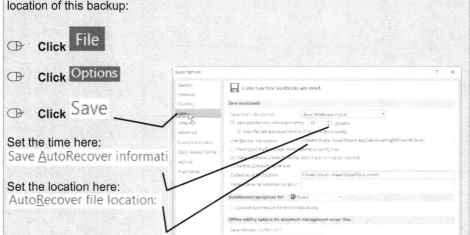

Notes

Write your notes down here.

3. Tables

If you want to begin a new worksheet, it may not be necessary to start from scratch and set it up yourself. There are many templates available for *Excel* that feature commonly used calculations and summaries. In many cases, you can also import data from other programs or computers into *Excel*.

A worksheet can often be quite large and may contain multiple complex summaries. By turning an individual summary into a table, you can adjust it without changing the rest of the worksheet. Cells, columns and rows that you insert do not change the entire worksheet, but only the selected table. You can design tables with different styles, so they are clearly recognizable. If you have a very large table, it can also be sorted and filtered so that you can easily view the pertinent information you need.

This chapter will teach you how to:

- download a template;
- import data;
- sort data;
- turn data into a table;
- select a table style;
- add rows and columns to a table;
- delete duplicates;
- sort within a table;
- filter data;
- use custom filters;
- name cells and tables;
- use *Go To*;
- find and replace data;
- convert a table into a range.

3.1 Downloading Templates

In the previous chapters you learned how to create a new *Excel* worksheet and how to open and edit worksheets that were already saved. There are lots of standard templates available that can be used for a variety of purposes. These are divided into different categories. Here is how you open a template in the *Personal* category:

☞ **Open** *Excel* ⁶⁶¹

You will see a few suggested templates right away. Select a different category:

☞ **Click** Personal

☞ **Click a template, for example**

Personal money tracker

You will see information about the template:

☞ **Click** Create

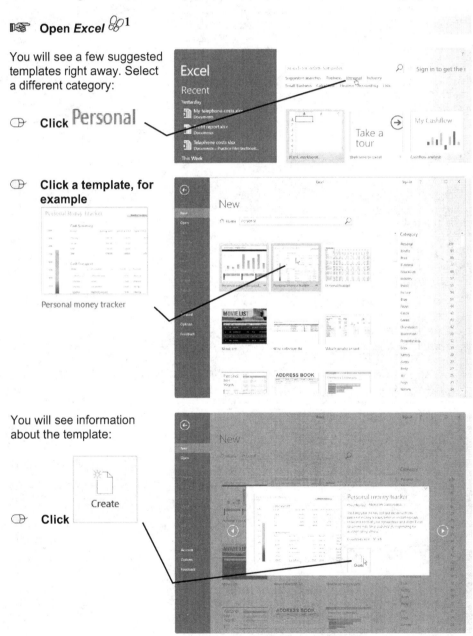

The template will be
downloaded and opened in
Excel:

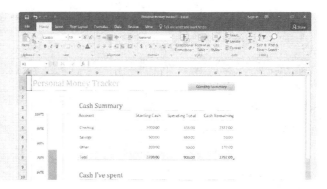

Templates are normal *Excel* workbooks created by specialists and nicely formatted.
Many companies also use their own templates to create summaries. You can edit the
templates as a normal workbook. For now, you do not have to do this and you can
simply close the template:

☞ Click **File**

☞ Click **Close**

A message may appear that
asks if you want to save your
changes:

☞ **If necessary, click**
Don't Save

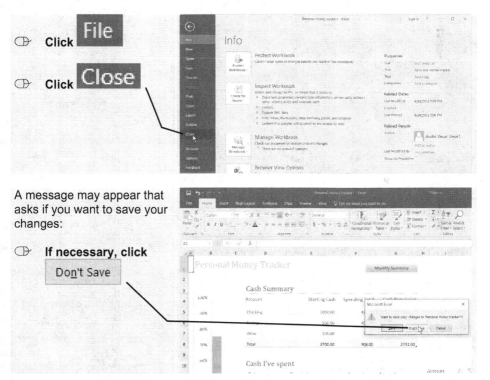

3.2 Importing Data

If the data you need has been created in another program, you may be able to import it
into the worksheet.

☞ **Open the** 🗎 Sales report.csv **practice file from the** *Practice Files Textbook*
Excel folder ⨒⁵⁰

You will see this summary:

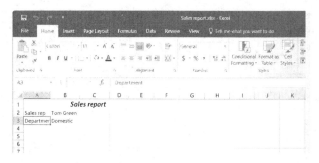

☞ **Save the folder in the *(My) Documents* folder with the name *Sales report Green* ௸33**

The sales data from *Tom Green* is listed in a text file. This text file may have been created on another computer, but you can still import the data from that file into cell A5:

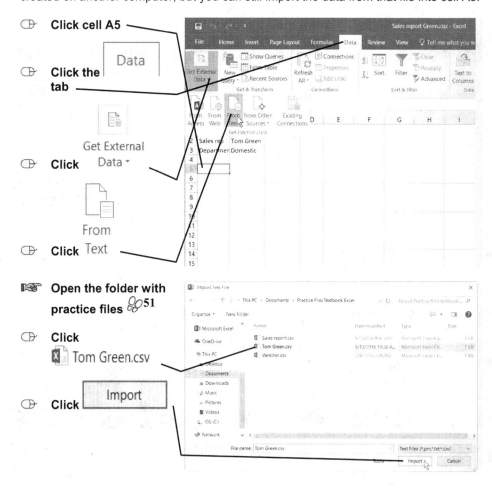

↻ **Click cell A5**

↻ **Click the** Data **tab**

↻ **Click** Get External Data ▾

↻ **Click** From Text

☞ **Open the folder with practice files ௸51**

↻ **Click** 🗎 Tom Green.csv

↻ **Click** Import

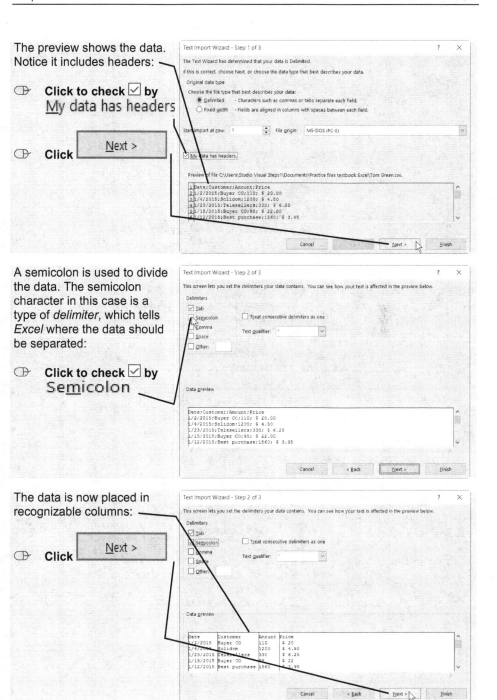

The preview shows the data. Notice it includes headers:

☞ **Click to check ☑ by**
   My data has headers

☞ **Click** Next >

A semicolon is used to divide the data. The semicolon character in this case is a type of *delimiter*, which tells *Excel* where the data should be separated:

☞ **Click to check ☑ by**
   Semicolon

The data is now placed in recognizable columns:

☞ **Click** Next >

Text, numbers and the date will automatically be recognized.

☞ **Click** Finish

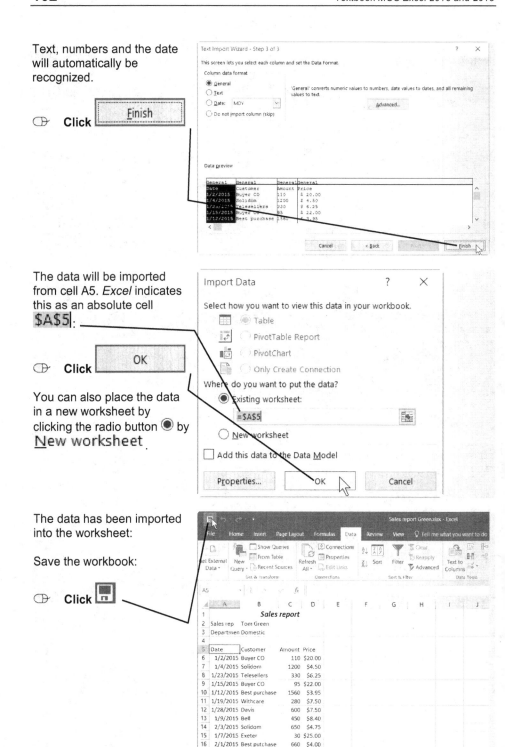

The data will be imported from cell A5. *Excel* indicates this as an absolute cell $A$5:

☞ **Click** OK

You can also place the data in a new worksheet by clicking the radio button ⦿ by New worksheet.

The data has been imported into the worksheet:

Save the workbook:

☞ **Click** 💾

3.3 Sorting

As you may know by now, *Excel* can do more than calculate numbers. You can also sort data in various ways. For example, you can sort the rows by customer name:

☞ **If necessary, click the**
Home **tab**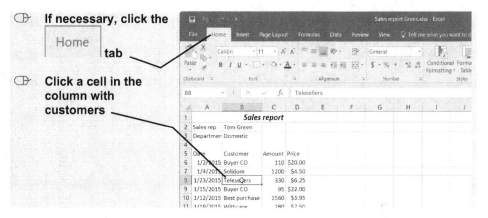

☞ **Click a cell in the**
column with
customers

🖐 Please note:

The selected cell determines what column will be sorted.

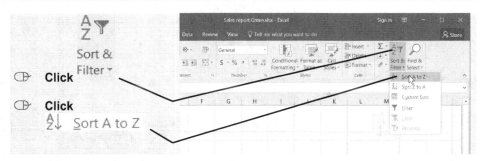

Sort &
Filter ▾

☞ **Click**

☞ **Click**
A↓ Sort A to Z

The customers have been
sorted in descending order:

The other cells in the rows
have also been sorted.

	A	B	C	D	E	F	G	H
1		*Sales report*						
2	Sales rep	Tom Green						
3	Departmen	Domestic						
4								
5	Date	Customer	Amount	Price				
6	1/9/2015	Bell	450	$8.40				
7	1/12/2015	Best purchase	1560	$3.95				
8	2/1/2015	Best purchase	660	$4.00				
9	1/2/2015	Buyer CO	110	$20.00				
10	1/15/2015	Buyer CO	95	$22.00				
11	1/28/2015	Davis	600	$7.50				
12	1/7/2015	Exeter	30	$25.00				
13	1/4/2015	Solidom	1200	$4.50				
14	2/3/2015	Solidom	650	$4.75				
15	1/23/2015	Telesellers	330	$6.25				
16	1/19/2015	Withcare	280	$7.50				

🖐 Please note:

Notice that only the orders have been sorted. The first few rows of data above have not. *Excel* sorts the area between two empty rows. A sort area therefore must not contain empty rows.

You can also sort in descending order. You can do that now with the numbers:

☞ **Click the column with amount**

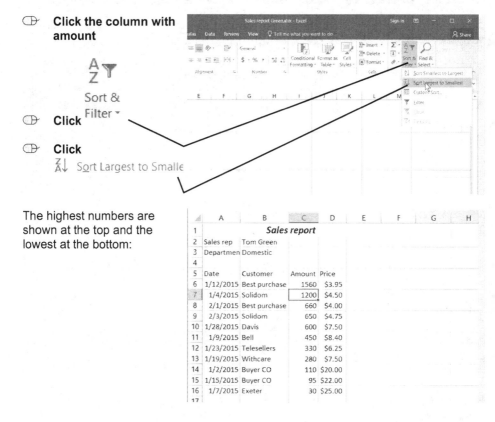

$\begin{array}{c} A \\ Z \end{array}$ ▼

Sort &

☞ **Click** Filter ▾

☞ **Click**

$\begin{array}{c} Z \\ A \end{array}$↓ Sort Largest to Smalle

The highest numbers are shown at the top and the lowest at the bottom:

	A	B	C	D
1		*Sales report*		
2	Sales rep	Tom Green		
3	Departmen	Domestic		
4				
5	Date	Customer	Amount	Price
6	1/12/2015	Best purchase	1560	$3.95
7	1/4/2015	Solidom	1200	$4.50
8	2/1/2015	Best purchase	660	$4.00
9	2/3/2015	Solidom	650	$4.75
10	1/28/2015	Davis	600	$7.50
11	1/9/2015	Bell	450	$8.40
12	1/23/2015	Telesellers	330	$6.25
13	1/19/2015	Withcare	280	$7.50
14	1/2/2015	Buyer CO	110	$20.00
15	1/15/2015	Buyer CO	95	$22.00
16	1/7/2015	Exeter	30	$25.00
17				

3.4 Working with Tables

Excel regards a worksheet as one whole. If you insert a column, then all the other columns shift to the right. Sometimes that is not the intention: you may only want to insert a column in a part of the rows. Look what happens when you insert a column labelled *District* between the *Date* and *Customer* columns:

☞ **Click the *Customer* column**

The new column should be inserted before that column.

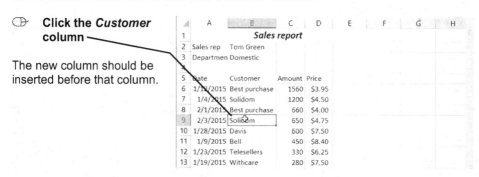

⌨ **By** 🔲 **Insert , click** ▾

⌨ **Click**
🔲 **Insert Sheet Colu**

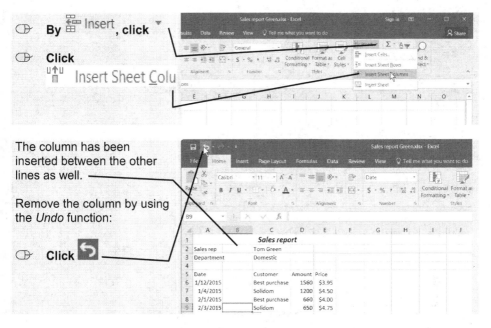

The column has been inserted between the other lines as well.

Remove the column by using the *Undo* function:

⌨ **Click** ↩️

If you only want to insert a column in the sales summary section of the worksheet (from row 5 downwards), you first have to convert that section into a table:

⌨ **Click the tab** | Insert

⌨ **Click** Table

Excel recognizes the table at once. Notice it has a green dotted line around it:

⌨ **Click** | OK

Please note: when you have a table without headers, you can remove the check ☑ by My table has headers.

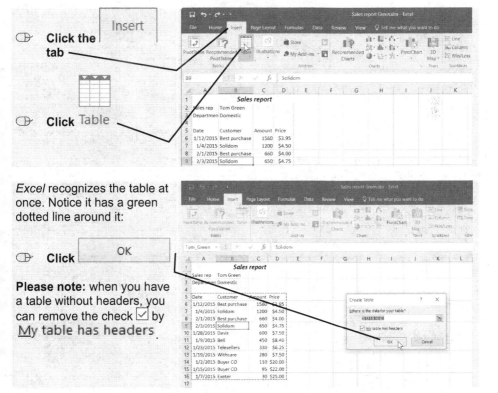

If you see this window:

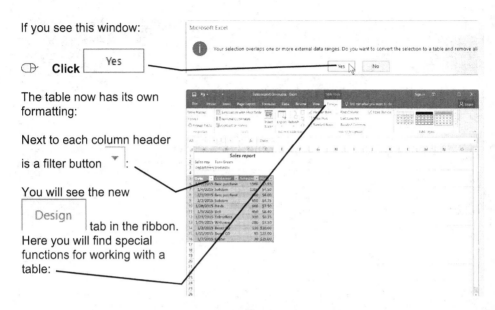

⊕ **Click** Yes

The table now has its own formatting:

Next to each column header

is a filter button ▼ :

You will see the new

Design tab in the ribbon. Here you will find special functions for working with a table:

You can easily adjust the formatting of this table:

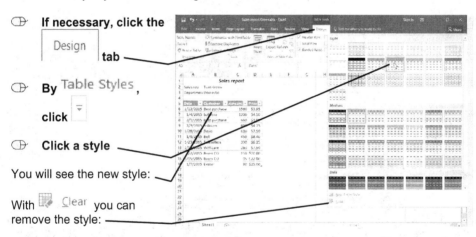

⊕ **If necessary, click the** Design **tab**

⊕ **By** Table Styles,

click ▼

⊕ **Click a style**

You will see the new style:

With ◱ Clear you can remove the style:

If you add new rows to the table, the table will grow automatically:

⊕ **Click D16**

This is the last cell of the table.

⌨ **Press** Tab

A row has been added to the table:

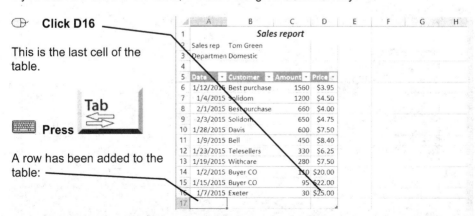

	A	B	C	D	E	F	G	H
1			*Sales report*					
2	Sales rep	Tom Green						
3	Departmen	Domestic						
4								
5	Date	Customer	Amount	Price				
6	1/12/2015	Best purchase	1560	$3.95				
7	1/4/2015	Solidom	1200	$4.50				
8	2/1/2015	Best purchase	660	$4.00				
9	2/3/2015	Solidom	650	$4.75				
10	1/28/2015	Davis	600	$7.50				
11	1/9/2015	Bell	450	$8.40				
12	1/23/2015	Telesellers	330	$6.25				
13	1/19/2015	Withcare	280	$7.50				
14	1/2/2015	Buyer CO	110	$20.00				
15	1/15/2015	Buyer CO	95	$22.00				
16	1/7/2015	Exeter	30	$25.00				
17								

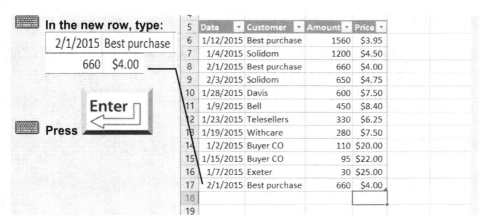

In the new row, type:

2/1/2015	Best purchase
660	$4.00

Press Enter

	Date	Customer	Amount	Price
5				
6	1/12/2015	Best purchase	1560	$3.95
7	1/4/2015	Solidom	1200	$4.50
8	2/1/2015	Best purchase	660	$4.00
9	2/3/2015	Solidom	650	$4.75
10	1/28/2015	Davis	600	$7.50
11	1/9/2015	Bell	450	$8.40
12	1/23/2015	Telesellers	330	$6.25
13	1/19/2015	Withcare	280	$7.50
14	1/2/2015	Buyer CO	110	$20.00
15	1/15/2015	Buyer CO	95	$22.00
16	1/7/2015	Exeter	30	$25.00
17	2/1/2015	Best purchase	660	$4.00
18				
19				

HELP! Another empty row appears.

When you press **Tab** instead of **Enter** by the price, then another empty row will be inserted below the table. Use ↩ (Undo) in the Quick Access toolbar to delete that row.

In the upper left corner of the window:

Click ↩

14	1/2/2015	Buyer CO	110	$20.00
15	1/15/2015	Buyer CO	95	$22.00
16	1/7/2015	Exeter	30	$25.00
17	2/1/2015	Best purchase	660	$4.00
18				
19				

You can also enlarge the table by inserting an additional column:

Drag the corner point ◢ **in the last cell one column to the right**

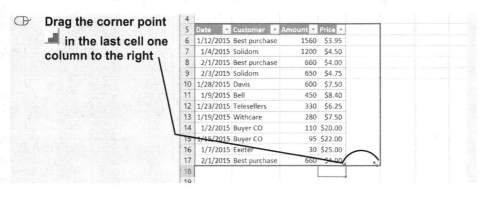

	Date	Customer	Amount	Price
4				
5				
6	1/12/2015	Best purchase	1560	$3.95
7	1/4/2015	Solidom	1200	$4.50
8	2/1/2015	Best purchase	660	$4.00
9	2/3/2015	Solidom	650	$4.75
10	1/28/2015	Davis	600	$7.50
11	1/9/2015	Bell	450	$8.40
12	1/23/2015	Telesellers	330	$6.25
13	1/19/2015	Withcare	280	$7.50
14	1/2/2015	Buyer CO	110	$20.00
15	1/15/2015	Buyer CO	95	$22.00
16	1/7/2015	Exeter	30	$25.00
17	2/1/2015	Best purchase	660	$4.00
18				
19				

This will be the column *Total*:

👉 **Click** Column

⌨ **Type:** Total

⌨ **Press** Enter

The total is the amount times the price:

⌨ **Type:** =

👉 **Click in cell C6**

⌨ **Type:** *

👉 **Click in cell D6**

Notice that instead of the cell indication, the name of the column is inserted:

⌨ **Press** Enter

The formula will automatically be copied to the next lines in the table:

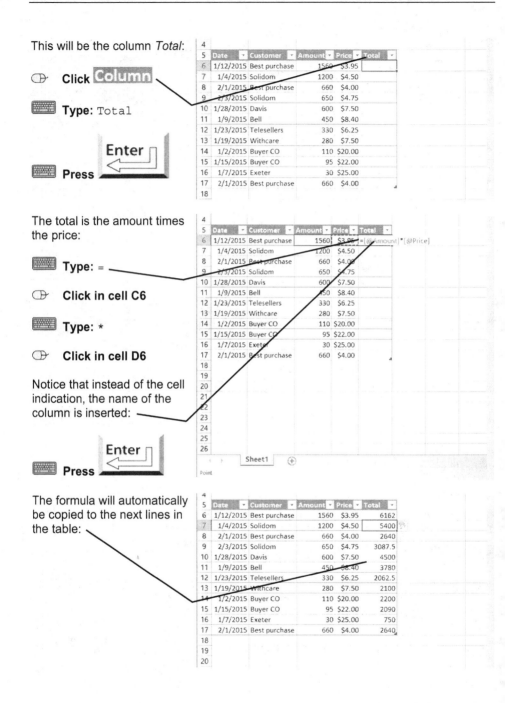

The numbers in the *Total* column should be formatted as currency:

☞ **Select cells E6:E17**
🐾19

☞ **Click** $

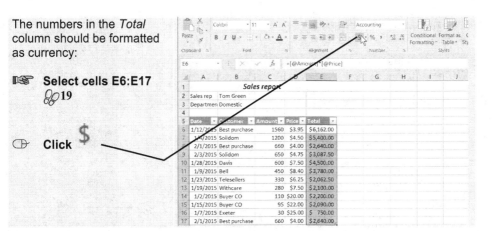

You can insert a row or column in the data table without it being inserted in the rest of the worksheet. Insert a new column between the *Date* and *Customer* columns:

☞ **Click the *Customer* column**

The column must be inserted before that column.

☞ **By 🔳 Insert, click ▾**

☞ **Click**
   Insert Table Columns to the Left

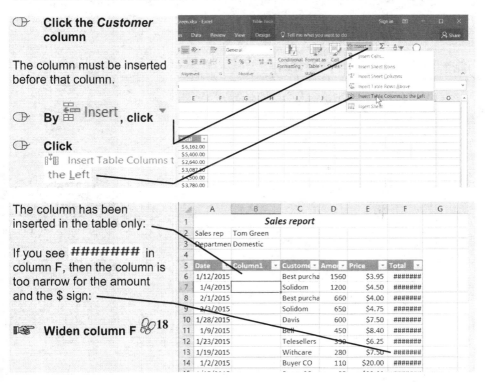

The column has been inserted in the table only:

If you see ####### in column F, then the column is too narrow for the amount and the $ sign:

☞ **Widen column F** 🐾18

Change the name of the new column to *District*:

⊕ **Click** `Column1`

⌨ **Type:** District

⌨ **Press** Enter

	Date	District	Custome	Amo	Price	Total
5						
6	1/12/2015		Best purcha	1560	$3.95	$6,162.00
7	1/4/2015		Solidom	1200	$4.50	$5,400.00
8	2/1/2015		Best purcha	660	$4.00	$2,640.00
9	2/3/2015		Solidom	650	$4.75	$3,087.50
10	1/28/2015		Davis	600	$7.50	$4,500.00
11	1/9/2015		Bell	450	$8.40	$3,780.00
12	1/23/2015		Telesellers	330	$6.25	$2,062.50
13	1/19/2015		Withcare	280	$7.50	$2,100.00
14	1/2/2015		Buyer CO	110	$20.00	$2,200.00
15	1/15/2015		Buyer CO	95	$22.00	$2,090.00
16	1/7/2015		Exeter	30	$25.00	$ 750.00
17	2/1/2015		Best purcha	660	$4.00	$2,640.00
18						

⌨ **Fill the *District* column in as shown**

	Date	District	Custome	Amo	Price	Total
4						
5						
6	1/12/2015	north	Best purcha	1560	$3.95	$6,162.00
7	1/4/2015	south	Solidom	1200	$4.50	$5,400.00
8	2/1/2015	north	Best purcha	660	$4.00	$2,640.00
9	2/3/2015	south	Solidom	650	$4.75	$3,087.50
10	1/28/2015	north	Davis	600	$7.50	$4,500.00
11	1/9/2015	north	Bell	450	$8.40	$3,780.00
12	1/23/2015	south	Telesellers	330	$6.25	$2,062.50
13	1/19/2015	north	Withcare	280	$7.50	$2,100.00
14	1/2/2015	south	Buyer CO	110	$20.00	$2,200.00
15	1/15/2015	south	Buyer CO	95	$22.00	$2,090.00
16	1/7/2015	north	Exeter	30	$25.00	$ 750.00
17	2/1/2015	north	Best purcha	660	$4.00	$2,640.00
18						

💡 **Tip**

Inserting rows
You can also insert a row into a table as follows. A new row is always inserted above the cell where the pointer is.

⊕ **Click the desired row**

⊕ **By** 🔲 Insert **, click** ▼

⊕ **Click** 🔲 Insert Cells...

The now row has been inserted:

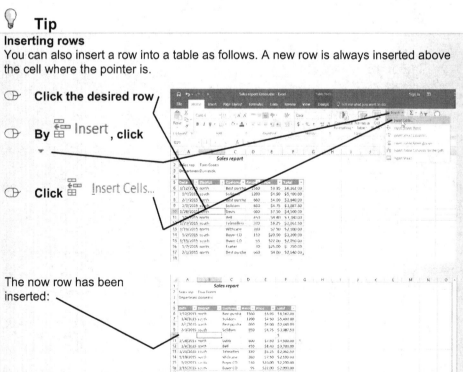

3.5 Removing Duplicate Data

A table may contain one or more duplicate rows. This happens sometimes after copying rows. *Excel* can remove these automatically with the *Remove Duplicates* option. Before creating summaries, it is a good idea to remove any duplicates so the data is not shown twice:

☞ **If necessary, click the table**

Row 8 is the same as row 17:

☞ **Click the** Design **tab**

☞ **Click** ▤·▤ Remove Duplicate

Please note: if the range has not been converted to a table, you can delete duplicates by clicking ▤·▤ on the Data tab.

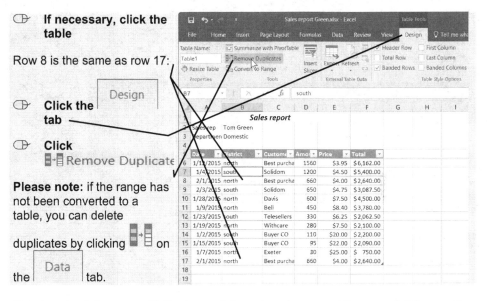

You can check for rows with the same date and customer and the same total amount:

All columns have a check mark ☑. You do not need to have all columns checked:

☞ **Remove the check marks ☑ by** District, Amount **and** Price

☞ **Click** OK

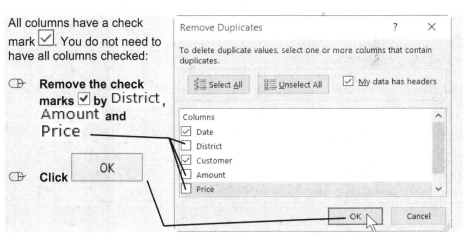

Excel has removed the last row:

⊕ **Click** OK

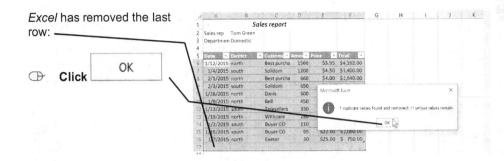

3.6 Multiple Sorting

The filter button above a column allows you to quickly sort data in a table. You can sort the orders by date, for instance:

⊕ **By Date click** ▼

⊕ **Click**
A↓ Sort Oldest to New

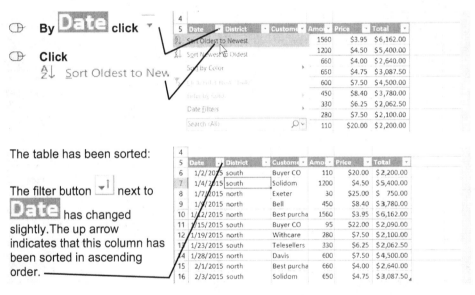

The table has been sorted:

The filter button ▼↑ next to **Date** has changed slightly. The up arrow indicates that this column has been sorted in ascending order.

You can also sort multiple columns at once. For example, to view the orders per *customer* by *district*. This will allow you to see the orders grouped per district and in each district, the orders grouped per customer.

⊕ **If necessary, click the table**

In the Home tab:

Sort & Filter

⊕ **Click** Filter ▼

⊕ **Click** Custom Sort...

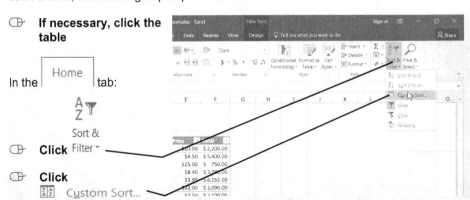

In order to sort both by district and by customer, add a new sorting level:

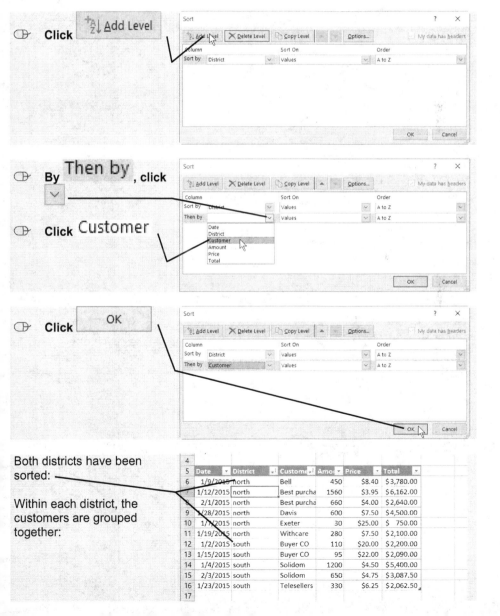

Please note:

Notice the orders are not sorted by date anymore. If you sort one attribute at a time, then any previous sorting is cancelled. Therefore always use 🔼 Custom Sort... if you want to have a table sorted by multiple items.

3.7 Filtering

In order to view the results of a single district in a large table, you can use a filter. You will see only the orders of the specified district, e.g. the south district:

☞ **By** District **, click**
▾↑

☞ **Remove the check mark ☑ by** north

☞ **Click** OK

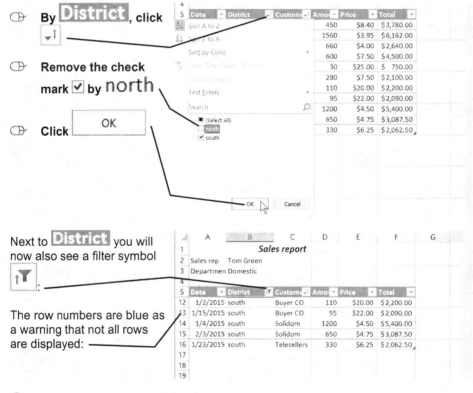

Next to District you will now also see a filter symbol
↑▼ :

The row numbers are blue as a warning that not all rows are displayed: ──────

Tip

Filtering by multiple columns
After you have filtered by one column, you can still filter by other columns.

There is an easy way to have the *Total* column added up in a table to know the total of the *South* district:

☞ **Click the** Design **tab**

☞ **Click to check** ☑ **by** Total Row

You will see **########** underneath the column:

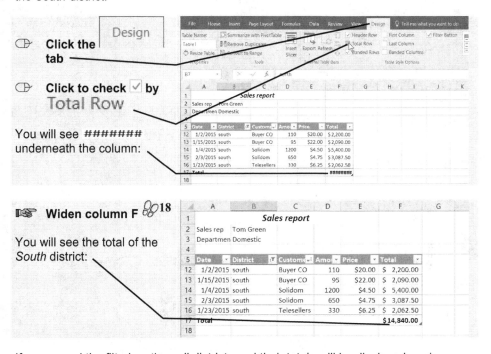

👉 **Widen column F** 👁️**18**

You will see the total of the *South* district:

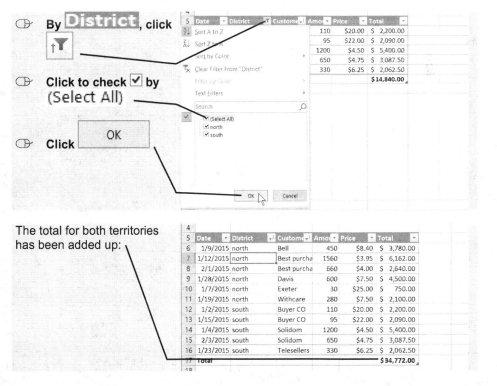

If you cancel the filtering, then all districts and their totals will be displayed again:

☞ **By** District **, click** ↑▼

☞ **Click to check** ☑ **by** (Select All)

☞ **Click** OK

The total for both territories has been added up:

3.8 Custom Filters

You can use filtering to find lines that meet certain conditions. This is how to find all totals equalling $3000,00 or greater:

- By **Total**, click ▼
- Click Number Filters
- Click Greater Than Or Equal

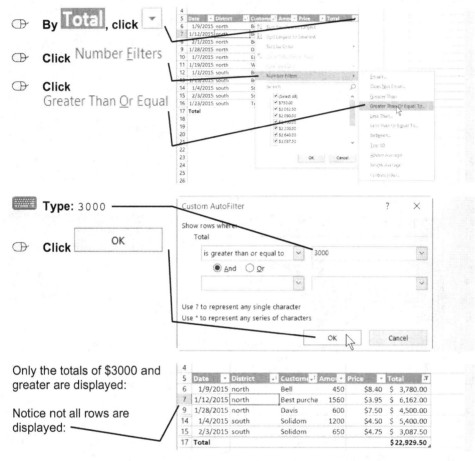

- Type: 3000
- Click OK

Only the totals of $3000 and greater are displayed:

Notice not all rows are displayed:

	Date	District	Customer	Amount	Price	Total
6	1/9/2015	north	Bell	450	$8.40	$ 3,780.00
7	1/12/2015	north	Best purcha	1560	$3.95	$ 6,162.00
9	1/28/2015	north	Davis	600	$7.50	$ 4,500.00
14	1/4/2015	south	Solidom	1200	$4.50	$ 5,400.00
15	2/3/2015	south	Solidom	650	$4.75	$ 3,087.50
17	Total					$ 22,929.50

It is also possible to display only the best three (or any other number):

- By **Total**, click 🔽
- Click Number Filters
- Click Top 10...

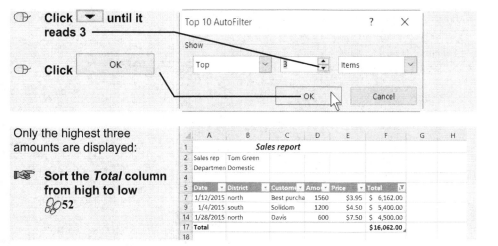

⬧ **Click ▼ until it reads 3**

⬧ **Click OK**

Only the highest three amounts are displayed:

☞ **Sort the *Total* column from high to low**
⚮52

If you want to see all rows again:

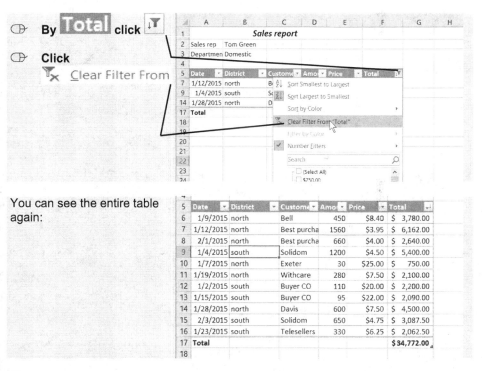

⬧ **By Total click**

⬧ **Click**
   🔽✕ Clear Filter From

You can see the entire table again:

 Please note:

If you have filtered by multiple columns, you will need to clear those filters as well in order to view the entire table again. Only when all row numbers appear in black again, you can view the entire table.

A custom filter presents even more possibilities. This allows you, for example, to find all totals between $1000,00 and $3000,00:

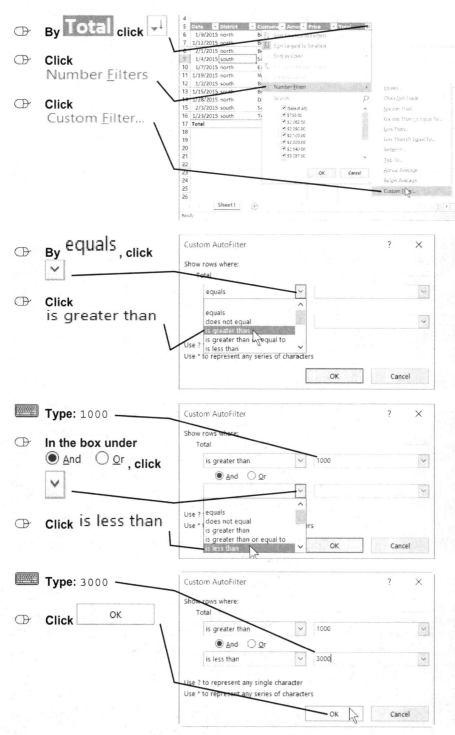

⟶ By **Total** click ⌄↓

⟶ **Click**
Number Filters

⟶ **Click**
Custom Filter...

⟶ By equals, click ⌄

⟶ **Click**
is greater than

⟶ **Type:** 1000

⟶ **In the box under**
⦿ And ○ Or , click
⌄

⟶ **Click** is less than

⟶ **Type:** 3000

⟶ **Click** [OK]

Only the totals between 1000 and 3000 are visible:

	A	B	C	D	E	F	G
1			*Sales report*				
2	Sales rep	Tom Green					
3	Departmen	Domestic					
4							
5	Date	District	Custome	Amo	Price	Total	
8	2/1/2015	north	Best purcha	660	$4.00	$ 2,640.00	
11	1/19/2015	north	Withcare	280	$7.50	$ 2,100.00	
12	1/2/2015	south	Buyer CO	110	$20.00	$ 2,200.00	
13	1/15/2015	south	Buyer CO	95	$22.00	$ 2,090.00	
16	1/23/2015	south	Telesellers	330	$6.25	$ 2,062.50	
17	Total					$11,092.50	
18							

 Please note:

Filtering and sorting only happens at the moment you give the command. If you change data or add rows later on, you will need to filter or sort again.

If you deactivate all filter buttons in the table, all rows will be displayed again as well. You do not have to deactivate the filters for each column separately:

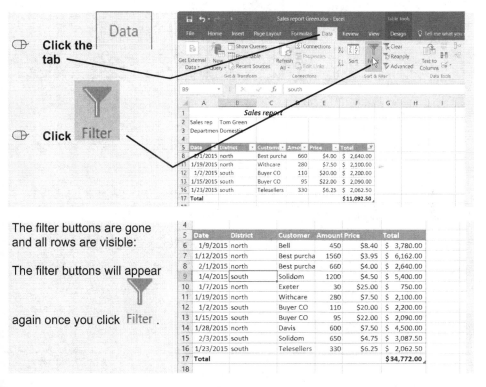

⊕ **Click the tab** | Data

⊕ **Click** Filter

The filter buttons are gone and all rows are visible:

The filter buttons will appear

again once you click Filter.

	A	B	C	D	E	F
4						
5	Date	District	Customer	Amount	Price	Total
6	1/9/2015	north	Bell	450	$8.40	$ 3,780.00
7	1/12/2015	north	Best purcha	1560	$3.95	$ 6,162.00
8	2/1/2015	north	Best purcha	660	$4.00	$ 2,640.00
9	1/4/2015	south	Solidom	1200	$4.50	$ 5,400.00
10	1/7/2015	north	Exeter	30	$25.00	$ 750.00
11	1/19/2015	north	Withcare	280	$7.50	$ 2,100.00
12	1/2/2015	south	Buyer CO	110	$20.00	$ 2,200.00
13	1/15/2015	south	Buyer CO	95	$22.00	$ 2,090.00
14	1/28/2015	north	Davis	600	$7.50	$ 4,500.00
15	2/3/2015	south	Solidom	650	$4.75	$ 3,087.50
16	1/23/2015	south	Telesellers	330	$6.25	$ 2,062.50
17	Total					$34,772.00
18						

3.9 Cell and Table Name

If there is more than one table in a workbook, it is a good idea to give the table a name. You can then use the *Go To* or *Search* functions to easily jump to the desired table.
You can enter a name for a table using the *Design* tab:

☞ **If necessary, click the table**

☞ **Click the** Design **tab**

☞ **By** Table Name: , **click** Table1

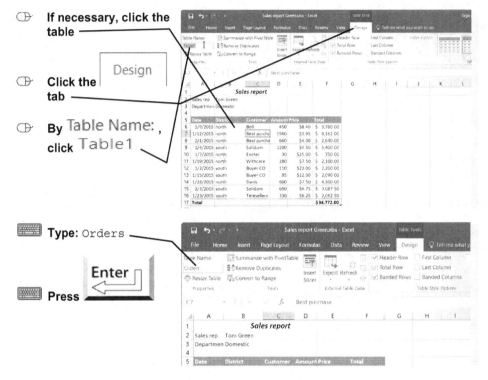

⌨ **Type:** Orders

⌨ **Press** Enter

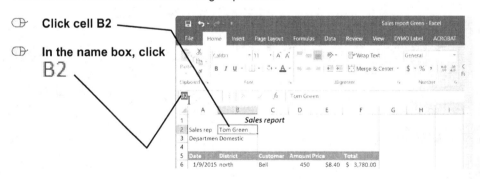

You can also name a cell or selected group of cells:

☞ **Click cell B2**

☞ **In the name box, click** B2

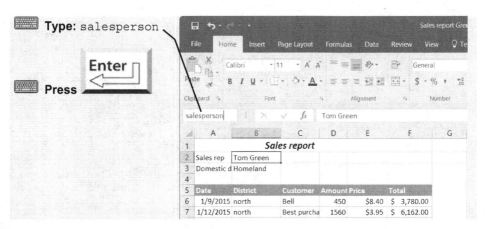

3.10 Go To

With the *Go To* function, you can jump easily to the specified section of the table:

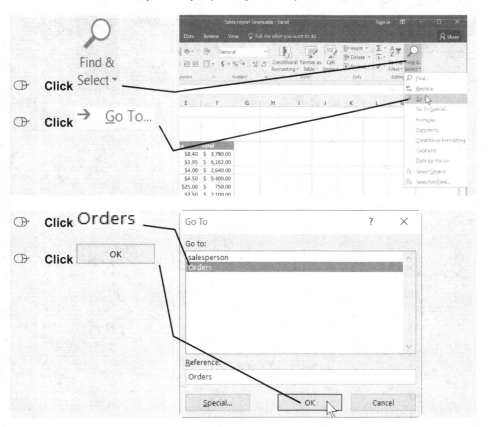

The *Orders* table has been selected:

	A	B	C	D	E	F	G	H
1			*Sales report*					
2	Sales rep	Tom Green						
3	Departmen	Domestic						
4								
5	Date	District	Customer	Amount	Price	Total		
6	1/9/2015	north	Bell	450	$8.40	$ 3,780.00		
7	1/12/2015	north	Best purcha	1560	$3.95	$ 6,162.00		
8	2/1/2015	north	Best purcha	660	$4.00	$ 2,640.00		
9	1/4/2015	south	Solidom	1200	$4.50	$ 5,400.00		
10	1/7/2015	north	Exeter	30	$25.00	$ 750.00		
11	1/19/2015	north	Withcare	280	$7.50	$ 2,100.00		
12	1/2/2015	south	Buyer CO	110	$20.00	$ 2,200.00		
13	1/15/2015	south	Buyer CO	95	$22.00	$ 2,090.00		
14	1/28/2015	north	Davis	600	$7.50	$ 4,500.00		
15	2/3/2015	south	Solidom	650	$4.75	$ 3,087.50		
16	1/23/2015	south	Telesellers	330	$6.25	$ 2,062.50		
17	Total					$ 34,772.00		
18								

3.11 Find and Replace

If a cell you are looking for does not have a name, you can use the standard search function:

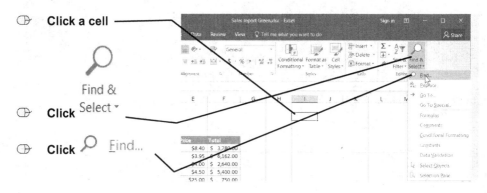

☞ **Click a cell**

🔍

Find &
☞ **Click** Select ▾

☞ **Click** 🔍 Find...

🏹 **Please note:**

If the *Orders* table is selected or if multiple cells are selected, then *Excel* will only search within the currently selected area.

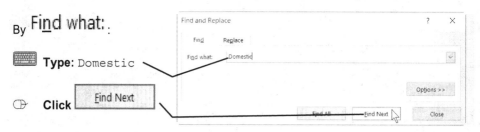

By **Find what:**.

⌨ **Type:** Domestic

☞ **Click** Find Next

The cell with *Domestic* is found:

If the word you are searching for appears more often, you can use **Find Next** to continue searching.

Now search for one or more words to automatically replace it by another word:

⊕ **Click the Replace tab**

⌨ **By Find what:, type: Solidom**

⌨ **By Replace with:, type: Bergalo**

⊕ **Click Find Next**

The first word is found:

⊕ **Click Replace**

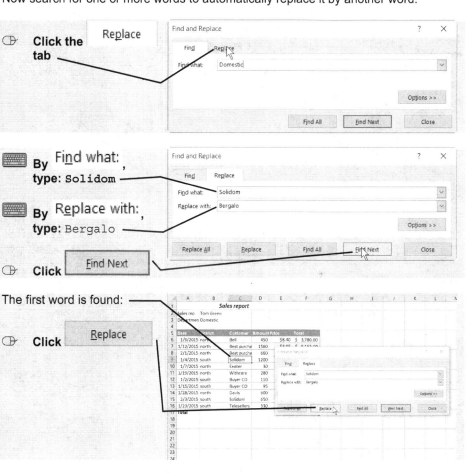

The word is replaced and the
next word is found:

Replace that as well:

⊕ **Click** Replace

The next word will also be
replaced:

⊕ **Click** Replace
    again

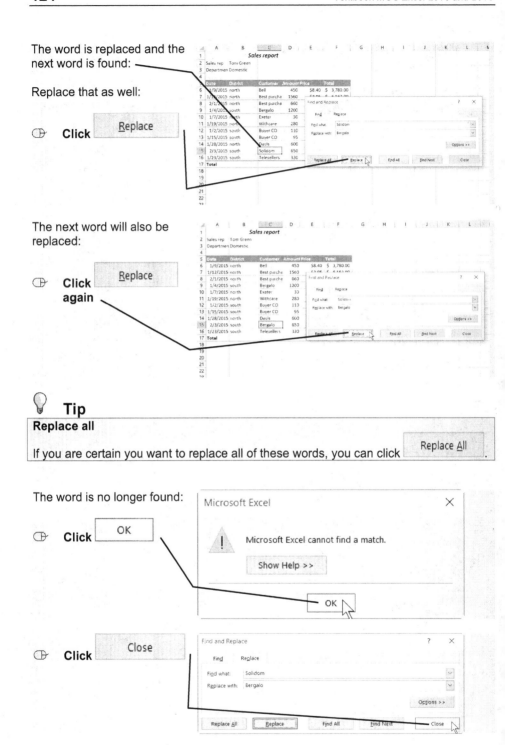

💡 Tip

Replace all

If you are certain you want to replace all of these words, you can click Replace All .

The word is no longer found:

⊕ **Click** OK

Microsoft Excel

⚠ Microsoft Excel cannot find a match.

Show Help >>

OK

⊕ **Click** Close

Find and Replace

Find   Replace

Find what: Solidom

Replace with: Bergalo

Options >>

Replace All   Replace   Find All   Find Next   Close

Before you continue, save the workbook:

Click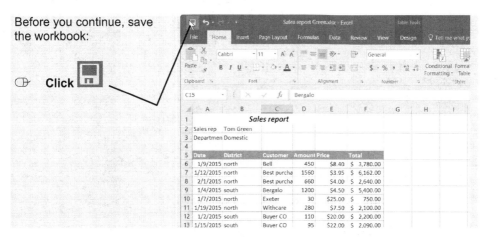

3.12 From Table to Range

Tables can be converted back into a so called normal range. Special table functions will be disabled and the data is displayed in standard worksheet cells again. You can do that as follows:

Click the tab | Design

Click Convert to Range

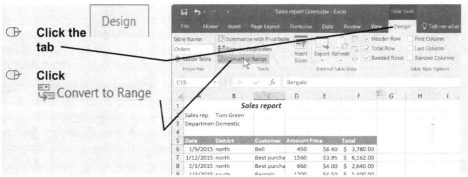

🍃 Please note:

A cell must be selected in order to see the | Design | tab.

Click Yes

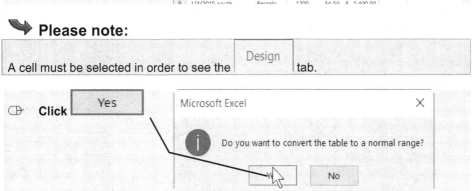

Microsoft Excel

Do you want to convert the table to a normal range?

Yes   No

The table has been
converted:

The table style has been
preserved, but table functions
no longer work.

⊕ **Click**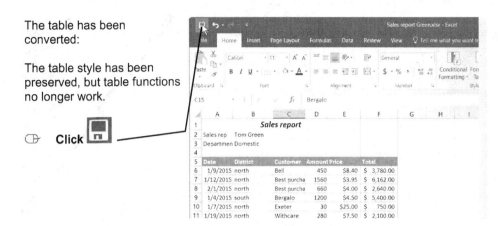

This chapter has shown you how to work with tables and how you can easily and
conveniently filter and sort data. You can practice a bit more with what you have
learned in the following section.

☞ **Close** *Excel* ${}^{\mathscr{O}\!\!\mathscr{O}16}$

3.13 Exercise

To learn how to quickly apply what you have just learned, you can do the following review exercise. Forgot how to carry out an action? Then look it up using the number next to the footsteps 👣[1] in the appendix *How Do I Do That Again?*

Exercise: Tables

In this exercise you will practice, amongst other things, sorting and filtering in tables.

☞ Open *Excel.* 👣[1]

☞ Open a blank workbook. 👣[2]

☞ Import the *weather.csv* file. 👣[53]

☞ Save the workbook with the name Temperature and precipitation 👣[33]

☞ Sort the places in alphabetical order. 👣[54]

☞ Convert the summary into a table. 👣[55]

☞ Set a different table style. 👣[56]

☞ Select cells B2:C7. 👣[19]

☞ Centre the selected cells. 👣[57]

☞ Add a new row 👣[58] and enter this data | Kansas city | 83 | 5.5 |. 👣[17]

☞ Sort the places from a to z with the filter button. 👣[52]

☞ Filter the top 5 of precipitation. 👣[60]

☞ Filter the places by a temperature above 15 degrees. 👣[59]

☞ Clear the filter by the precipitation. 👣[61]

☞ Rename the table to June 👣[62]

☞ Show the row totals to calculate the total precipitation. 👣[63]

☞ Clear the filter by the temperature. 👣[61]

☞ Click cell H16.

☞ Use *Go To* to jump to the table. ℰℰ^{64}

☞ Above Florida, add a table row ℰℰ^{67} and type the following data
   Atlanta   88   4 ℰℰ^{17}

☞ Sort the places again with the filter button. ℰℰ^{52}

☞ Use custom sorting to sort the table ascending by temperature and then
   ascending by precipitation. ℰℰ^{72}

☞ Use the *Replace* function to replace 82 by 84. ℰℰ^{65}

☞ Convert the table to a range. ℰℰ^{66}

☞ Close *Excel* and save the changes. ℰℰ^{16}

3.14 Tips

💡 **Tip**

Table design

The | Design | tab contains a number of options to format the table:

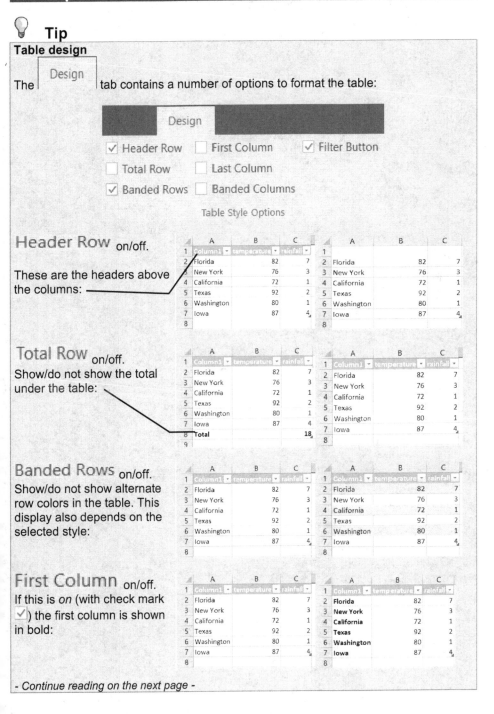

Design

☑ Header Row   ☐ First Column   ☑ Filter Button

☐ Total Row   ☐ Last Column

☑ Banded Rows   ☐ Banded Columns

Table Style Options

Header Row on/off.

These are the headers above the columns:

Total Row on/off.

Show/do not show the total under the table:

Banded Rows on/off.

Show/do not show alternate row colors in the table. This display also depends on the selected style:

First Column on/off.

If this is *on* (with check mark ☑) the first column is shown in bold:

- Continue reading on the next page -

Last Column on/off.
If this is *on* (with check mark
✓) the last column is shown
in bold:

	A	B	C
1	Column1	temperature	rainfall
2	Florida	82	7
3	New York	76	3
4	California	72	1
5	Texas	92	2
6	Washington	80	1
7	Iowa	87	4
8			

	A	B	C
1	Column1	temperature	rainfall
2	Florida	82	7
3	New York	76	3
4	California	72	1
5	Texas	92	2
6	Washington	80	1
7	Iowa	87	4
8			

Banded Columns on/off.
Show/do not show alternate
column colors in the table.
This display also depends on
the selected style:

	A	B	C
1	Column1	temperature	rainfall
2	Florida	82	7
3	New York	76	3
4	California	72	1
5	Texas	92	2
6	Washington	80	1
7	Iowa	87	4
8			

	A	B	C
1	Column1	temperature	rainfall
2	Florida	82	7
3	New York	76	3
4	California	72	1
5	Texas	92	2
6	Washington	80	1
7	Iowa	87	4
8			

Filter Button on/off
Use this setting to show or
hide the filter buttons at the
top of the columns:

	A	B	C
1	Column1	temperature	rainfall
2	Florida	82	7
3	New York	76	3
4	California	72	1
5	Texas	92	2
6	Washington	80	1
7	Iowa	87	4
8			

	A	B	C
1	Column1	temperature	rainfall
2	Florida	82	7
3	New York	76	3
4	California	72	1
5	Texas	92	2
6	Washington	80	1
7	Iowa	87	4
8			

4. Analyzing Data

Drawing conclusions from the amounts and quantities on a worksheet in *Excel* is often not easy for outsiders. First, the structure and layout of the worksheet have to be considered, then the numbers have to be interpreted and only then can you draw conclusions. That is why spreadsheets often make use of charts showing proportions and trends at a glance.

You can create various charts in *Excel* with the *Quick Analysis* function. With a few clicks you can create a chart from the selected data which can then be adjusted in many ways. Furthermore, *Quick Analysis* offers functions to calculate averages, for example, or to highlight high and low values by colors.

Adding graphic objects, such as the company logo or additional texts can help to clarify the information on a worksheet. Particularly when a spreadsheet will be used for presentations to third parties, adding these objects gives it a more professional image.

In this chapter you will learn:

- what the *Quick Analysis* button is;
- to calculate totals and averages;
- to use the color scale;
- to highlight values with icons;
- what sparklines are;
- to make charts from a selected area;
- to add and remove chart elements;
- to adjust chart data;
- to change chart dimensions;
- to switch the display of rows and columns;
- to choose a different type of chart;
- to insert and adjust text boxes;
- to insert images;
- to insert SmartArt images.

4.1 Totals and Averages

With the *Quick analysis* button you can calculate totals and averages easily without formulas:

☞ **Open** *Excel* $\mathcal{QO}^1$

☞ **Open the practice file *Sales comparison* from the folder *Practice Files Textbook Excel* $\mathcal{QO}^{50}$**

You will see the following summary:

☞ **Select cells B3:C8** $\mathcal{QO}^{19}$

At the bottom right of the area you will see 🔲. This is the *Quick Analysis* button.

☞ **Click** 🔲

In the menu:

☞ **Click** Totals

This sheet has a number of functions to calculate a total, a subtotal or an average quickly. This is a fast way to use certain options. This way, you do not have to use the ribbon.

☞ **Place the pointer on** Average

Please note: do not click Average.

The average turnover per month is shown underneath the columns:

☞ **Place the pointer on the other options**

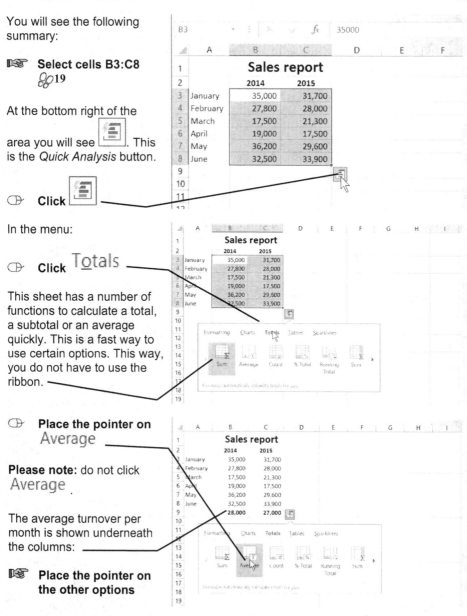

HELP! I have clicked.

If you click $Average$, the averages are placed in the cells and the menu disappears. Proceed as follows:

⊕ **Click** again

⊕ **Click** **Totals**

You can see how you can quickly and easily view the totals, numbers or averages of a summary, without having to enter formulas.

⊕ **Click**

You will see even more options:

☞ **Place the pointer on the other options**

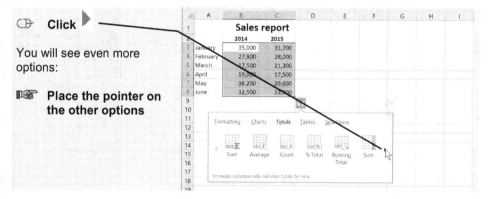

💡 **Tip**

Percentages
Often the figures of periods, departments or products are viewed as percentages in relation to the total. There is a very simple way to calculate such percentages:

⊕ **Click** % Total

The percentages will be calculated:

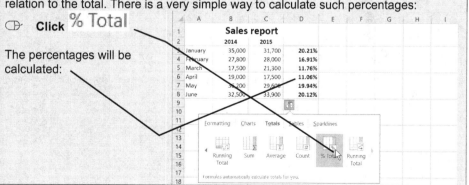

Now have the average turnover per month placed underneath the years:

⊕ **Click** ◀

⊕ **Click** Average

The average is shown
underneath the columns:

4.2 Colors and Icons

With colors, *Quick Analysis* can show information about the individual months:

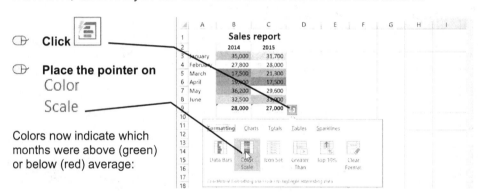

⊕ **Click**

⊕ **Place the pointer on**
    Color
    Scale

Colors now indicate which
months were above (green)
or below (red) average:

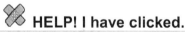 **HELP! I have clicked.**

If you click Scale, the colors are placed in the cells and the menu disappears. Proceed
as follows:

⊕ **Click**

        Color
⊕ **Click** Scale

        Clear
⊕ **Click** Format

The darker the color is, the greater the difference with the average. Months on or close to the average are (almost) white.

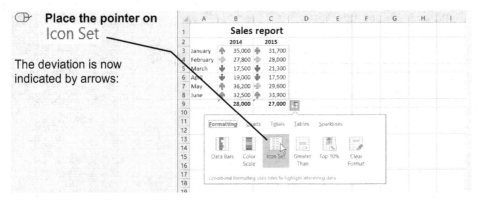

☞ Place the pointer on
Icon Set

The deviation is now indicated by arrows:

🖝 Also have a look at the other possibilities

- With Data Bars bars indicate how high the number is.
- With Greater Than the highest values become red.
- With Top 10% you can see 10% of the numbers with the highest values. In this case it is just a single number, but in the event of a large summary there will be more.

4.3 Sparklines

To see the course per month without having to compare all the numbers, *sparklines* can be of help. These are miniature charts within a single cell:

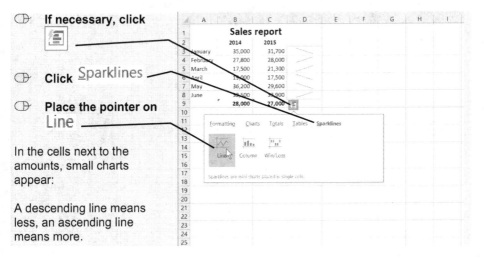

☞ If necessary, click

☞ Click Sparklines

☞ Place the pointer on
Line

In the cells next to the amounts, small charts appear:

A descending line means less, an ascending line means more.

Sparklines only show the trend and, unlike normal charts, do not tell us anything about the actual height of the values.

☞ **Place the pointer on**
   Column —

A bar indicates the highest
value:

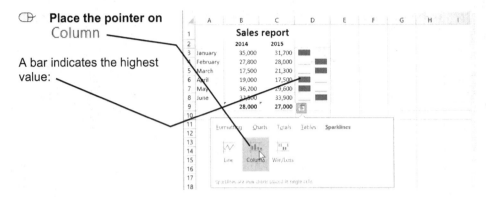

In this example, the sparkline Profit/loss does not provide any useful information.

💡 **Tip**

Look at the result
As with formulas, you should also check charts carefully to make sure the displayed information is correct and usable before you draw any conclusions.

4.4 Charts

The clearest way to show data is often a chart. A chart shows you directly what the course, ups and downs are.
You can create a number of frequently used charts with *Quick Analysis*, too:

☞ **Click** Charts

☞ **Place the pointer on**
   Clustered
   Column —

The chart shows the values,
but you cannot tell from
which month and which year.

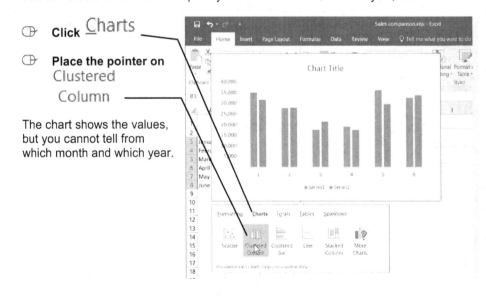

To create a chart, it is necessary not only to select the figures themselves, but also the legend (row and column titles) belonging to the chart.

⊕ **Click an empty cell**

The chart disappears.

☞ **Select cells A2:C8**

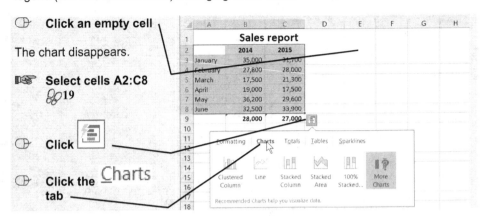

⊕ **Click**

⊕ **Click the** Charts
   tab

💡 **Tip**

Other charts
You will now see other charts than last time. *Quick Analysis* adjusts the possible charts to the selected area.

⊕ **Place the pointer on**
   Clustered
   Column

The months and years now also show in the chart:

Create the chart:

   Clustered
⊕ **Click** Column

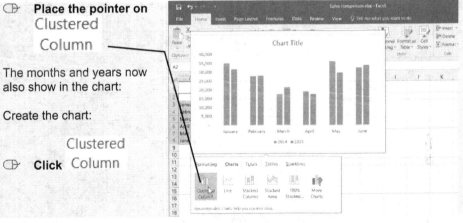

The chart has been inserted on the worksheet:

Notice the additional tabs for charts:

Tip

Moving a chart

If the chart is in the wrong place and, for example, covers a part of the summary, then you can move the chart:

☞ **Place the pointer on the chart area**

The pointer changes into

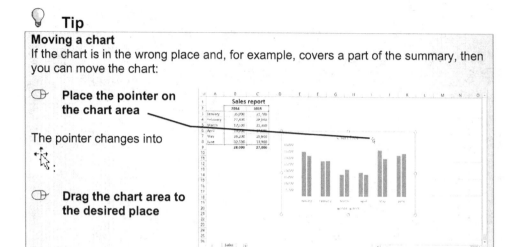

☞ **Drag the chart area to the desired place**

4.5 Chart Elements

To better understand a chart, the captions (legend) are important. In this example, these are the months and years. A clear chart title also helps to quickly understand what the chart is about. This is how to add titles:

☞ **Click** +

The data with a check mark ☑ are shown in the chart. In order to add titles:

☞ **Check the box ☑ by** Axis Titles

Next to the vertical and below the horizontal axis, you will see Axis Title:

Replace this text by the explanation for that axis:

☞ **Double-click** Axis Title

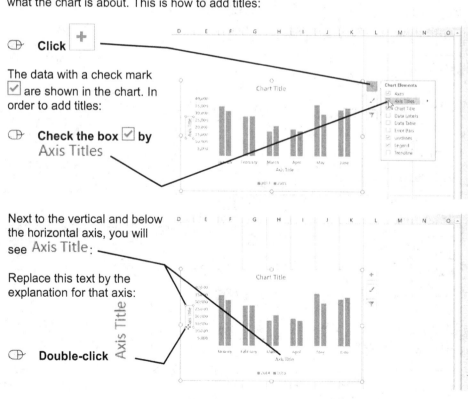

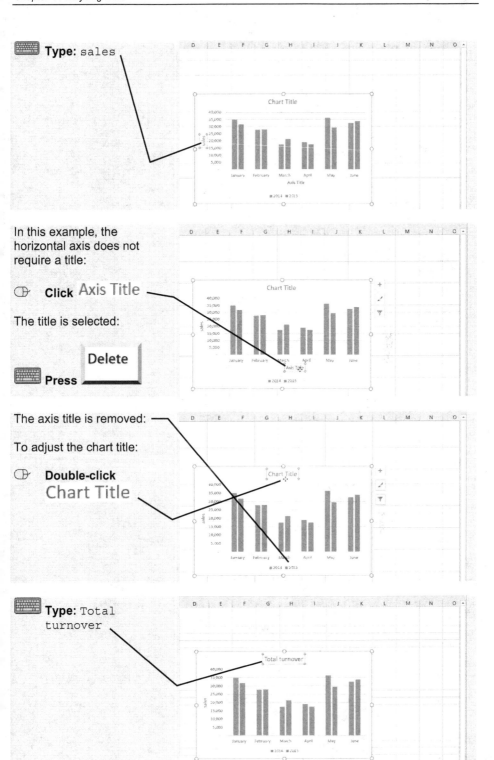

Type: sales

In this example, the horizontal axis does not require a title:

Click Axis Title

The title is selected:

Press Delete

The axis title is removed:

To adjust the chart title:

Double-click Chart Title

Type: Total turnover

You can format titles and legend the same way you can format cells or other texts:

🖰 **Click**
   Total turnover

The frame is selected:

🖰 **Click**
   Total turnover
   three times

You will see the tools
to format the text:

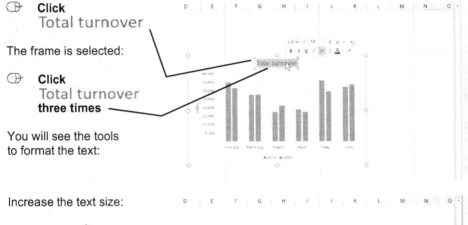

Increase the text size:

🖰 **Click A twice**

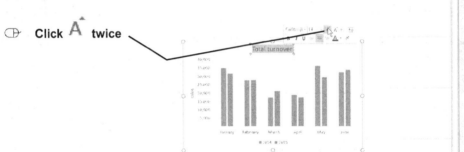

➡ Please note:

If the title consists of several words, you need to click three times.

Change the text color:

🖰 **By A , click ▾**

🖰 **Click a color**

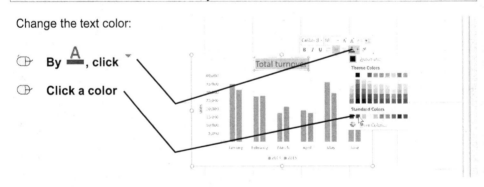

It is possible that the *Format Chart Title* pane is open. Close it:

☞ **If necessary, in the pane, click** ✕

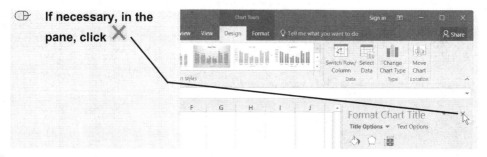

In order to clarify values, you can also specify them in the chart columns:

☞ **Click on the edge of the chart**

☞ **Click** ➕

☞ **Place the pointer on** Data Labels

You will see the turnover amounts above the columns:

In this graph, that is very unclear.

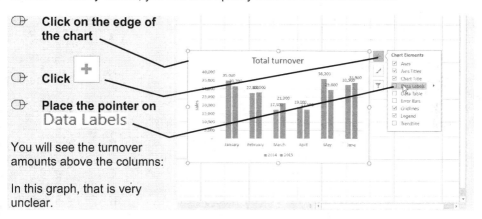

A data table is clearer:

☞ **Click to check** ☑ **by** Data Table

The figures are now in a table below the chart:

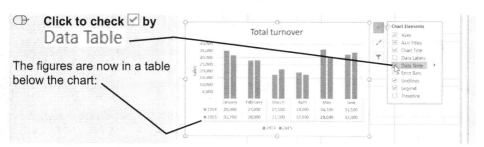

You can choose from several shapes and colors to format the chart:

☞ **Click** 🖌

To see the effect:

⊕ **Place the pointer on some examples**

In order to change the colors:

⊕ **Click** Color

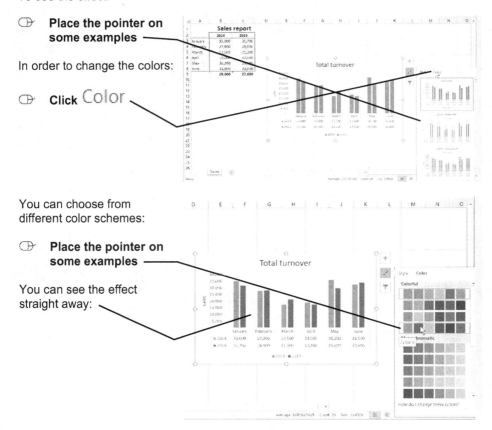

You can choose from different color schemes:

⊕ **Place the pointer on some examples**

You can see the effect straight away:

You can also indicate what you do and do not want to show in the chart. First select the original color of the chart:

⊕ **Click** Color 1

⊕ **Click** 🔻

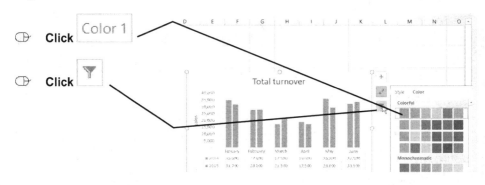

You will see the years and
months that are shown in the
chart.

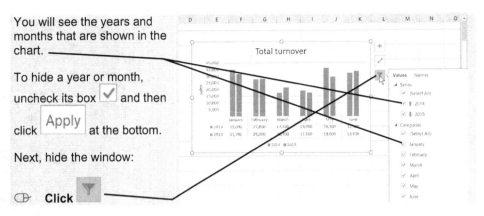

To hide a year or month,
uncheck its box ✓ and then
click Apply at the bottom.

Next, hide the window:

◯ **Click**

✖ HELP! I do not see any values.

If you do not see years and months, then do the following:

◯ **Click the chart**

◯ **Click** ▼

4.6 Adjusting Chart Data

When amounts in the summary change, then the chart also changes.

◯ **If necessary, drag the scroll bar to the left**

◯ **Click cell C8**

⌨ **Type:** 26,000

⌨ **Press** Enter

The chart has been adjusted:

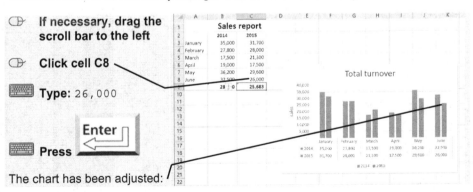

When the figures of a new year are announced, they can be entered in the summary:

☞ **If necessary, move the chart** ✂75

⌨ **Enter the data for 2016**

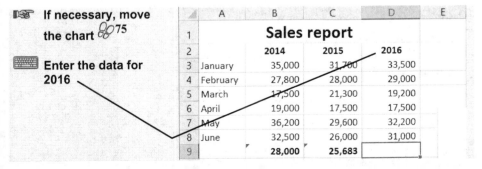

	A	B	C	D	E
1		Sales report			
2		2014	2015	2016	
3	January	35,000	31,700	33,500	
4	February	27,800	28,000	29,000	
5	March	17,500	21,300	19,200	
6	April	19,000	17,500	17,500	
7	May	36,200	29,600	32,200	
8	June	32,500	26,000	31,000	
9		28,000	25,683		

☞ **Copy the formula from C9 to D9** ✂25

The graph is not changed. The new column is outside the area from which the graph is created. Add the data for 2016 to the chart:

👉 **Click the chart**

👉 **Click** [🔽]

👉 **Click** Select Data...

👉 **Click** [🔲 Add]

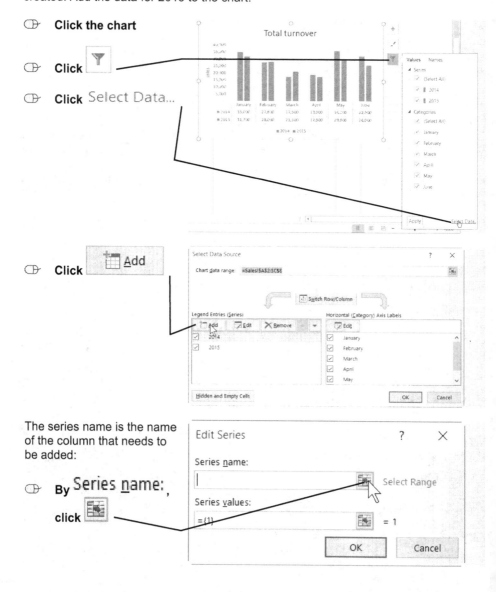

The series name is the name of the column that needs to be added:

👉 **By** Series name:, click 🔲

The series name is the year 2016:

☞ **Click in cell D2**

The cell is completed:

☞ **Click**

The series values are the amounts that need to be displayed in the chart.

☞ By **Series values**, click

☞ **Select cells D3:D8**
&&19

☞ **Click**

☞ **Click** OK

The series 2016 has been added:

☞ **Click** OK

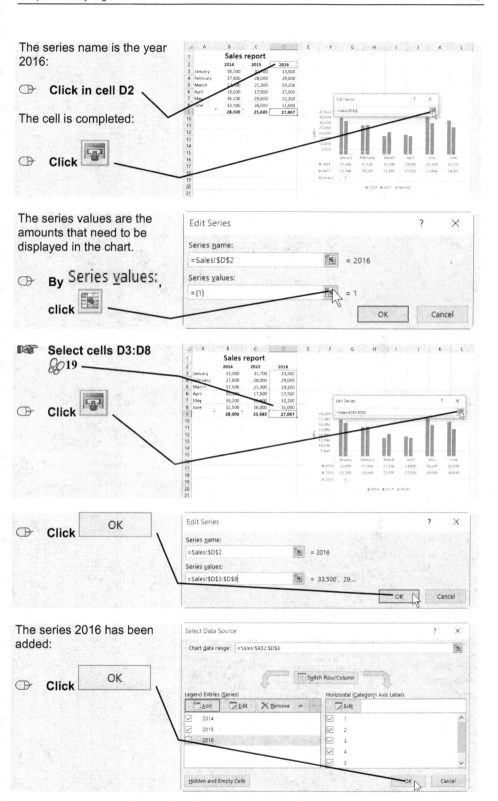

The chart and table have been extended with the figures for 2016:

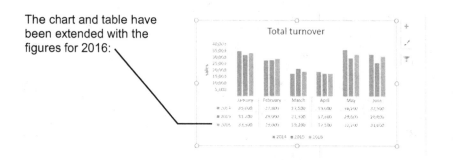

💡 Tip

Another way to add data to a chart
You can also add the data in the new column by

dragging the corner point ◼ in the desired
cell, so that the new column or row is added.

	A	B	C	D
1		Sales report		
2		2014	2015	2016
3	January	35,000	31,700	33,500
4	February	27,800	28,000	29,000
5	March	17,500	21,300	19,200
6	April	19,000	17,500	17,500
7	May	36,200	29,600	32,200
8	June	32,500	26,000	31,000
9		28,000	25,683	27,067
10				

4.7 Changing Chart Dimensions

If there is a lot of data in the chart, you can increase the size of the chart to make it easier to read:

☞ **Click the chart**

You can change the size by dragging a corner point:

☞ **Place the pointer on a corner point of the chart**

The pointer changes to a diagonal arrow ↖↘ :

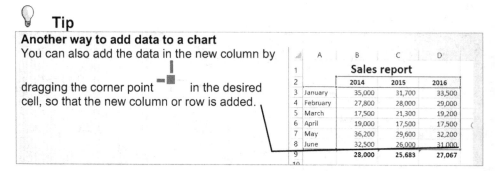

You can increase the size of the chart by dragging outwards. If you drag inwards, the size of the chart is reduced. Now increase the size of the chart:

☞ **Drag a corner point outwards**

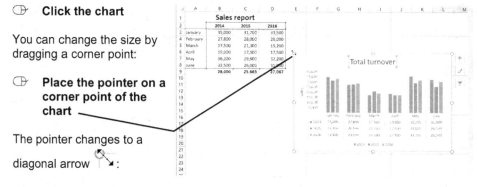

The size of the chart has been increased:

In this example the data can no longer be seen clearly:

Tip

Moving a chart

If the chart covers a part of the summary, then you can move the chart:

☞ **Place the pointer on the chart area**

The pointer changes into

🔖:

☞ **Drag the chart area to the desired place**

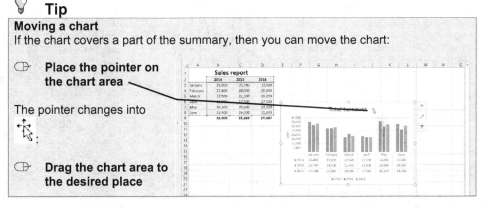

If there is a lot of data on a worksheet or if the chart is large, you better place the chart on a separate worksheet. This is how to do it:

☞ **Click the** Design **tab**

☞ **Click** Move Chart

☞ **Click the radio button** ⦿ **by** New sheet:

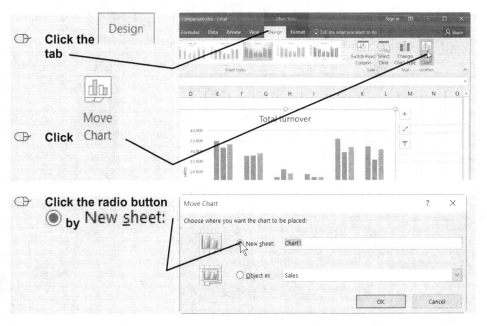

Change the name of this sheet:

⌨ **Type:** Chart 2014-2016

⬚ **Click** OK

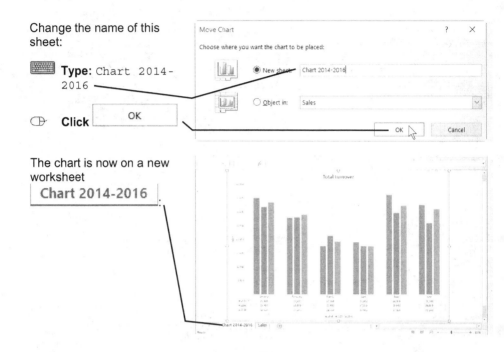

The chart is now on a new worksheet

Chart 2014-2016

4.8 Switching Rows and Columns

A chart can be clearer when the rows and columns are switched. Now have a quick look how that looks here:

⬚ **If necessary, click the** Design **tab**

⬚ **Click** Switch Row/ Column

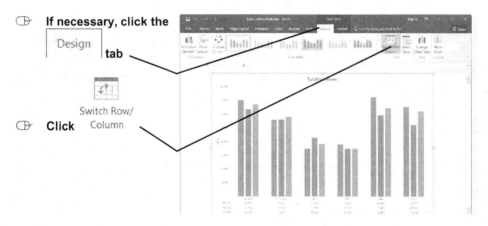

The rows and columns have been switched:

Please note: if the rows and columns have not yet been switched now, you need to click in the chart area.

The chart is less clear like this. Undo the change:

⊕ **Click**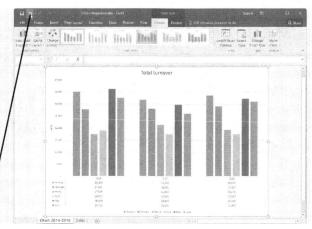

The columns are displayed by month again:

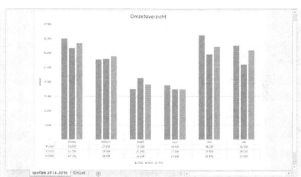

4.9 Changing Chart Type

There are various chart types. Depending on the type of data you can choose the type that is the most clear. You can still change the type of chart for an existing chart as well:

On the | Design | tab:

⊕ **Click** Change Chart Type

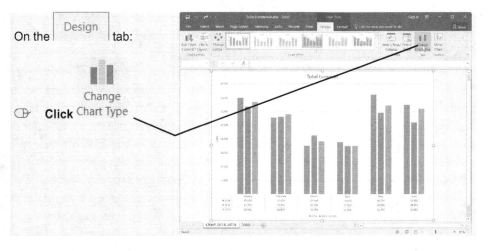

☞ **Click** ◔ Pie

You will see an example:

☞ **Click** [OK]

The chart is a circle:

A circle is not suitable to display data in multiple columns (here: the years). So you change the chart again:

Change
☞ **Click** Chart Type

☞ **Click** ▥ Column

Choose a different kind of columns:

☞ **Click**

At the bottom of the window:

☞ **Click** [OK]

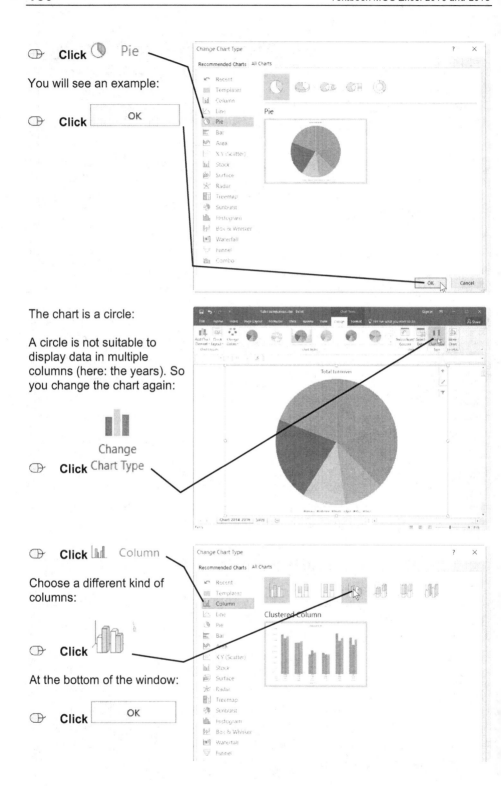

The chart now has a 3D-effect:

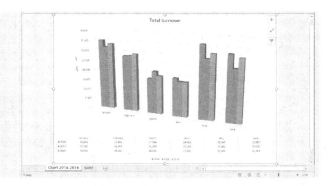

4.10 Changing the Scale

The turnover on the vertical axis is displayed in increments of 5000 dollar. Change it to 2500:

☞ **Double-click**
20,000

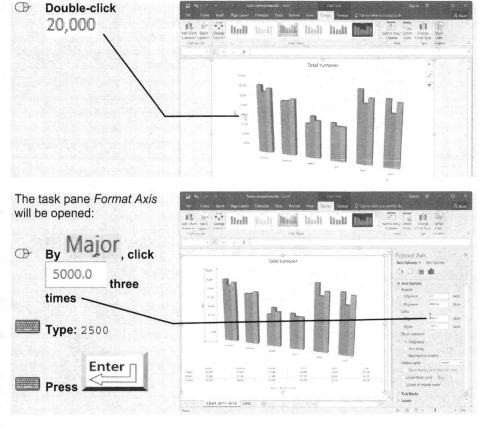

The task pane *Format Axis* will be opened:

☞ **By Major, click**
5000.0 **three times**

⌨ **Type:** 2500

⌨ **Press** Enter

There are now more numbers on the vertical axis and more grid lines in the chart:

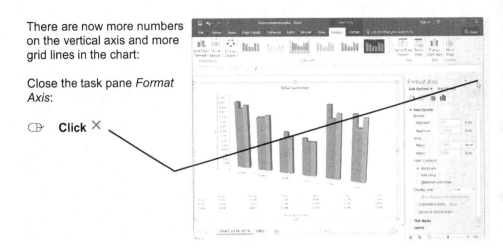

Close the task pane *Format Axis*:

☞ **Click** ✕

By selecting a new style you can change the appearance of the chart.

☞ **Click**
(Style 3)

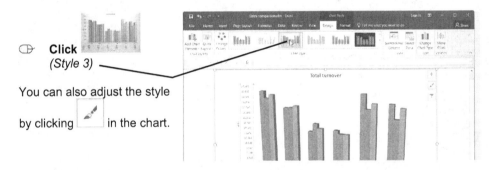

You can also adjust the style

by clicking 🖌 in the chart.

The style is applied.

The chart now has a grey background:

The previous format was nicer. Undo this action:

☞ **Click** ↶

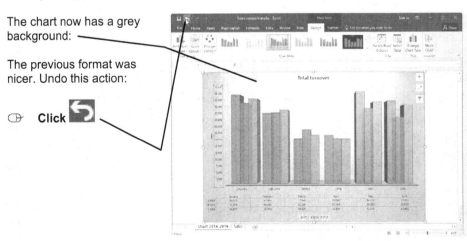

Apply a shape style to the chart area:

⊕ **If necessary, click the**
    background of the
    chart

⊕ **Click the** Format
    tab

⊕ **By** Shape Styles,

    click ⯆

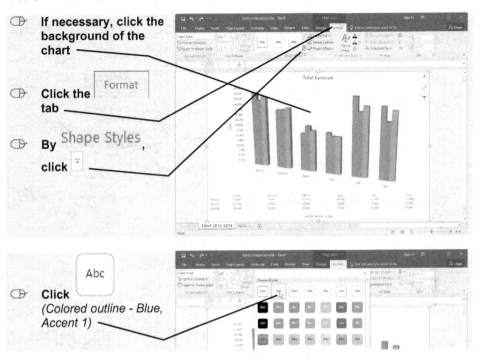

⊕ **Click** Abc
    (Colored outline - Blue,
    Accent 1)

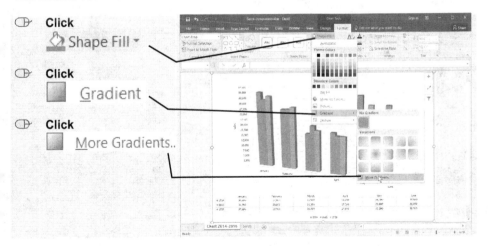

The chart is outlined in blue. This is how to set a background with a color transition:

⊕ **Click**
    Shape Fill ▾

⊕ **Click**
    Gradient

⊕ **Click**
    More Gradients..

The task pane *Format Chart Area* will be opened:

☞ **Click the radio button**
   ⊙ **by** G̲radient fill

☞ **By** P̲reset gradients,

   click [ ]▼

☞ **Click**
   (Light gradient - Accent 1)

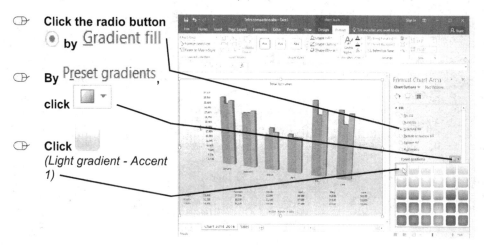

The color transition is applied to the chart.

☞ **Close the task pane *Format Chart Area*** ✂️[145]

4.12 Formatting Chart Elements

The chart is made up of shapes and texts which can be formatted. This is how to adjust the format of the horizontal axis:

☞ **Click** February

The text on the horizontal axis is selected:

☞ **Click the** [Home] **tab**

☞ **Click B**

The text is now shown in bold. Now adjust the font size:

☞ **Click** A̋ **until you see** 12

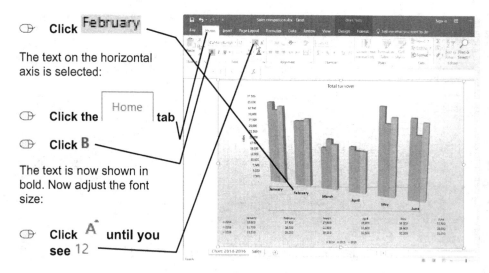

The text on the horizontal axis is now in bold with a font size of 12 points.

Copy this format to the vertical axis:

☞ **Click** 🖌

☞ **Click a number in the vertical axis**

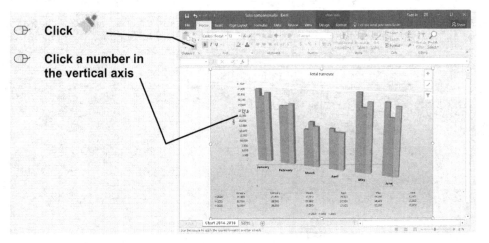

The format of the vertical axis is adjusted. Finally, apply a WordArt style to the chart title:

☞ **Click the chart title**

☞ **Click the** Format **tab**

☞ **Click** Quick Styles ▾

☞ **Click** A *(Gradient Fill - Blue, Accent 5, Reflection)*

The chart title has been adjusted:

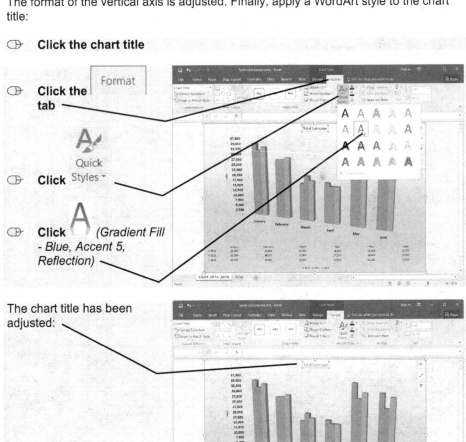

4.13 Inserting a Text Box

In order to clarify a summary on a worksheet, you can insert different types of objects. With a text box you can insert a text at a random place. You do not have to put the text in a cell then. This is possible both in a graph and on the normal worksheet. Now insert a text box on the worksheet with the summary:

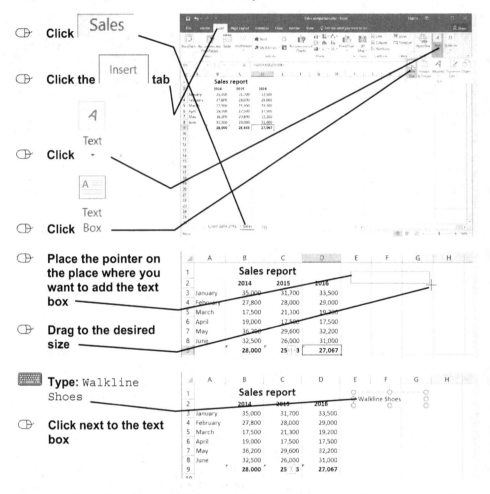

➪ **Click** Sales

➪ **Click the** Insert **tab**

➪ **Click** A Text ▾

➪ **Click** Box Text

➪ **Place the pointer on the place where you want to add the text box**

➪ **Drag to the desired size**

⌨ **Type:** Walkline Shoes

➪ **Click next to the text box**

The advantage of a text box is that you can place it anywhere and can also move it easily:

➪ **Click the text**

The text box is selected.

➪ **Drag the text box to another place**

⊕ **Rotate the text box slightly by dragging**

You can format text and the text box in different ways to make them stand out more or decorate them:

To do this, the text box has to be selected:

⊕ **If necessary, click the text**

⊕ **Click the** Format **tab**

⊕ **By** Shape Styles, **click** ⏷

⊕ **Click a style**

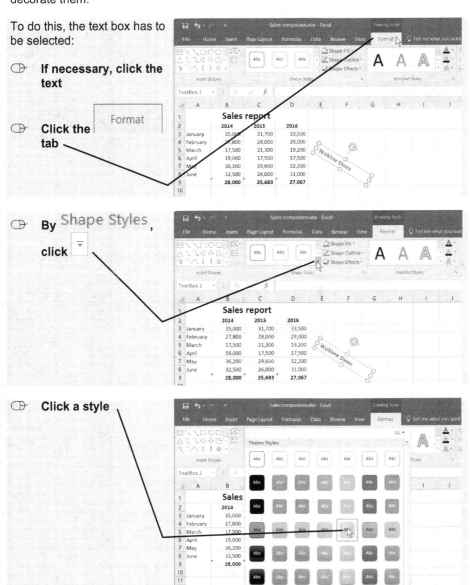

The text box has the chosen style:

To apply a shape effect:

⊕ **Click**
    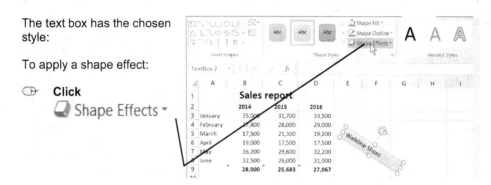
    Shape Effects ▾

💡 **Tip**

Choose colors by yourself

With ▨ Shape Fill ▾ and ✏ Shape Outline ▾ you can choose the color of the shape and the outline by yourself.

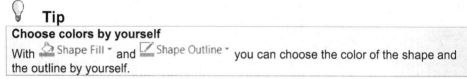

⊕ **Click** ▢ Glow

⊕ **Click an effect**

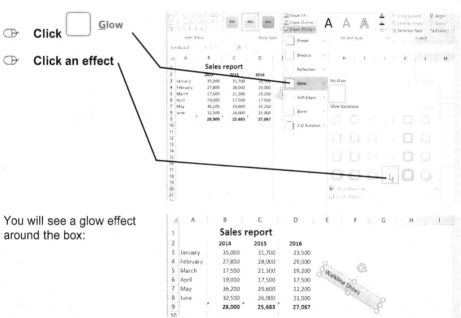

You will see a glow effect around the box:

You can also format the text itself. You can set a special format with WordArt. To do this, the whole text has to be selected:

⊕ **Click the text three times**

The whole text is selected:

⊕ **By** WordArt Styles ,

    click ▢

➔ **Click a style**

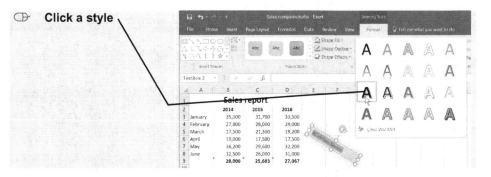

You can change the size of a text box by dragging the sizing handle:

➔ **Drag the sizing handle in the middle on the right side until the text fits the box exactly**

Cancel the selection of the text box:

➔ **Click an empty cell**

💡 **Tip**

Exact measurements
If the text box must have a fixed size, for example for a label, you can enter the dimensions:

On the right side of the tab:

To adjust the height:

➔ **By ↕⬚, click ▲▼**

To adjust the width:

➔ **By ↔, click ▲▼**

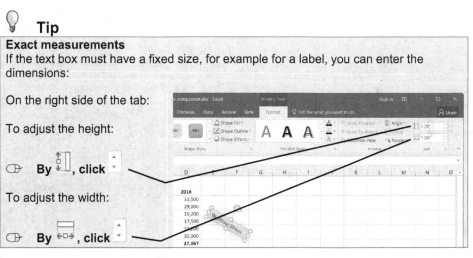

4.14 Inserting a Picture

Except text, you can also insert pictures. These pictures have to be stored on your computer.

☞ **Click the** `Insert` **tab**

☞ **Click** Illustrations ▾

☞ **Click** Pictures

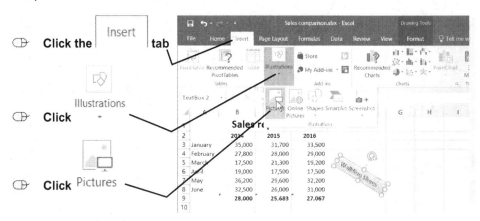

☞ **Open the folder with practice files** ⌘51

In the folder with practice files:

☞ **Click** Clogs.jpg

☞ **Click** `Insert` ▼

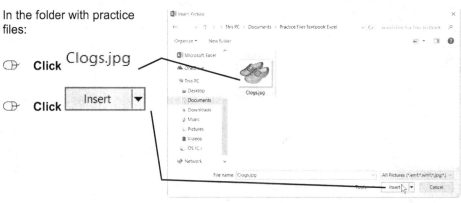

The picture has been inserted on the worksheet:

☞ **Move the image under the table** ⌘75

☞ **By** Picture Styles **, click a style**

The picture will get a border:

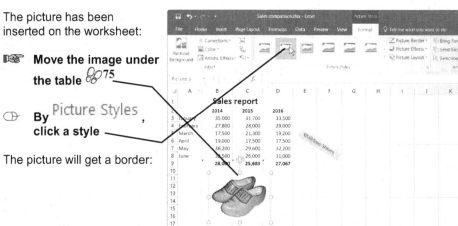

Give the border a color:

⊕ **Click** Picture Border ▼

⊕ **Click a color**

The border will get the
chosen color:

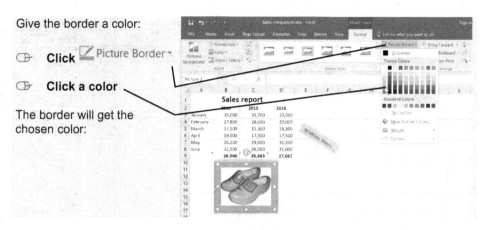

 Tip

Size and position
You can enlarge, reduce and move pictures just like you learned for text boxes and
charts.

For pictures, you can choose artistic or color effects:

⊕ **Click**
   Artistic Effects ▼

⊕ **Click an effect**

⊕ **Click** Color ▼

⊕ **Click a color effect**

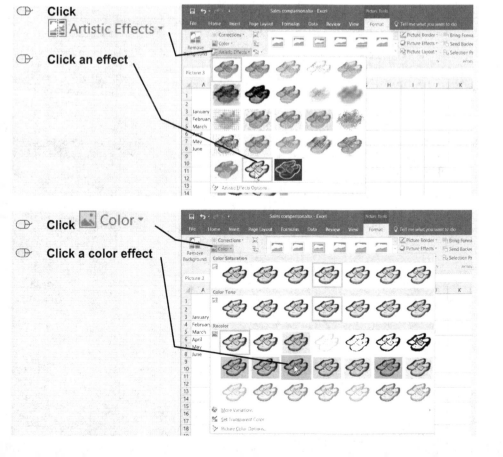

With one click you undo all effects:

⊕ **Click**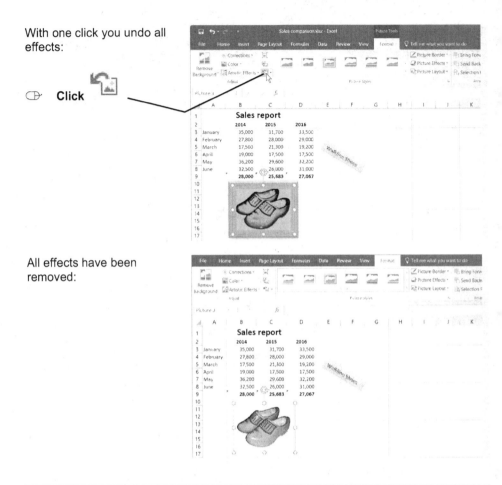

All effects have been removed:

4.15 SmartArt Illustrations

To create professional diagrams and summaries, you can use SmartArt illustrations. These are a large number of symbols in which you can place a (short) text.

⊕ **Click an empty cell**

⊕ **Click the** Insert **tab**

Illustrations

⊕ **Click** ▾

⊕ **Click** SmartArt

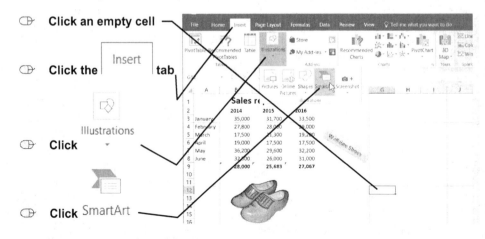

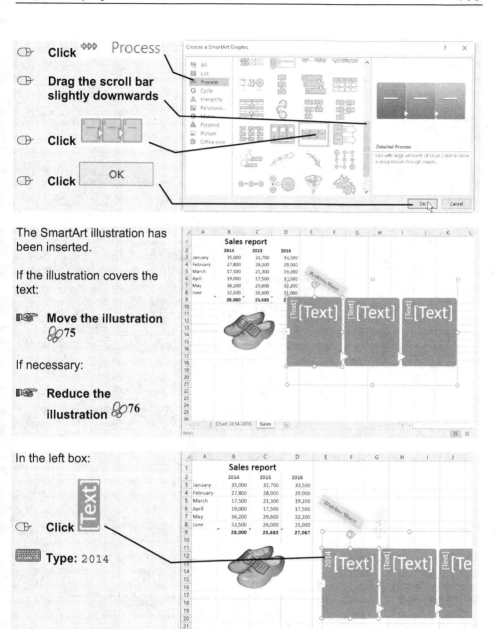

⊕ **Click** ⁘ Process

⊕ **Drag the scroll bar slightly downwards**

⊕ **Click**

⊕ **Click** OK

The SmartArt illustration has been inserted.

If the illustration covers the text:

☞ **Move the illustration** &75

If necessary:

☞ **Reduce the illustration** &76

In the left box:

⊕ **Click**

⌨ **Type:** 2014

In the left box:

👆 **Click** [Text]

⌨ **Type:** 28,000

👉 **Also type the data for 2015 and 2016 in the next boxes**

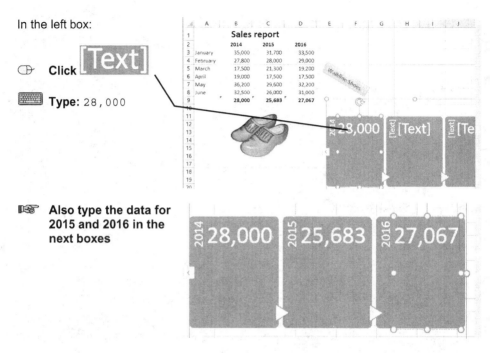

Just like with pictures and text boxes, you can change the format:

On the | Design | tab:

👆 **Click** Change Colors ▾

👆 **Click a color scheme**

To change the style:

👆 **By** SmartArt Styles,

click

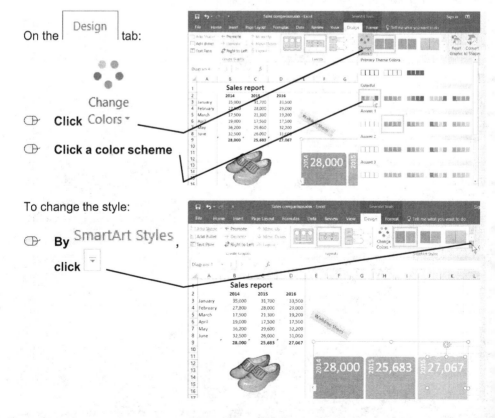

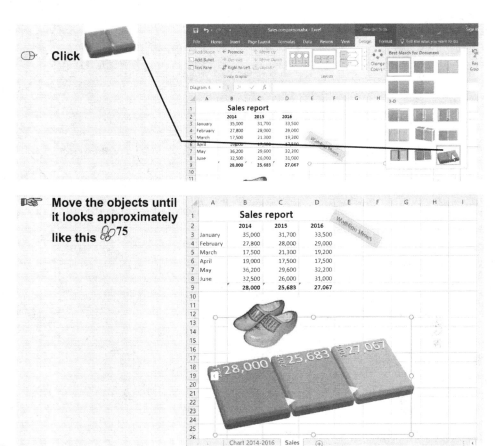

⊕ **Click**

☞ **Move the objects until it looks approximately like this** ✂️⁷⁵

💡 **Tip**

Adding a shape
If you need more SmartArt shapes, you can add extra boxes.

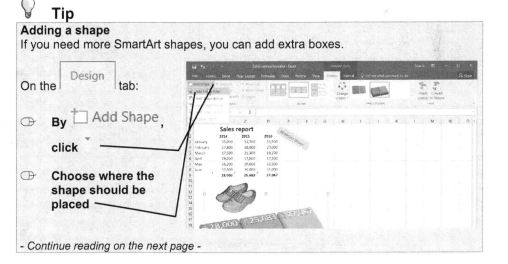

On the | Design | tab:

⊕ **By** ⬚ Add Shape,

   click ▾

⊕ **Choose where the shape should be placed**

- Continue reading on the next page -

The extra shape has been added:	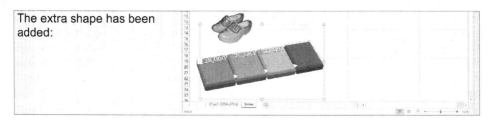

📝 **Save the workbook in the (*My*) *Documents* folder with the name** Walkline shoes 🐾³³

In this chapter you have learned to insert graphic elements such as charts, texts or objects that allow you to clarify the figures of the worksheet. This helps others to faster understand the summary.

📝 **Close *Excel*** 🐾¹⁶

4.16 Exercise

To learn how to quickly apply what you were taught, you can try the following review exercise. Forgot how to carry out an action? Then look it up using the number next to the footsteps 🐾¹ in the appendix *How Do I Do That Again?*

Exercise: Analyzing data

In this exercise you will use *Quick Analysis* and create a chart.

☞ Open *Excel.* 🐾¹

☞ Open the practice file *Vehicle fleet* from the folder *Practice Files Textbook Excel.* 🐾50

☞ Save the workbook with the name `Auto costs 2015` in the (*My*) *Documents* folder. 🐾33

☞ Select cells B2:D5. 🐾19

☞ Calculate the averages using *Quick Analysis.* 🐾77

☞ Let the values show icons. 🐾78

☞ Select cells A1:D5. 🐾19

☞ Create a chart with a stacked column. 🐾79

E
insurance
290
360
320

☞ In column E, type: 400 .

☞ Add Column E to the chart. 🐾80

☞ Change the chart title to `Car costs` 🐾81

☞ In the preview pane *Format Chart Title*, click ✕.

☞ Change the chart to a grouped bar chart.

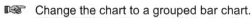

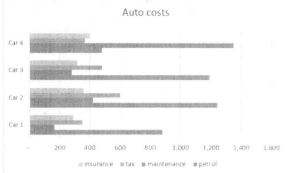

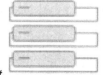

☞ Reduce the chart to half the size. ✂76

☞ Place the chart on a separate worksheet. ✂83

☞ Add the data table to the chart. ✂84

☞ Select *Style 10* for the chart. ✂95

☞ Change the format of the horizontal axis to bold and font size 11. ✂171

☞ Copy this format to the vertical axis. ✂154

☞ Below the table on Sheet1, add a text box with 2015 ✂85

☞ Rotate the text until it is vertical. ✂86

☞ Place the text to the right of the table. ✂75

☞ Change the style of the text box. ✂87

☞ Select the text. ✂88

☞ Choose a WordArt style. ✂89

☞ Select cells B2:E5. ✂19

☞ Have the totals calculated and replace the old data. ✂90

☞ Insert the SmartArt shape *Vertical Box List* .✂91

☞ Add a shape. &⁹²

☞ Inside the shapes, type:

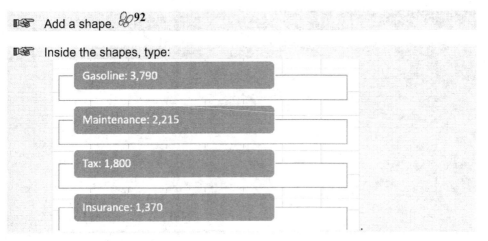

Gasoline: 3,790

Maintenance: 2,215

Tax: 1,800

Insurance: 1,370

☞ Close *Excel* and save the changes. &¹⁶

4.17 Background Information

Which chart?

In *Excel* you can choose from different types of charts. Which chart is most suitable largely depends on the type of data that has to be displayed. An association, for example:

The member distribution can be shown very well in a *pie chart*:

The circle shows the ratio between the member categories, but it does not give any information about the actual number.

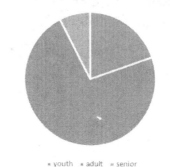

If you want to display the growth of the number of members, a *line chart* is more suitable.

The line represents the increase or decrease in the number of members:

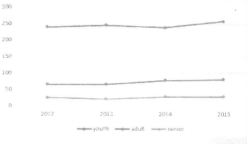

To display the distribution of the members per year, you can use a bar or column chart.

You can see the distribution of the member categories per year:

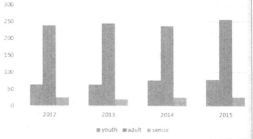

In a grouped column chart, the years are grouped per category so you can easily see the course:

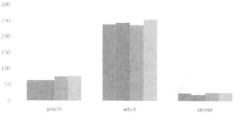

- Continue reading on the next page -

To also see the course of the total number of members, you can use a *stacked column chart*:

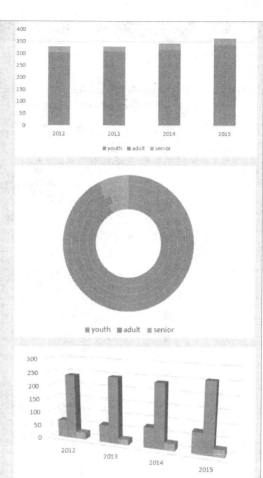

There are variants for each type of chart. These present the data in a slightly different way, but are essentially the same as the basic models.

So instead of a circle you can also choose a *ring chart*:

For column or bar charts, often three-dimensional charts are used:

Sometimes it is not immediately clear which type of chart is most suitable for your data. If so, then start with a simple standard chart, such as a column chart and then

use the button Change Chart Type on the Design tab by Chart Tools to also view the other types.

4.18 Tips

 Tip

Moving objects to the foreground or background
Objects such as pictures are sometimes partially overlapping.

In this case, there is an object in the background that is covered by the object in the foreground:

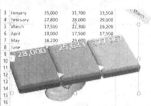

For example, to place the picture of the clogs before the SmartArt illustration, this what you need to do:

☞ **Click the** `Format` **tab**

☞ **By** `Bring Forward`, **click** ▼

☞ **Click** `Bring to Front`

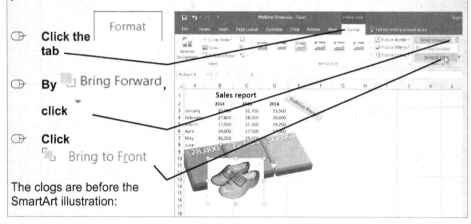

The clogs are before the SmartArt illustration:

 Tip

Changing chart colors
You can change the colors of the chart by choosing another color scheme. But you can also choose the color of an element by yourself:

☞ **Right-click a column**

All columns of that year are selected.

☞ **Click** `Fill`

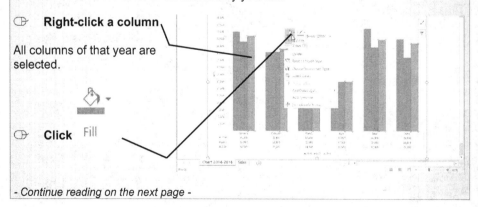

- *Continue reading on the next page -*

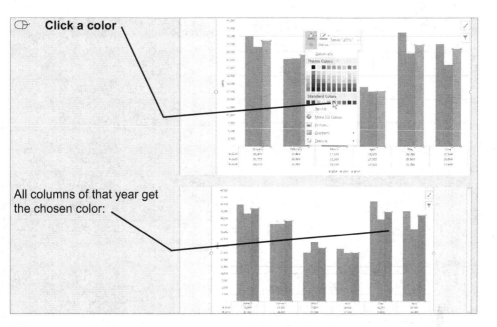

Click a color

All columns of that year get the chosen color:

💡 Tip

Make a chart by yourself

In this chapter, you have created charts with the *Quick Analysis* button. You can also use the ribbon to create charts from a selected area:

👉 Select the cells for the chart ℰℰ19

☞ Click the | Insert | tab

☞ By the chart type, click ˅

☞ Click the chart

The chart has been inserted on the worksheet:

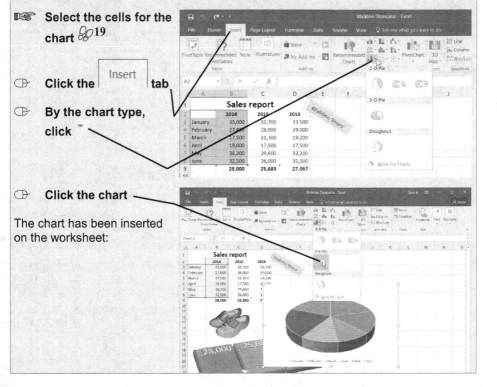

Notes

Write your notes down here.

5. Functions

Excel provides many pre-defined formulas called functions. You started working with some of the simpler functions such as *SUM* in the previous chapters. Functions can help you save time creating formulas as you only need to supply the values but not the operators, such as +, -, *, or /. You will often use a *wizard* (window) to enter these values (arguments). With *Excel's* powerful built-in functions, you can perform logical operations, and more complex statistical or scientific calculations.

Excel classifies its functions in different categories, such as financial, statistical, mathematical, date/time, etc. Many of these functions may at first seem difficult to understand. But if you start slow and go one step at a time, you will be surprised at how much easier it becomes working with functions.

In addition to the mathematical functions there are also text functions. For example, you can merge cells containing text, select specific parts of a text string or convert text to upper or lower case.

In this chapter you will learn to use some of the most popular functions by adjusting a grading list worksheet. The method used for all functions is essentially the same. As you become more comfortable working with functions, you can explore new ones on your own.

In this chapter you will learn how to:

- indicate a cell range;
- find formulas;
- count the number of values in a range;
- calculate an average of selected cells;
- search for the highest or lowest value;
- highlight cells that meet certain conditions;
- count the number of cells with text;
- count the number of cells meeting a certain condition;
- calculate the average of cells meeting a certain condition;
- calculate the total of cells meeting a certain condition;
- use the *IF* function;
- validate cell entries;
- select parts of a text string;
- merge cell texts;
- convert text to upper case or lower case;
- delete any spaces.

5.1 Cell Range

When you use a function, you first need to specify the cells where the formula is to be applied. This is called the cell range. You began to work with a cell range already in the first chapter of this book. The cell range is indicated in the same way in both formulas and functions:

A single cell	A1 or C5
A group of joint cells	A1:A12 or B3:H15
An absolute cell	$B$5
A group of joint absolute cells	$B$5:$H$15
A cell on a different worksheet in the same workbook	Turnover!B9
A cell in a different workbook	[Sales.xlsx]January!B15

 Tip

Click the cells
The risk of errors is very large if you type complex references by yourself. Therefore, when entering a formula, it is better to click the cell or select the cell range with the mouse. This is especially useful if this is a cell on a different worksheet or in another workbook.

You will use the same method of notation of the cells or cell range both in arithmetic formulas and in the functions you will learn to use in this chapter.

5.2 Formulas Tab

The first function that you already have learned about in *Chapter 1 Setting up Excel and Basic Functions* is the *SUM* function on the │ Home │ tab. This and all other functions can be found on the │ Formulas │ tab.

☞ **Open** *Excel* ⏏1

☞ **Open the** *Grading list* **workbook** ⏏50

☞ **Save the list with the name** Class 2A **in the (***My***) *Documents* folder** ⏏33

This workbook shows the grades for a number of subjects per student:

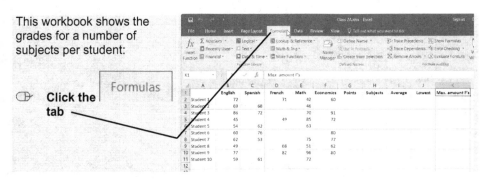

☞ **Click the** *Formulas* **tab**

You will find all the functions in the *Function Library* group. These are divided into categories. If you know a function's category, you can select it:

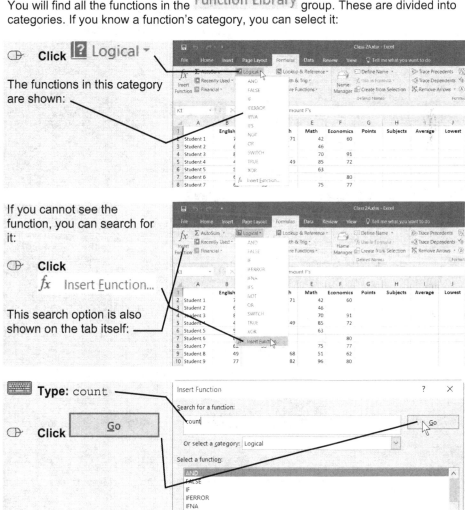

☞ **Click** 🔲 *Logical ▾*

The functions in this category are shown:

If you cannot see the function, you can search for it:

☞ **Click** *fx Insert Function...*

This search option is also shown on the tab itself:

⌨ **Type:** count

☞ **Click** *Go*

The functions with *numbers* are listed at the top:

☞ **Click** Cancel

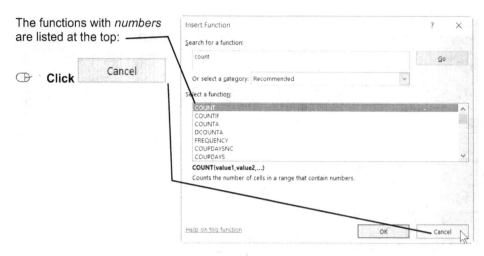

A number of frequently used functions can also be found by Σ AutoSum.

☞ **Click cell G2**

☞ **By** Σ **AutoSum**, **click** ▾

☞ **Click** Σ **Sum**

The cells with numbers next to it are selected automatically.

The selection ends at the first empty cell:

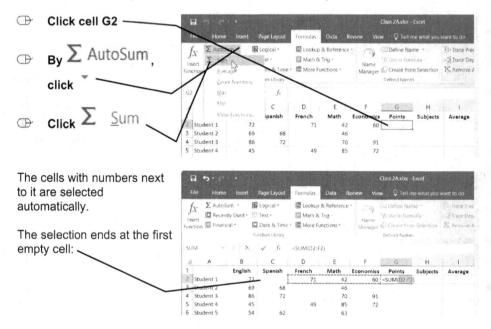

The grade for English that is shown before the empty cell has to be selected, too:

☞ **Select cells B2:F2**
∂∂19

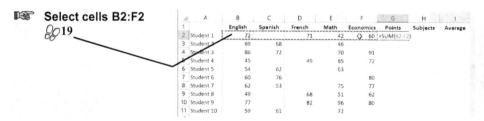

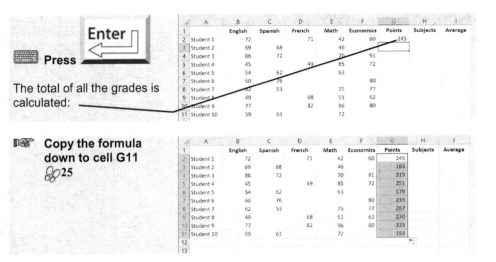

Press [Enter ↵]

The total of all the grades is calculated:

☞ **Copy the formula down to cell G11**
✂ 25

5.3 COUNT Function

Not every student has the same number of subjects. The number of subjects per student is calculated with the COUNT function:

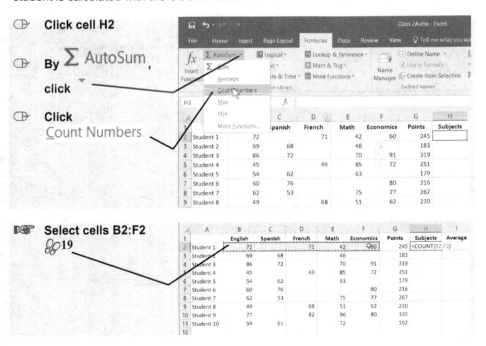

☞ **Click cell H2**

☞ **By Σ AutoSum, click** ▾

☞ **Click** <u>C</u>ount Numbers

☞ **Select cells B2:F2**
✂ 19

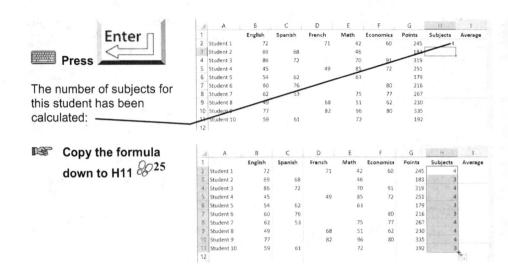

Press `Enter`

The number of subjects for this student has been calculated: —

☞ **Copy the formula down to H11** ✂25

5.4 AVERAGE Function

The average grade per subject of each student is calculated with the *AVERAGE* function:

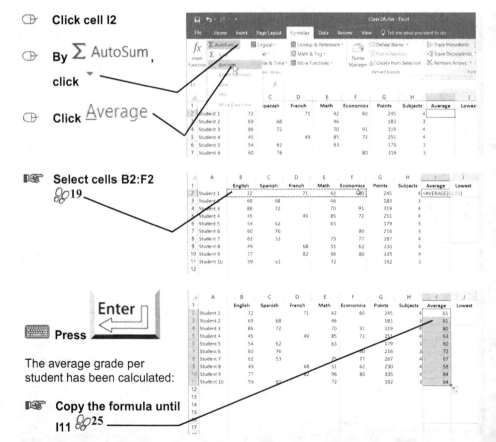

👆 **Click cell I2**

👆 **By Σ AutoSum,** click ▾

👆 **Click Average**

☞ **Select cells B2:F2** ✂19

Press `Enter`

The average grade per student has been calculated:

☞ **Copy the formula until I11** ✂25

It is a good idea to check whether this is the correct average. Do this for student 1:
- Achieved grades: 72+71+42+60 = 245. This is the same as in the *Points* column.
- The number of subjects is 4.
- The average grade is 245 divided by 4 or 61.25. Rounded off, that's 61.

The average grade per subject can also be calculated like this:

☞ **Click cell B12**

☞ **By Σ AutoSum,**

 click ▼

☞ **Click** <u>Average</u>

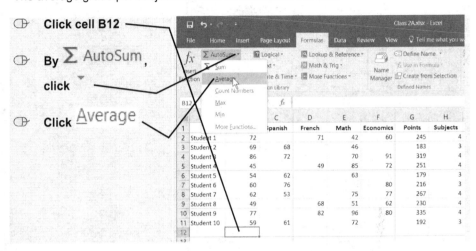

The correct range is selected:

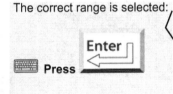

⌨ **Press** ⏎ Enter

☞ **Copy the formula until F12**

The average grade per subject has been calculated:

	A	B	C	D	E	F	G	H
1		English	Spanish	French	Math	Economics	Points	Subjects
2	Student 1	72		71	42	60	245	4
3	Student 2	69	68		46		183	3
4	Student 3	86	72		70	91	319	4
5	Student 4	45		49	85	72	251	4
6	Student 5	54	62		63		179	3
7	Student 6	60	76			80	216	3
8	Student 7	62	53		75	77	267	4
9	Student 8	49		68	51	62	230	4
10	Student 9	77		82	96	80	335	4
11	Student 10	59	61		72		192	3
12		63	65	68	60	75		
13								

🔖 Please note:

There is no grade shown for a subject the student is not taking. Should there have been a zero there, then that zero counts for the calculation of the average. The average will then be lower. Cells that do not count should be completely empty in such a case.

If you have typed something in it, then empty the cell by pressing ⟩ **Delete**

5.5 MIN and MAX Functions

It can also be important to know the lowest grade. Let's say, for example, that a student cannot pass a course if the grade is less than 45. You can do this type of calculation with the *MIN* function:

☞ **Click cell J2**

☞ **By Σ AutoSum ,**

   click ▾

☞ **Click Min**

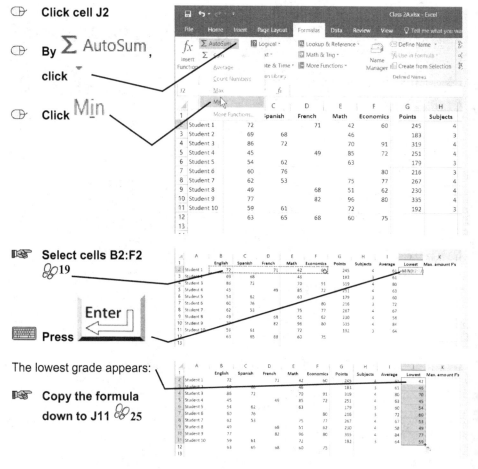

☞ **Select cells B2:F2**
   ⌨19

   Enter

⌨ **Press**

The lowest grade appears:

☞ **Copy the formula**
   down to J11 ⌨25

🐾 **Please note:**

Just as in the previous section, it is important here as well that there is no zero for the subjects a student does not take. Otherwise, the lowest grade would always be zero.

💡 **Tip**

Highest grade

With the *MAX* function, you can determine the highest grade in the same way.

5.6 Conditional Formatting

Notice only student 1 has a grade of less than 45. Thus, this student would not pass the course. To make this more visibly apparent, you can highlight that grade with a color:

 Please note:

The range of cells J2 to J11 should be selected and not just the cell that needs to be colored now. If a grade changes, another student may receive a grade of 45 or less.

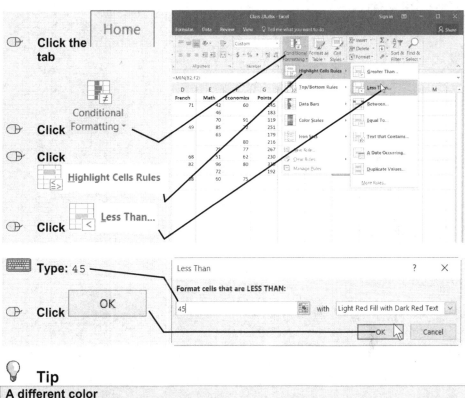

⊕ **Click the** *Home* **tab**

⊕ **Click** *Conditional Formatting ▾*

⊕ **Click** *Highlight Cells Rules*

⊕ **Click** *Less Than...*

⌨ **Type:** 45

⊕ **Click** *OK*

💡 **Tip**

A different color

The cells which meet this condition become light red with a red text. You can also choose a different color:

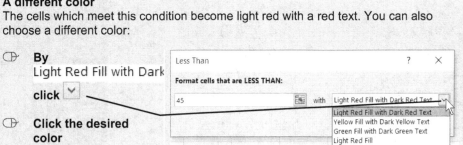

⊕ **By** *Light Red Fill with Dark...* **click** ⌄

⊕ **Click the desired color**

Click cell K2

The grade from student 1 is highlighted in red:

Even if a grade changes, the average is calculated directly:

In cell B9, type: 42

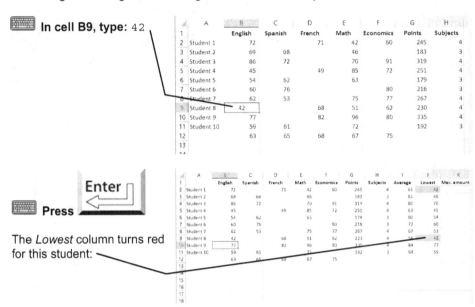

Enter

Press

The *Lowest* column turns red for this student:

5.7 COUNTA Function

You can use the *COUNT* function to count the number of cells that contains a number. To count the total numbers of cells with text *or* numbers, you need a different function called *COUNTA*. This function is not located under *AutoSum*, but you can find it like this:

Click cell A12

Click the Formulas tab

fx Insert

Click Function

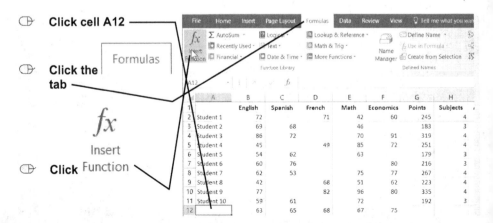

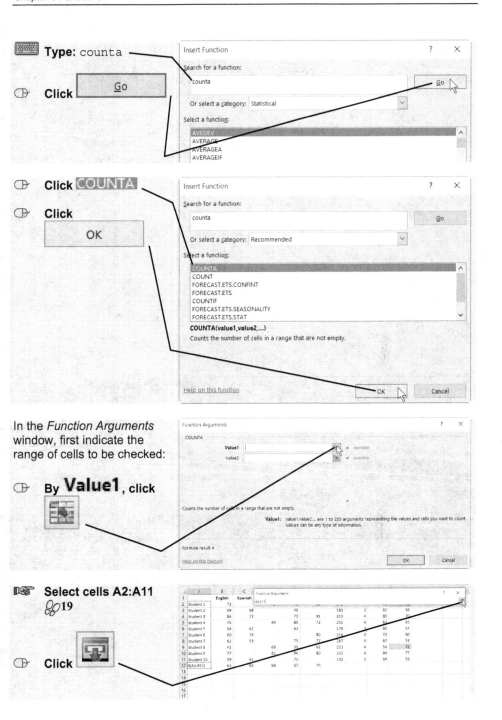

Type: counta

Click Go

Click COUNTA

Click OK

In the *Function Arguments* window, first indicate the range of cells to be checked:

By **Value1**, click

Select cells A2:A11

Click

The selection has been filled in:

☞ **Click**

OK

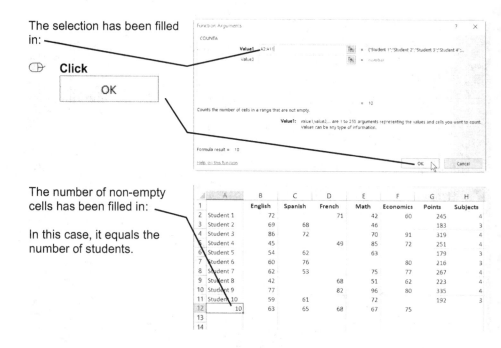

The number of non-empty cells has been filled in:

In this case, it equals the number of students.

5.8 COUNTIF Function

For various functions, it is possible to use an *IF* condition. Only the cells that meet a certain condition will be used with the function.

If a requirement to pass this semester is that only one grade must be less than 50, then you can use the COUNTIF function to determine the number of grades less than 50 per student:

☞ **Click cell K2**

☞ **If necessary, click the**

Formulas

tab

fx

Insert

☞ **Click** Function

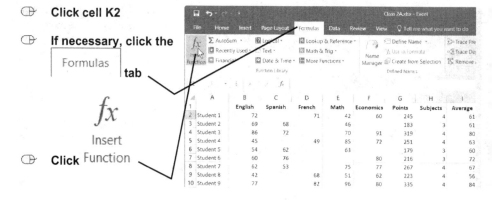

Type: `countif`

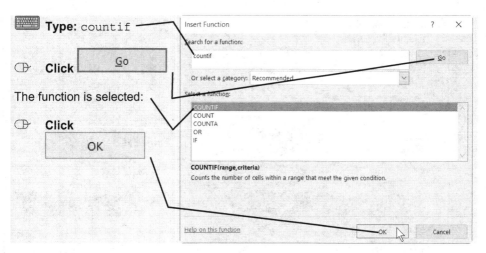

Click [Go]

The function is selected:

Click [OK]

💡 **Tip**

Function description
Sometimes there are functions that may seem very similar to one another. If you click the name of the function, you can see a brief description for it:

Click a function

You will see the description:

If necessary, you can view more information, including examples:

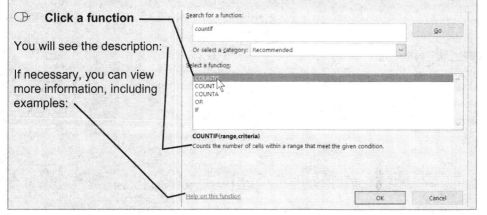

First indicate the range of cells to be checked:

By **Range**, click

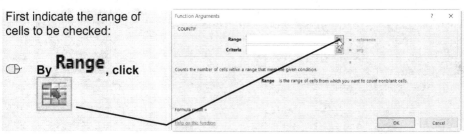

☞ **Select cells B2:F2**
🐾19

Click

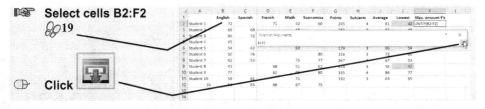

The range has been filled in. The condition is *less than 50*:

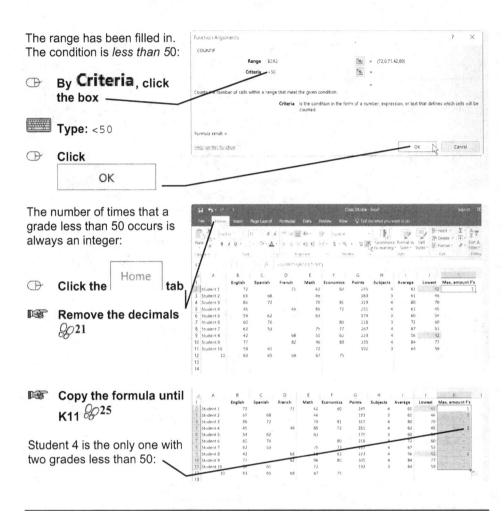

🖱 By **Criteria**, click the box

⌨ Type: <50

🖱 Click

OK

The number of times that a grade less than 50 occurs is always an integer:

🖱 Click the [Home] tab

☞ Remove the decimals 🦶21

☞ Copy the formula until K11 🦶25

Student 4 is the only one with two grades less than 50:

5.9 AVERAGEIF and SUMIF Functions

Functions with ranges and criteria nearly all work in the same way. You can use them to perform all kinds of calculations in a simple way. For instance, if you want to know what is the average of all grades greater than or equal to sixty, then this is how to calculate that:

⌨ In cell A14, type:
Average passing

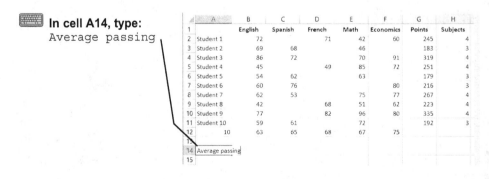

⊕ **Click cell C14**

⊕ **Click the** Formulas **tab**

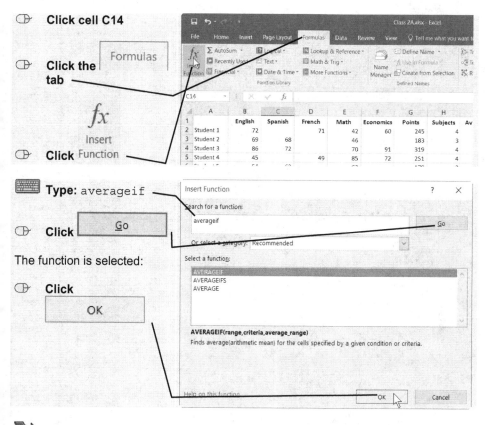

⊕ **Click** Insert Function

⌨ **Type:** averageif

⊕ **Click** Go

The function is selected:

⊕ **Click** OK

👆 Please note:

Notice that the names of functions can also be very similar. For example AVERAGEIF and AVERAGEIFS. Pay close attention to which function is selected. If necessary, click the appropriate function before you click OK.

First indicate the range of cells the function must check:

⊕ **By** Range**, click**

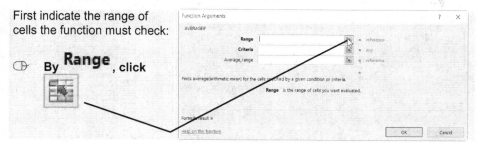

Select all grades:

☞ **Select cells B2:F11** ℅19

⊕ **Click**

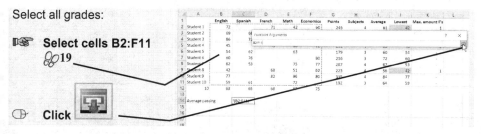

The condition is *greater than or equal to 60*:

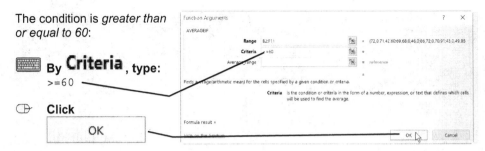

 By **Criteria**, type:
>=60

⊕ **Click**

| OK |

Comparisons
For conditions and comparisons, the mathematical signs are used:

=   Equal to
>   Greater than
<   Less than

These can also be used in combinations:

>=   Greater than or equal to
<=   Less than or equal to
<>   Unequal to

The average satisfactory grade is 72.925926:

	A	B	C	D	E	F	G	H
1		English	Spanish	French	Math	Economics	Points	Subjects
2	Student 1	72		71	42	60	245	4
3	Student 2	69	68		46		183	3
4	Student 3	86	72		70	91	319	4
5	Student 4	45		49	85	72	251	4
6	Student 5	54	62		63		179	3
7	Student 6	60	76			80	216	3
8	Student 7	62	53		75	77	267	4
9	Student 8	42		68	51	62	223	4
10	Student 9	77		82	96	80	335	4
11	Student 10	59	61		72		192	3
12	10	63	65	68	67	75		
14	Average passing	72.925926						

 Tip

Input fields
In the *Function Arguments* window, there are often fields that must be filled in. These are the required fields. Other fields may be left blank. These fields can be used for more detailed conditions, but are not required.

The fields shown in **bold** text are required:

Field names that are not bold, are optional:

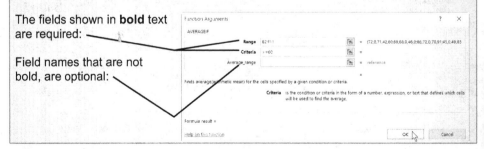

If you want to calculate the total number of points of all students with an unsatisfactory grade, then you can calculate it in the same way with *SUMIF*:

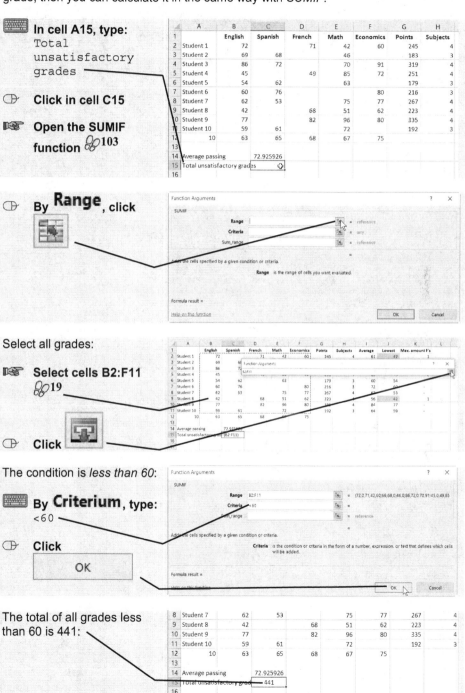

In cell A15, type:
Total
unsatisfactory
grades

☞ **Click in cell C15**

🖙 **Open the SUMIF**
function 🦶103

☞ **By Range, click**

Select all grades:

🖙 **Select cells B2:F11**
🦶19

☞ **Click**

The condition is *less than 60*:

By Criterium, type:
<60

☞ **Click**
OK

The total of all grades less than 60 is 441:

This figure in itself is not very meaningful, because it says nothing about the number of unsatisfactory grades. You could calculate that number using the *COUNTIF* function.

5.10 IF Function

Sometimes the content of a cell has to be dependent on the content of another cell. You can have this done automatically with the *IF* function.

For example, you can put the temperature in a cell and have the word "frost" appear opposite it, if it is below thirty-two degrees Fahrenheit.
If the temperature is thirty-two degrees Fahrenheit or above, the word "thaw" can appear:

	A	B
1	Temperature (F):	
2	41	thaw
3	33.8	thaw
4	28	frost

In this exercise, you use the function to determine whether someone needs to repeat a exam in a certain subject. Here, a repeat exam has to be taken if the average grade is below 60. Enter the formula as follows:

In cell L1, type:
Repeat exam

Widen column L until the text fits $\mathscr{L}$18

Click cell L2

Open the function IF $\mathscr{L}$103

Click cell I2

The average grade is in cell I2.

After cell I2, type: <60

By Value_if_true, **type:** repeat exam

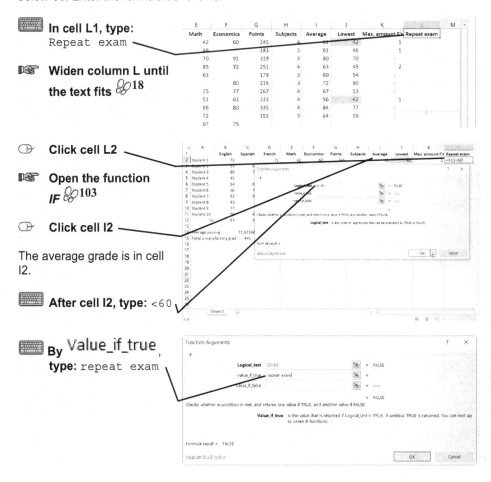

If you leave Value_if_false completely blank, the cell will show a zero or a dash. Therefore, type a space so the cell remains blank:

By Value_if_false, click the box ─

Press the space bar

Click

OK

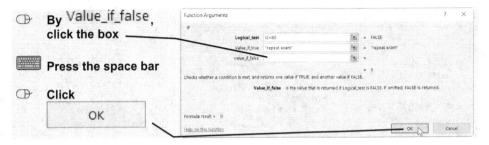

The average grade of student 1 is 61, so no repeat exam is necessary. Now, check the other students:

Copy the formula until L11 ✂25

The status for students 5 and 8 shows *repeat exam*: ↖

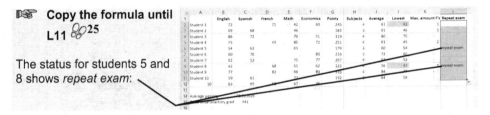

The average grade of student 8 is 56, so a repeat exam is necessary. The average grade of student 5 is 60, but it still shows *repeat exam*. This is because *Excel* rounds the numbers on the screen to one decimal. The actual grade of student 5 in this case is less than 60, but it is rounded to 60.

If you increase the number of decimals in the column with average grades, the grade is shown more accurately:

Select cells I2:I11 ✂19

Click the Home tab ─

Click the .00

You will see that the average grade of student 5 is not 60 but 59.7. ─

Excel calculates with this actual figure, which is why student 5 also has to take a repeat exam.

Click 🔲 ─

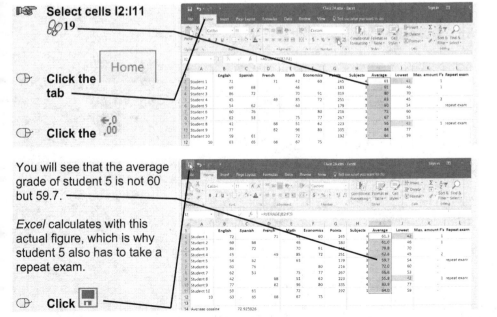

Tip

Setting the accuracy
You can set the accuracy for calculations in *Excel* to the desired numbers of decimals.

Close the workbook, but keep *Excel* open:

⊕ **Click** File

⊕ **Click** Close

5.11 Data Validation

To help prevent you from entering wrong data in certain cells, you can use data validation. Data validation allows you to set:

- what values are allowed to be entered;
- an input message with instructions, if necessary;
- what should happen if an invalid value is entered.

☞ **Open the *Text functions* practice file from the *Practice Files Workbook Excel* folder** &&50

☞ **Save the file with the same name in the (*My*) *Documents* folder** &&33

The age must be entered in cell B6. The minimum age should be 18 years old. For this purpose, you will set up data validation:

⊕ **Click cell B6**

⊕ **Click the** Data **tab**

⊕ **Click**

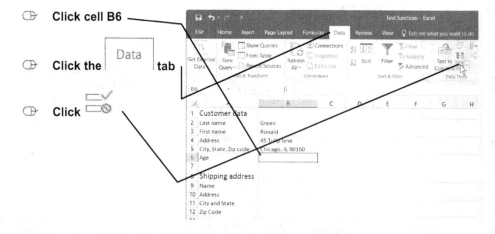

The default value is that any value is allowed. Change this setting:

⊕ By <u>A</u>llow: , click

⊕ **Click**
Whole number

⊕ By <u>D</u>ata: , click

The minimum age is 18 years old:

⊕ **Click**
greater than or equ

⌨ By <u>M</u>inimum: ,
type: 18

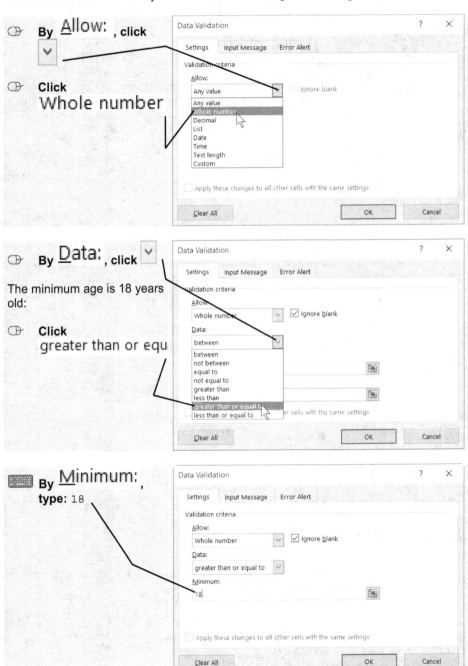

You can set an input message for this cell, so that the person who is typing the age in this cell knows that the minimum age is 18 years old:

⊕ **Click the** Input Message **tab**

⌨ **By** Title: **, type:** Please note!

⌨ **By** Input message: **, type:** Minimum age is 18 years old

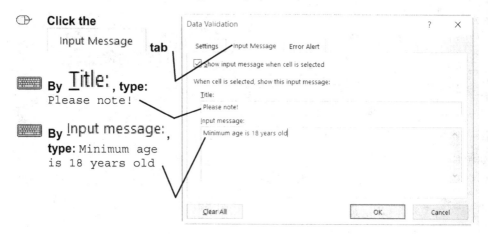

On the *Error Alert* tab, you can set an error message that will be shown if the age is less than 18 years old:

⊕ **Click the** Error Alert **tab**

⌨ **By** Title: **, type:** Invalid

⌨ **By** Error message: **, type:** Age too low

⊕ **Click** OK

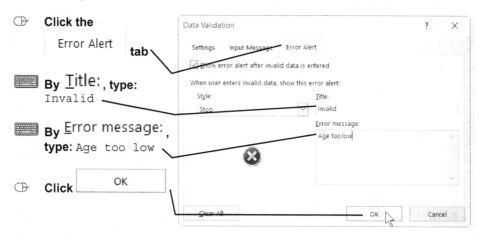

💡 **Tip**

Other options
If it is not necessary to stop when an invalid value is entered, you can also choose from a small warning or information window:

⊕ **By** Style: **, click** ⌄

⊕ **Click the desired type**

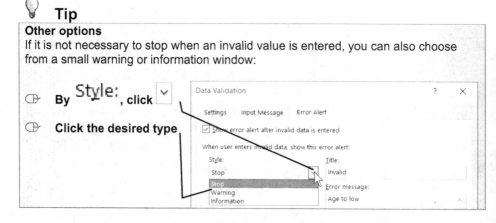

Since cell B6 is still selected, the input message appears directly:

Type: 15

Press Enter

The error message appears:

Click Retry

Type: 18

Press Enter

That age is accepted.

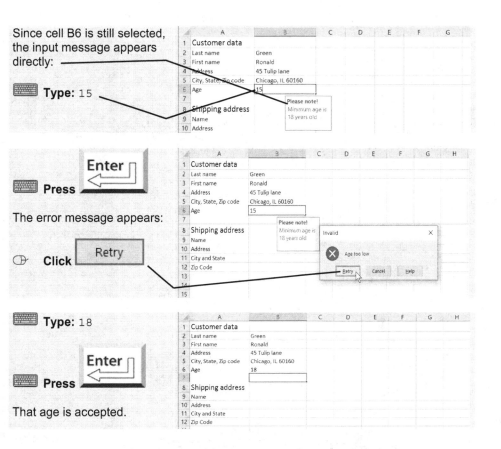

5.12 Text Functions

In this chapter you have been working with various arithmetic functions. There are also a number of functions available for working with text. You can start using some of these text functions to place the address details in a mailing list in a different format.

The first name and last name should be placed next to each other in the mailing list. To do this, you can use the *CONCAT* function:

Click cell B9

Click the Formulas **tab**

Click 🅰 Text ▾

Click CONCAT

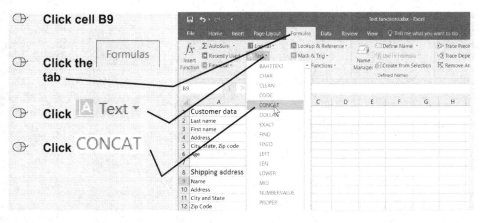

💡 Tip

Inserting a function

fx

Insert

If you know the name of the function, you can use the Function button to look it up.

The first name comes before the last name, so first you select the first name:

☞ **Click in cell B3**

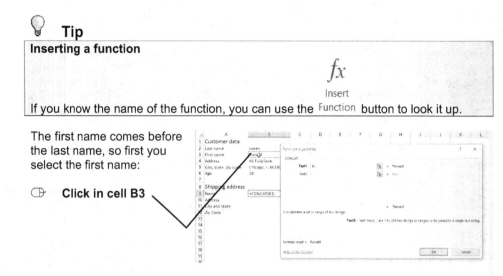

The first name should be followed by a space:

☞ **By** Text2 **, click the box**

A new box appears automatically: Text3

⌨ **Press the space bar**

☞ **Click the box by** Text3

Select the last name:

☞ **Click in cell B2**

☞ **Click** OK

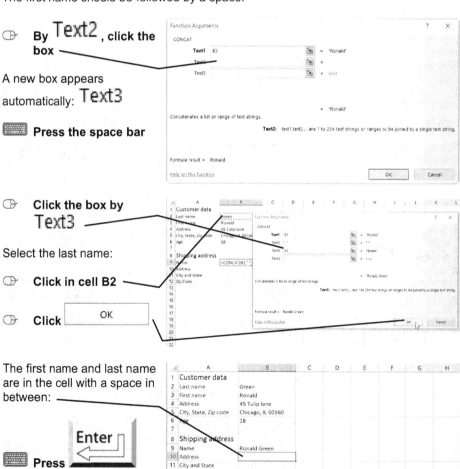

The first name and last name are in the cell with a space in between:

⌨ **Press** Enter

5.13 Converting Text to Upper Case or Lower Case

You can convert text to upper case with the *UPPER* function or to lower case with the *LOWER* function. In the shipping address, change the street name to upper case:

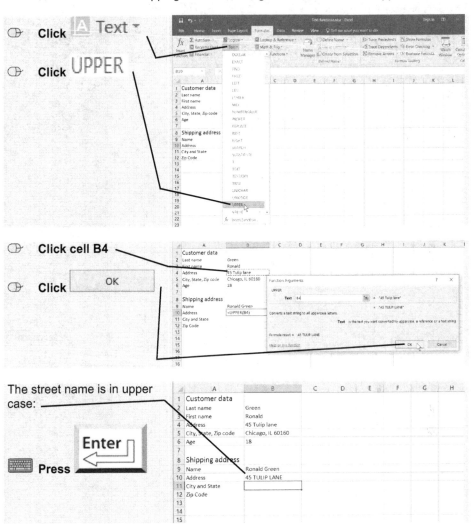

Click Text ▾

Click UPPER

Click cell B4

Click OK

The street name is in upper case:

Press Enter

5.14 Selecting Part of a Text String

The city, state and zip code are listed in a single cell and need to be shown separately in the shipping address. In order to do this, first copy the first eleven characters (the city plus the state abbreviation) to the shipping address with the *Left* function:

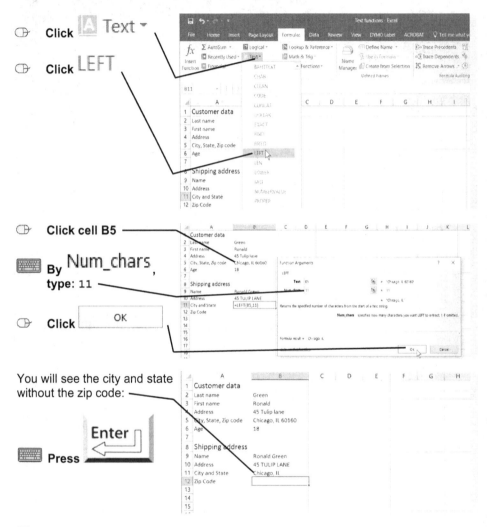

☞ **Click** 🅰 Text ▾

☞ **Click LEFT**

☞ **Click cell B5**

⌨ By **Num_chars**,
    type: 11

☞ **Click** | OK |

You will see the city and state without the zip code:

⌨ **Press** Enter ⏎

🢗 Please note:

The operations described in this section are correct only if you have a city name and state name consisting of eleven characters, as in "Chicago, IL" (includes the comma and a space) and a ZIP code of 5 characters. If the data used in other examples contains more or less characters, keep in mind that the function will then need to be altered.

With the *Right* function, you can split a specified number of characters from the right. You can copy the zip code to the shipping address with the *Right* function:

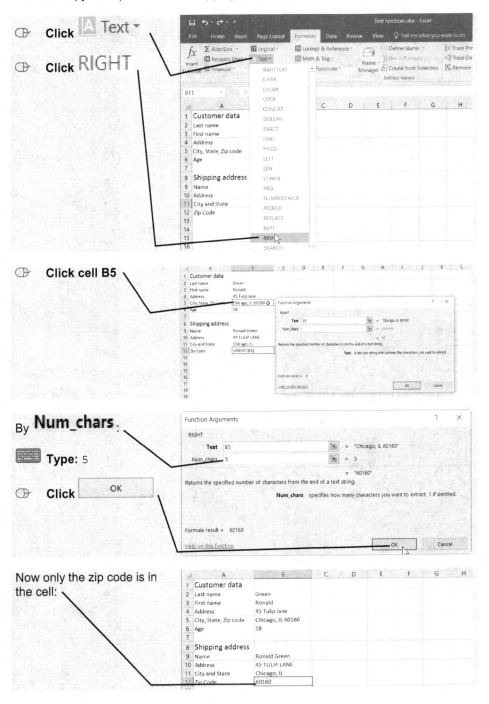

Click Text ▾

Click RIGHT

Click cell B5

By **Num_chars**.

Type: 5

Click OK

Now only the zip code is in the cell:

If there are too many spaces in a cell, you can delete them with the *TRIM* function. To see how this works, first insert a number of extra spaces between the street name and the house number in the customer data:

⊕ **Click cell B4**

⊕ **In the formula bar, click between the house number and the street name**

⌨ **Press the space bar a number of times**

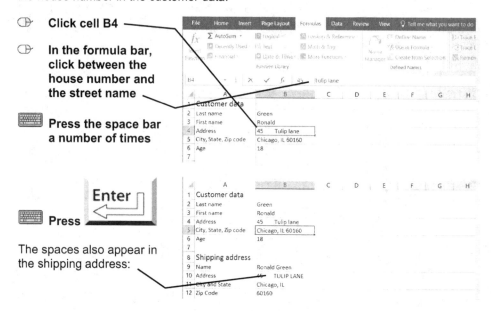

Enter

⌨ **Press**

The spaces also appear in the shipping address:

You can use a formula to delete the excess spaces. To show this, in this example you will use the formula in cell B14:

⊕ **Click cell B14**

You can show the street name here without the extra spaces:

⊕ **Click** **Text ▾**

⊕ **Drag the scroll bar downwards**

⊕ **Click** **TRIM**

⊕ **Click cell B4**

⊕ **Click** **OK**

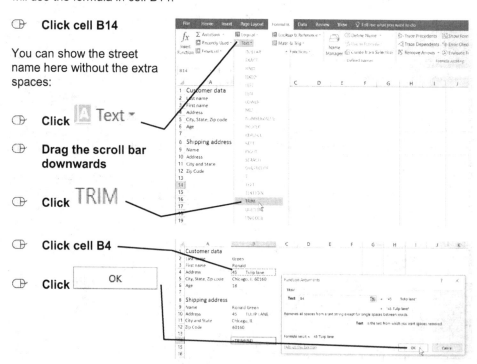

The extra spaces have been removed:

	A	B	C	D	E	F	G	H
1	Customer data							
2	Last name	Green						
3	First name	Ronald						
4	Address	45 Tulip lane						
5	City, State, Zip code	Chicago, IL 60160						
6	Age	18						
7								
8	Shipping address							
9	Name	Ronald Green						
10	Address	45 TULIP LANE						
11	City and State	Chicago, IL						
12	Zip Code	60160						
13								
14		45 Tulip lane						
15								

In this chapter you have worked with functions for calculations and text. You have learned how to set up the range of cells to be checked and how to specify certain conditions. You will use this same method for all functions of *Excel*.

☞ **Close *Excel* and save the changes** ✂ 16

5.15 Exercise

To practice a little more with what you have just learned, you can do the following review exercise. If you have forgotten how to do something, use the number beside the footsteps to look it up in the appendix *How Do I Do That Again?* &1 at the end of the book.

Exercise: Functions

In this exercise you will work with some basic functions.

☞ Open *Excel.* &1

☞ Open the *Functions* file. &50

☞ Save the workbook with the name Chapter 5 in the *(My) Documents* folder. &33

☞ Open the *SUM* function. &104

☞ In cell B8, calculate the total sales for January. &23

☞ Copy the formula from B8 up to D8. &25

☞ In cell E3, use *SUM* to calculate the total sales for Customer A. &23

☞ Copy the formula from E3 up to E8. &25

☞ In cell B10, calculate the number of orders for January. &105

☞ Copy the formula from B10 up to D10. &25

☞ In cell B11, search for the lowest order in January. &106

☞ Copy the formula from B11 up to D11. &25

☞ In cell B12, search for the highest order in January. &107

☞ Copy the formula from B12 up to D12. &25

☞ In cell B13, calculate the average order size in January. &108

☞ Copy the formula from B13 up to D13. &25

☞ Click the | Home | tab.

☞ Set cell D13 not to use any decimals. &21

☞ Click the | Formulas | tab.

☞ Click cell C15.

☞ Open the *SUMIF* function. ✂103

☞ In cell C15, calculate the total of the orders in January to March with an order amount <u>less than</u> 500. ✂109

☞ Click cell C16.

☞ Open the *COUNTIF* function. ✂103

☞ In cell C16, calculate the number of the orders in January to March with an order amount <u>less than</u> 500. ✂110

☞ Click the | Home | tab.

☞ Select cells B3:D7. ✂19

☞ Highlight the cells with an order amount <u>greater than</u> 500 in green. ✂111

☞ Go to Sheet2. ✂41

☞ Click the | Formulas | tab.

☞ Click cell A6.

☞ Use the *CONCAT* function to place the first name and last name in cell 6 with a space in between them. ✂112

☞ Click cell B6.

☞ Open the *IF* function. ✂103

☞ In cell B6, use the *IF* function to place:
"passed" if the grade in cell B4 is greater than 55,
"failed" if the grade in cell B4 is lower. ✂113

☞ Click cell B4.

☞ Use *DATA VALIDATION* to allow only decimal numbers from 1 to 10 in cell B4 and set an error message to be shown when the number is invalid. ✂114

☞ In cell B4, type a 0 and press **Enter** .

You will see the error message:

☞   Click .

☞   In cell B4, type a 4 and press 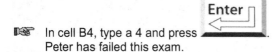.
Peter has failed this exam.

☞   In cell B4, type a 7 and press 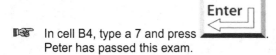.
Peter has passed this exam.

☞   Close the workbook and save the changes. ✂ [16]

5.16 Background Information

Calculation sequence
When you use more complex formulas it is important to keep the order of operations or calculation sequence in mind. This is the same as in mathematics. Excel uses the following sequence:
1. Raise to a power (with the character ^)
2. Multiply and divide (with * and /)
3. Add and subtract (with + and -)

If a formula contains multiple calculations, then those calculations will be performed from left to right in this sequence. For example:

50-10*4=   10*4=40
                50-40=10
50/5+10*4=   50/5=10
                10*4=40
                10+40=50

By putting calculations between parentheses, they will be prioritized. For example:
50/(10-5)*4   10-5=5
                50/5=10
                10*4=40

Without parentheses, the result would be:
50/10-5*4   50/10=5
                5*4=20
                5-20=-15

Nested functions
A function can also be applied within another function or formula. These are called nested functions. This often happens with the *IF* function in a conditional formula. A nested function looks like this, for example:

=IF(AVERAGE(B2:B4)<60;"failed"; "pass")

With this formula you can indicate whether a student has passed or failed an exam. The condition you enter for passing the exam is that the average grade may not be less than 60:

The *AVERAGE* function is as it were embedded in the *IF* function:

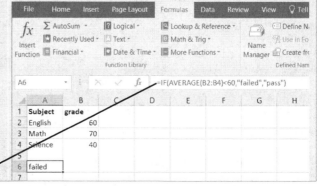

5.17 Tips

  Tip

Selecting faster

If you need to select cells in a function, you can do so directly without clicking 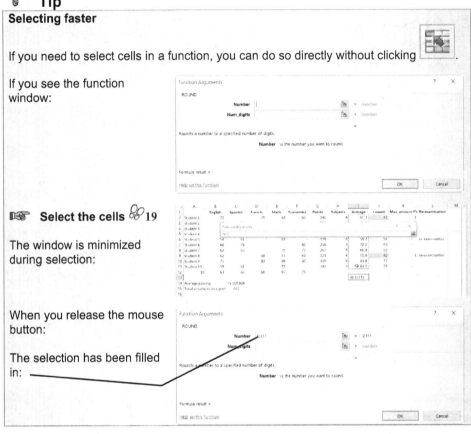.

If you see the function window:

 Select the cells 🕮19

The window is minimized during selection:

When you release the mouse button:

The selection has been filled in: —————

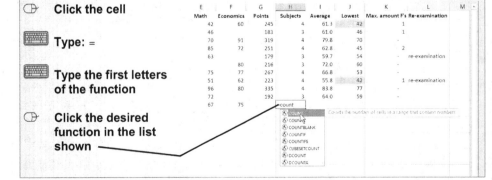 **Tip**

Go directly to the correct function
If you already know the name of the function, you can also type the = character in a cell and the first letters of the name of the function:

🖰 **Click the cell**

⌨ **Type:** =

⌨ **Type the first letters of the function**

🖰 **Click the desired function in the list shown** ———

6. Viewing and Saving

Excel is often used to process and keep track of large amounts of data. The worksheets in the latest versions of *Excel* can contain more than a million rows and over 16.000 columns. Such large summaries cannot be easily viewed at once. That is why there are various functions to make it easier to scroll through the data without losing the overview. By summarizing similar rows or columns with subtotals or by grouping them together, you can quickly view the outlines. If necessary, you can view the details. There are also several useful functions for printing the summary.

Macros help you to carry out common actions quickly, easily and flawlessly. With macros, you capture a number of successive actions in a small program, which you can "playback" with a key combination.

If you need to share your workbook with other people, there might be users with older versions of *Excel*. In that case, you can save the workbook in a so called compatible format, so that they can also open the file. And if you only want to share the information, you can create a file in PDF format. Others see the worksheet in print form, but cannot make any changes to it.

In this chapter you will learn how to:

- change the view by zooming;
- freeze panes;
- split the window;
- hide rows, columns and worksheets;
- use themes and styles;
- copy the format of a cell;
- print titles on each sheet;
- change the paper settings;
- determine the print area;
- place headers and footers on a page;
- set up subtotals;
- display details or only subtotals;
- group data;
- create formulas with cell names;
- display formulas in the worksheet;
- use macros;
- record and run macros;
- save a workbook with macros;
- save a workbook for older versions of *Excel*;
- create a PDF or XPS file;
- save files in the cloud.

6.1 Zooming In and Out

Worksheets are often larger than the screen window, so you can only see a part of the worksheet at any given time. There are several ways to get a better overview of worksheets that are larger than the screen. For example, by zooming:

☞ **Open *Excel*** 🦶¹

☞ **Open the *Languages* workbook** 🦶⁵⁰

☞ **Save the workbook with the same name in the (*My*) *Documents* folder** 🦶³³

You see a part of a long list:

The worksheet is shown in the default size.
The zoom level is shown in the lower right corner of the window

⊕ **Drag the slider slightly to the right**

The zoom level changes and the text is immediately increased in size:

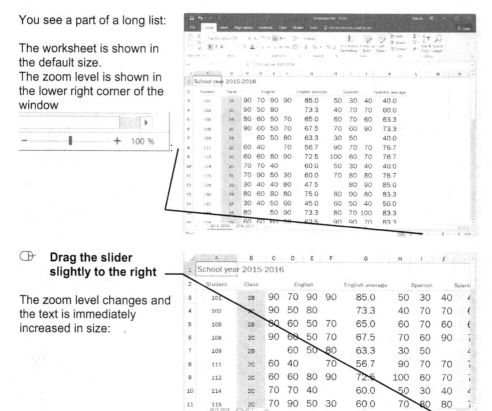

🐾 **Please note:**

The zoom level only changes the size on the screen. The print size does not change. The zoom level on the other worksheets in the workbook does not change either.

To see a larger part of the worksheet on the screen, reduce the zoom level:

 Drag the slider to the left until you see the bottom of the worksheet

The zoom level becomes smaller and the text is reduced in size:

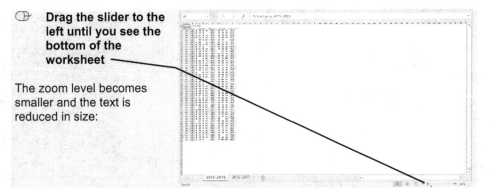

You will now see the entire worksheet, but the content is difficult or impossible to read.

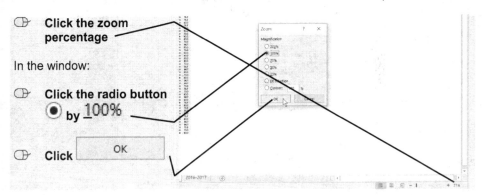

 Click the zoom percentage

In the window:

 Click the radio button
⊙ **by 100%**

 Click OK

Please note:

The zoom level of 100% is not always the most appropriate. The best zoom factor also depends on the size and resolution of the monitor and the data on the worksheet.

Only the first part of the worksheet is visible:

	Student	Class	English				English average	Spanish			Spanish average
1	School year 2015-2016										
2	Student	Class	English				English average	Spanish			Spanish average
3	101	2A	90	70	90	90	85.0	50	30	40	40.0
4	102	2C	90	50	80		73.3	40	70	70	60.0
5	106	2A	80	60	50	70	65.0	60	70	60	63.3
6	108	2C	90	60	50	70	67.5	70	60	90	73.3
7	109	2A		60	50	80	63.3	30	50		40.0
8	111	2C	60	40		70	56.7	90	70	70	76.7
9	112	2C	60	60	80	90	72.5	100	60	70	76.7
10	114	2C	70	70	40		60.0	50	30	40	40.0
11	115	2A	70	90	50	30	60.0	70	80	80	76.7
12	128	2A	30	40	40	80	47.5		80	90	85.0
13	130	2A	80	60	80	80	75.0	80	90	80	83.3
14	131	2A	30	40	50	60	45.0	60	50	40	50.0
15	133	2A	80		50	90	73.3	80	70	100	83.3
16	134	2A	60	60	60	70	62.5	90	90	70	83.3

6.2 Freezing Panes

To see the bottom part of the list, you can scroll down with the scroll bar:

☞   **Drag the scroll bar
downwards**

The column titles are no
longer visible:

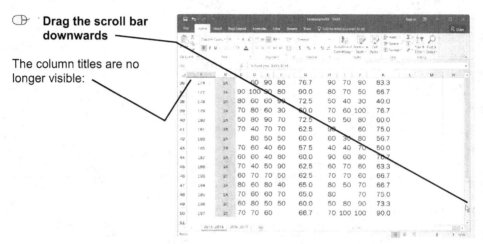

To keep the titles above the columns visible, you can *freeze* the upper rows:

☞   **Drag the scroll bar
upwards**

☞   **Click the** View **tab**

The titles are shown in the
top two rows:

☞   **Click cell A3**

☞   **Click** Freeze Panes ▾

☞   **Click** Freeze Panes

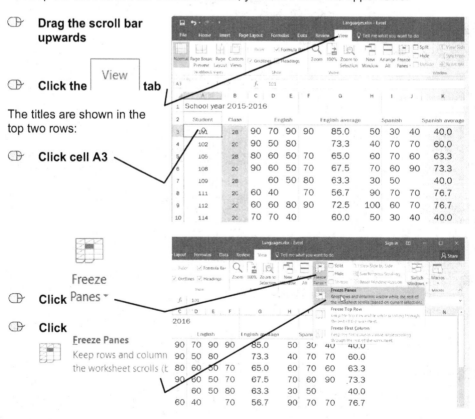

Drag the scroll bar downwards

The column titles will remain visible:

The dark line under the fixed rows indicates the panes are frozen:

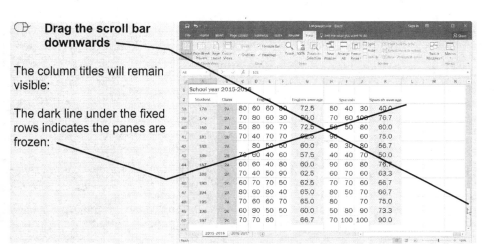

💡 Tip

Freezing panes

With **Freeze Panes** you decide by yourself how many rows or columns you want to freeze. With **Freeze Top Row** only the top row is frozen and with **Freeze First Column** only the first column.

If you want to freeze other columns as well, select the cell next to the column(s) to be frozen. To freeze both the first two rows and columns A and B:

☞ **Click cell C3**

Freeze
☞ **Click Panes ▾**

☞ **Click Freeze Panes**

If you scroll downwards now, the top two rows remain visible. If you scroll to the right, then column A and B remain visible.

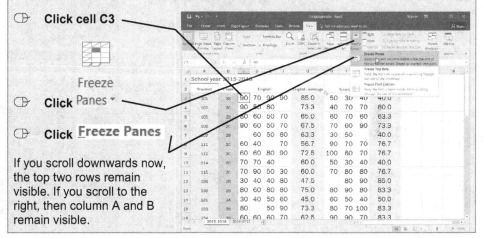

To unfreeze the panes:

Freeze
☞ **Click Panes ▾**

☞ **Click Unfreeze Panes**

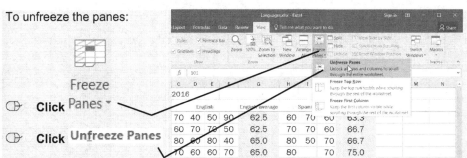

The panes have been unfrozen. The dark line is no longer visible:

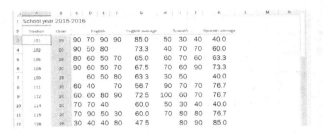

6.3 Splitting the Window

If you want to view different parts of a worksheet at the same time, you can split the *Excel* window. For instance, you can compare the average grades for English next to those for Spanish:

⊕ **Click cell H1**

⊕ **Click** ▭ **Split**

You will see a dark vertical line to the left of column H:

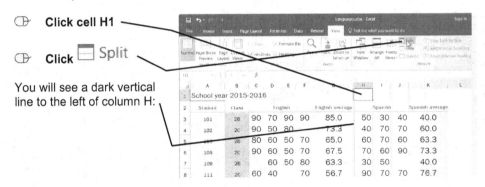

🍃 Please note:

If you select a cell in the middle of the worksheet, not in row 1 or column A, the window will be split in four parts.

Now slide the right part to the column with the average grades for English using the scroll bar:

In the bottom right part of the window:

⊕ **Click** ▶ **three times**

The averages are now shown next to each other.

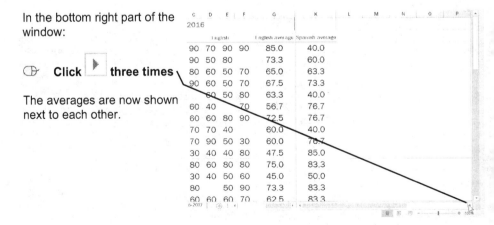

Undo the splitting:

⊕ **Click** Split

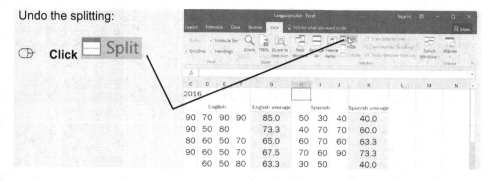

6.4 Hiding Rows, Columns and Worksheets

Sometimes things become clearer if you only see the relevant data. If you just want to see the average grades for English and Spanish, then you can hide the columns with separate grades. First hide the columns with the grades for English:

⊕ **Click the tab** Home

⊕ **Drag through the column titles C:F**

The columns C to F are now selected:

⊕ **Click** Format ▾

⊕ **Click** Hide & Unhide

⊕ **Click** Hide Columns

The columns C to F are hidden:

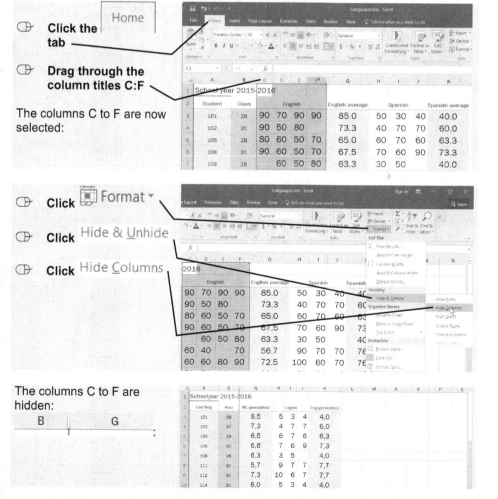

Tip

Not printing columns or rows
Hidden columns or rows will not be printed.

Now also hide columns H to
J:

⊕ **Select the columns
     H:J**

⊕ **Click** 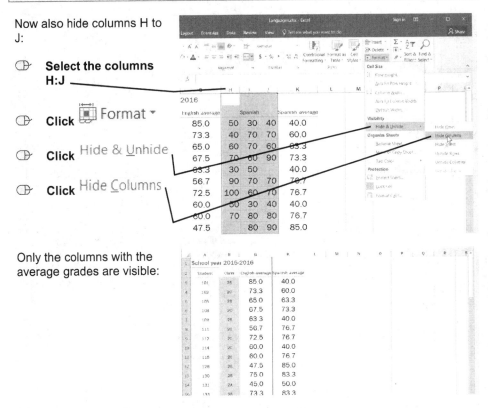 Format ▾

⊕ **Click** Hide & Unhide

⊕ **Click** Hide Columns

Only the columns with the
average grades are visible:

To unhide hidden columns, select the columns before and after:

⊕ **Select column B:G**

⊕ **Click** Format ▾

⊕ **Click** Hide & Unhide

⊕ **Click**
     Unhide Columns

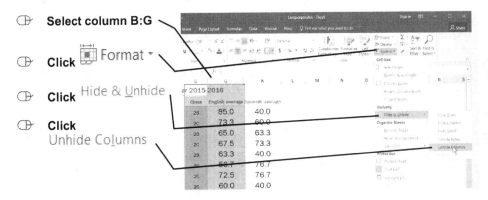

Hiding and unhiding rows is done in the same way.

You can also unhide all hidden rows or columns at once:

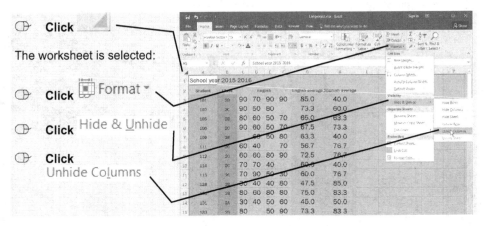

Click

The worksheet is selected:

Click ▣ Format ▾

Click Hide & Unhide

Click
    Unhide Columns

All hidden columns on the worksheet are visible again. If there are multiple worksheets, you can hide worksheets. First, open the worksheet you want to hide:

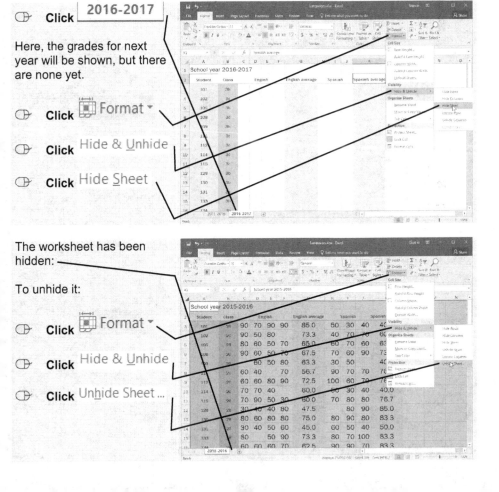

Click [2016-2017]

Here, the grades for next year will be shown, but there are none yet.

Click ▣ Format ▾

Click Hide & Unhide

Click Hide Sheet

The worksheet has been hidden:

To unhide it:

Click ▣ Format ▾

Click Hide & Unhide

Click Unhide Sheet ...

The correct worksheet is already selected:

Click OK

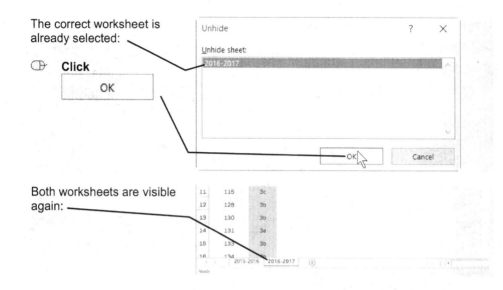

Both worksheets are visible again:

6.5 Colors, Styles and Themes

To make a worksheet more attractive and easier to read, you can use colors and other formatting features. This can be done in several ways. The easiest way to add color to cells is with a background color:

Select cells A2:K2 $\mathcal{G}_{\mathcal{G}}$19

By , click

Click a color, for example ▢ *(Orange, Accent 2, Lighter 40%)*

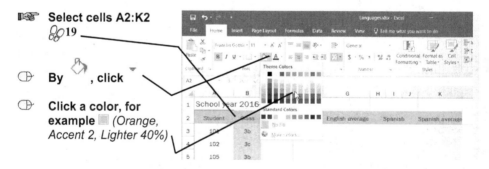

You can also choose a style. A style is a matching set of background colors, font types and sizes, sometimes supplemented by borders.

Click Cell Styles ▾

Click a style, for example
40% - Accent4

The style is applied to the selected cells:

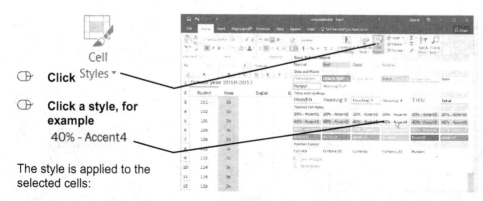

To display the entire worksheet in a similar style, you can use themes. All cells which are formatted with styles will then have a similar theme:

⊕ **Click the** Page Layout **tab**

⊕ **Click** Themes

⊕ **Click a theme, for example** Circuit

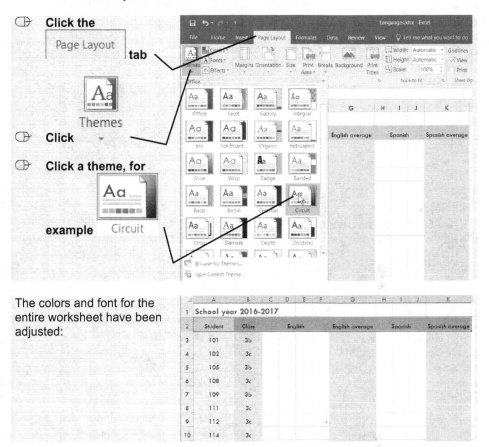

The colors and font for the entire worksheet have been adjusted:

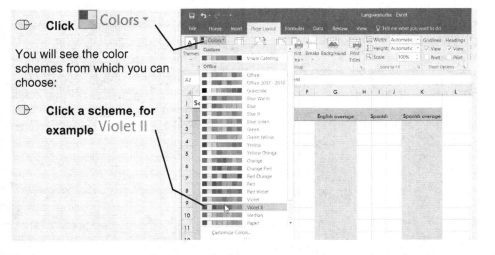

The color scheme, font type or special effects (such as borders and shadows) can still be adjusted when you use a theme:

⊕ **Click** Colors

You will see the color schemes from which you can choose:

⊕ **Click a scheme, for example** Violet II

The colors have been replaced by the colors of the chosen scheme:

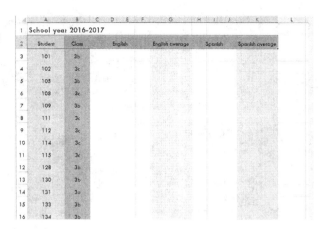

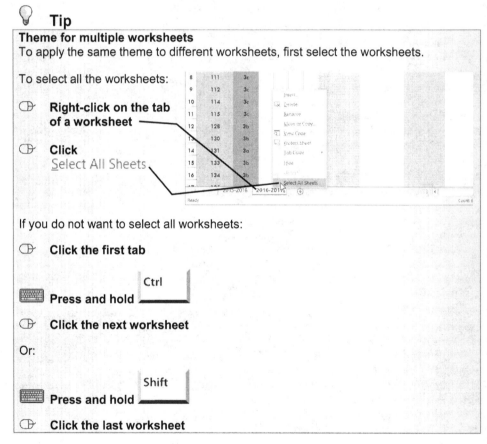

💡 **Tip**

Theme for multiple worksheets
To apply the same theme to different worksheets, first select the worksheets.

To select all the worksheets:

☞ **Right-click on the tab of a worksheet**

☞ **Click**
Select All Sheets

If you do not want to select all worksheets:

☞ **Click the first tab**

⌨ **Press and hold** Ctrl

☞ **Click the next worksheet**

Or:

⌨ **Press and hold** Shift

☞ **Click the last worksheet**

6.6 Copying the Formatting

If you want to set a similar style or formatting somewhere else on the worksheet or on a different worksheet, you can copy the formatting from the cell where this is already set. You will only copy the formatting, not the content of the cell.

In cell H2, type:
French

Enter

Press

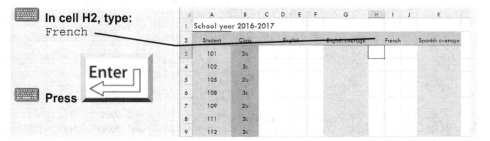

You will then copy the formatting of cell H2 to the other worksheet:

⊕ **Click cell H2**

⊕ **Click the** Home **tab**

⊕ **Click**

The pointer changes into 🔁:

⊕ **Click** 2015-2016

⊕ **Click** Spanish

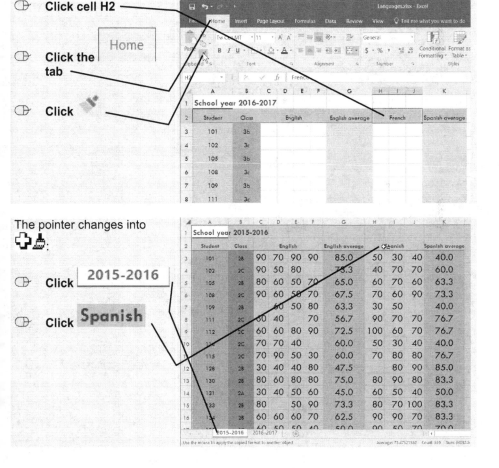

The cell now has the same formatting as the reference cell. The text is not changed:

You can undo this action:

☞ **Click**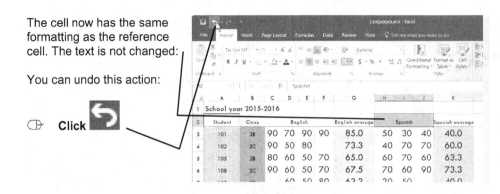

6.7 Printing Titles

In many cases, the worksheets or parts thereof will be printed on paper. You can see the layout in the print preview:

☞ **Click** File

☞ **Click** Print

You will see page 1 of the print preview:

In order to view the next page:

☞ **Click** ▶

The following pages do not show titles above the columns. You cannot tell what each column is about then:

You can adjust this:

☞ **Click** ⬅

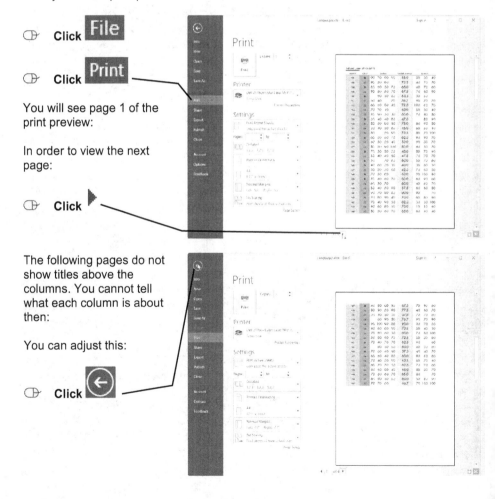

To repeat the titles on each page, you will need to use the *Print Titles* option:

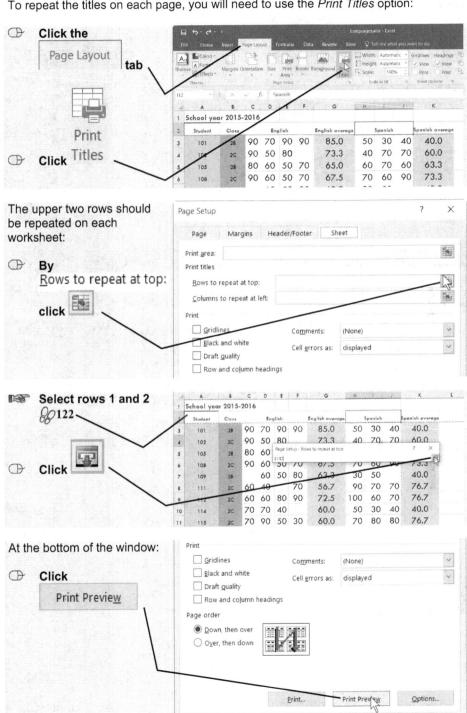

👆 **Click the** Page Layout **tab**

👆 **Click** Print Titles

The upper two rows should be repeated on each worksheet:

👆 **By** Rows to repeat at top:

click

👉 **Select rows 1 and 2** ℘℘122

👆 **Click**

At the bottom of the window:

👆 **Click** Print Preview

You will see the print
preview:

☞   **Click** ▶

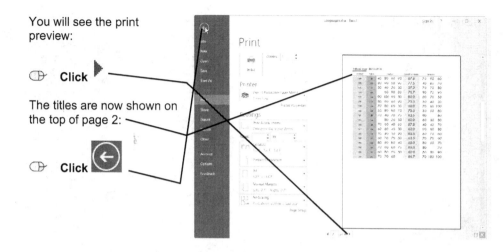

The titles are now shown on
the top of page 2:

☞   **Click** ⬅

6.8 Margins, Orientation and Paper Size

In order to print the data in the most efficient way, you may need to adjust some other
settings. *Excel* has several ways of doing this. On the *Page Layout* tab:

Margins

☞   **Click** ▾

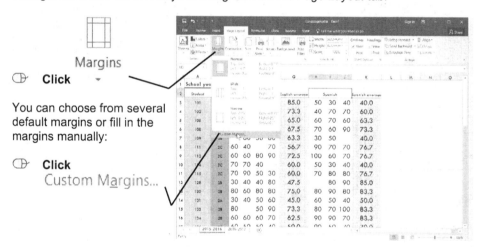

You can choose from several
default margins or fill in the
margins manually:

☞   **Click**
Custom Margins...

💡   **Tip**

Page border
After you have viewed the print preview once, you can see a dotted line that indicates
the page border, both on the side and the bottom of the worksheet:

⬚	A	B	C	D	E	F	G	H	I	J	K	L
1	School year 2015-2016											
2	Student	Class		English			English average		Spanish		Spanish average	
3	101	2B	90	70	90	90	85.0	50	30	40	40.0	
4	102	2C	90	50	80		73.3	40	70	70	60.0	
5	105	2B	80	60	50	70	65.0	60	70	60	63.3	
6	108	2C	90	60	50	70	67.5	70	60	90	73.3	
7	109	2B		60	50	80	63.3	30	50		40.0	

In this window you can define the margins:

Keep in mind the capabilities of your printer when doing so. Usually, printers cannot print a part of the margin.

In this example, you do not need to adjust anything:

☞ **Click**

Cancel

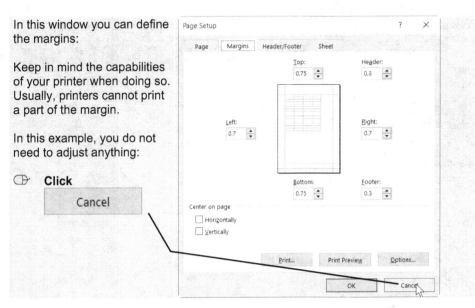

💡 **Tip**

Centering
If you want the worksheet to be printed in the middle of the page, you will need to select one or both of the *Center on page* options shown here.

☞ **Place a checkmark**
✔ by the desired
method

Note: centering is only visible if the data to be printed is smaller than one page.

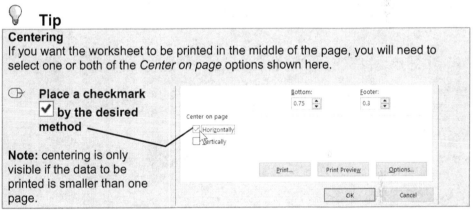

Many *Excel* summaries are wider than a vertical page. You can then choose to have the worksheet printed horizontally:

Orientation

☞ **Click**

You can choose from portrait or landscape printing.

It does not make any difference on the screen.

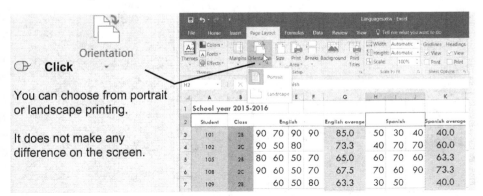

You can also change the default paper size for this worksheet:

Size

☞ **Click** ▾

You will see the list with paper sizes:

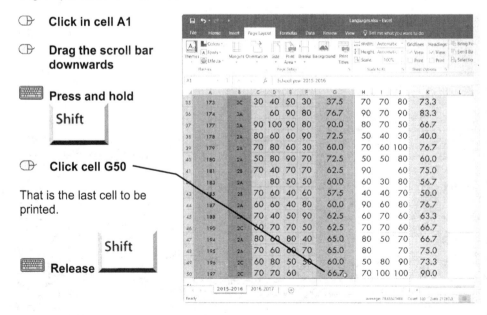

💡 **Tip**

Smaller margins
If you set a smaller paper size, you may need to adjust the margins. If you do not do that, you may only be able to print very little on a page. Again, keep the minimum margins of your printer in mind when doing so.

6.9 Print Area

By default, the entire worksheet is printed. If you want to print only a part of the worksheet, you can set a print area. Let's say, you just want to print the grades for English per student. First select the desired area:

☞ **Click in cell A1**

☞ **Drag the scroll bar downwards**

⌨ **Press and hold**
Shift

☞ **Click cell G50**

That is the last cell to be printed.

Shift
⌨ **Release**

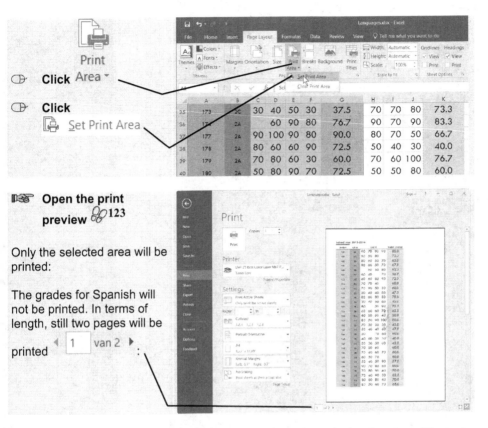

⊕ **Click** Area ⁻

⊕ **Click**
　🖶 Set Print Area

☞ **Open the print preview** 🔖123

Only the selected area will be printed:

The grades for Spanish will not be printed. In terms of length, still two pages will be printed ◀ 1 van 2 ▶ :

If there is just too much text for a single page, you can try reducing the size of the text so it can fit on a single page. Here is how you do that:

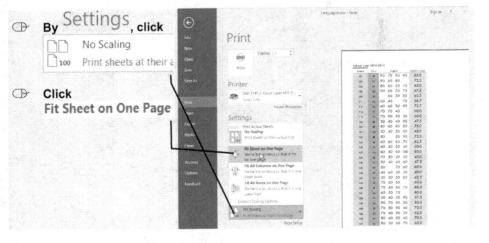

⊕ **By** Settings **, click**
　🗋 No Scaling
　🗋100 Print sheets at their a

⊕ **Click**
　Fit Sheet on One Page

💡 **Tip**

Set the increase or decrease manually

To set the increase or decrease yourself, press Custom Scaling Options... .

By _Adjust to:_ enter the desired print percentage:

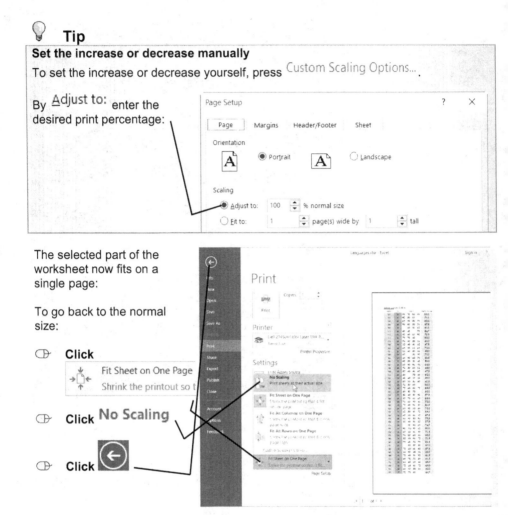

The selected part of the worksheet now fits on a single page:

To go back to the normal size:

☞ **Click**
   Fit Sheet on One Page
   Shrink the printout so t

☞ **Click No Scaling**

☞ **Click** ⬅

If later on, you want to print the columns for Spanish, you will first need to clear the print area:

☞ **Click** Print Area ▾

☞ **Click** Clear Print Area

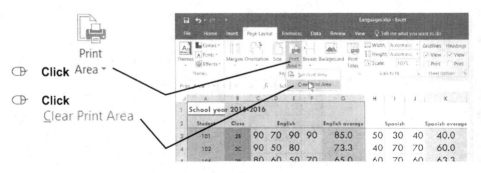

Tip

Printing a Workbook

By default, only the displayed worksheet is printed. To print the entire workbook:

In the print preview:

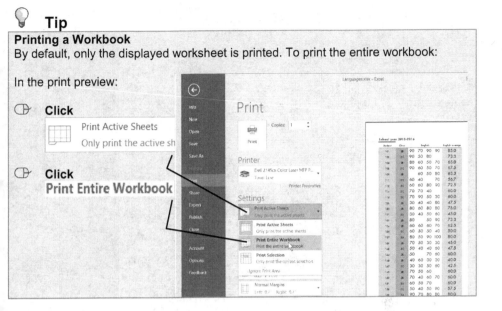

☞ **Click**

    Print Active Sheets

    Only print the active sh

☞ **Click**
Print Entire Workbook

6.10 Headers and Footers

Headers and footers are printed at the top or bottom of a page. They include, for example, the name of the document or a page number. This is how to set them:

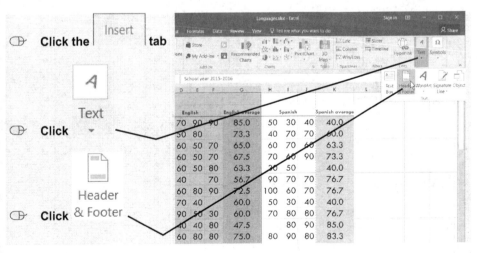

☞ **Click the** Insert **tab**

    A

    Text

☞ **Click** ▾

    Header

☞ **Click** & Footer

First type a header:

Type: Language Grade Summary

This text will be shown centered at the top of each page.

Then enter a footer:

Go to

☞ **Click** Footer

☞ **Click the left box**

Current

☞ **Click** Date

A field name appears &[Date]:

When printing, this will be replaced by the date.

☞ **Click the right box**

Type: Page

Type a space

This text will appear in the bottom right:

Page

☞ **Click** Number

A field name appears here as well:

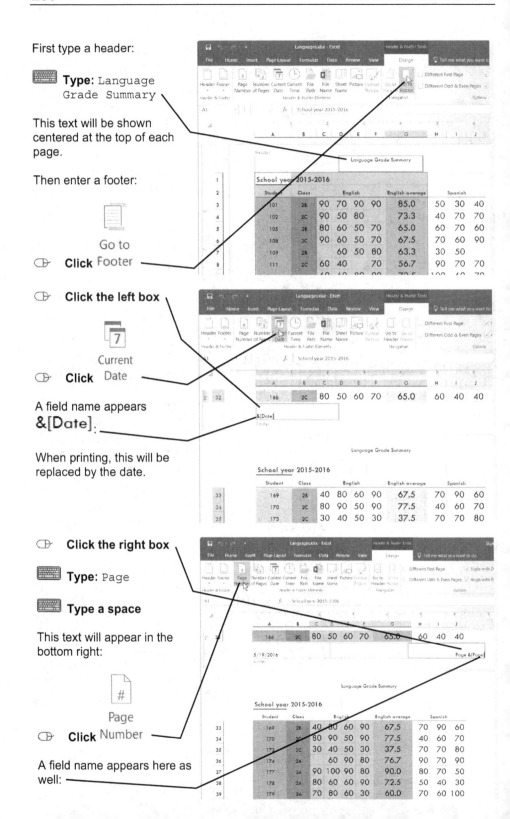

💡 Tip

Picture in header/footer

To insert a picture, for example a company logo, in the header or footer instead of text:

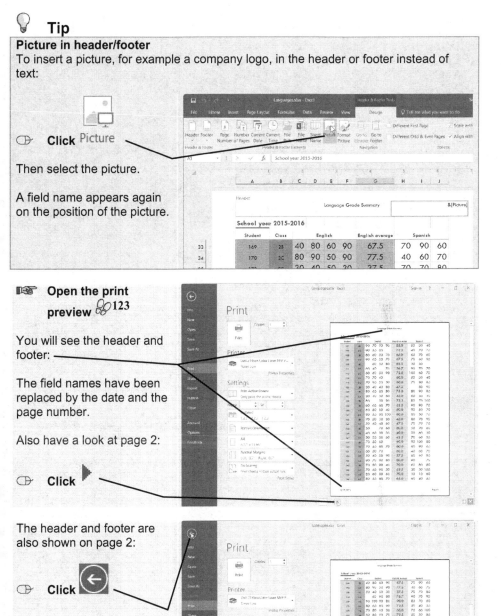

☞ **Click** Picture

Then select the picture.

A field name appears again on the position of the picture.

📖 **Open the print preview** 🦶123

You will see the header and footer:

The field names have been replaced by the date and the page number.

Also have a look at page 2:

☞ **Click** ▶

The header and footer are also shown on page 2:

☞ **Click** ⊙

💡 **Tip**

Headers and footers for the entire workbook
The headers and footers can be specified for each separate worksheet. If you want all worksheets in the workbook to have the same headers and footers, then first select all worksheets:

⊕ **Right-click a tab**

⊕ **Click**
   S̲elect All Sheets

Then enter the header or footer.

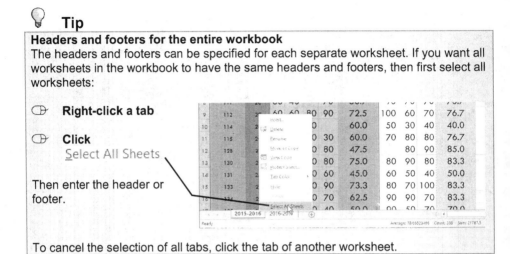

To cancel the selection of all tabs, click the tab of another worksheet.

The worksheet is shown in *Page Layout* view. Return to the normal view:

⊕ **Click the** View **tab**

⊕ **Click** Normal

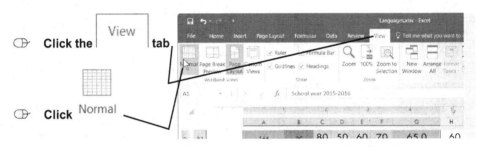

6.11 Subtotals

With the *Subtotals* function, long lists are grouped and summarized by subtotals. First you need to sort the data in the column you plan to summarize and set subtotals. If you want to see subtotals by class:

⊕ **Click the** Data **tab**

⊕ **Click a class in column B**

⊕ **Click** A↓Z

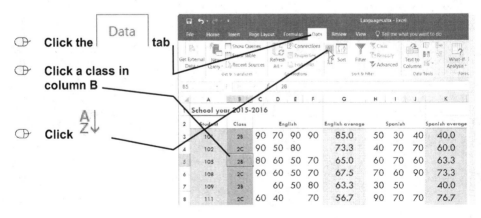

Because there is more data in the worksheet, you need to select all remaining cells that will affect the summary for which the subtotals are to be set:

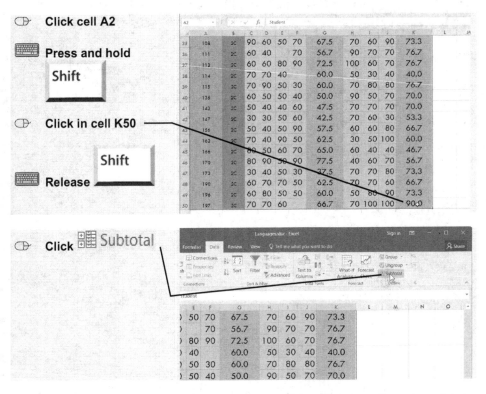

- ☞ **Click cell A2**
- ⌨ **Press and hold** Shift
- ☞ **Click in cell K50**
- Shift
- ⌨ **Release**
- ☞ **Click** Subtotal

You will see a message. *Excel* cannot determine which row contains the column labels:

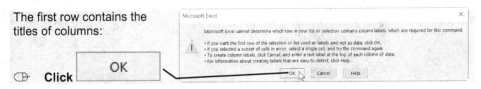

- The first row contains the titles of columns:
- ☞ **Click** OK

Next, indicate the column where you want to have subtotals. In this case, that is per class:

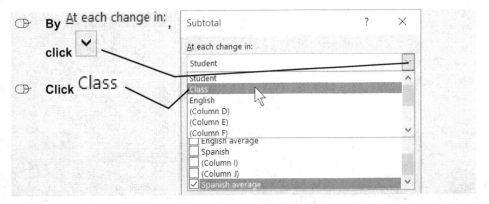

- ☞ **By** At each change in:, **click** ∨
- ☞ **Click** Class

By <u>U</u>se function: choose what you want to know per class, for example the average grade per subject:

⊕ **By <u>U</u>se function:**, **click** ∨

⊕ **Click** Average

With *Sum* you can calculate the totals per class.

With *Count* you can see the number of students per class.

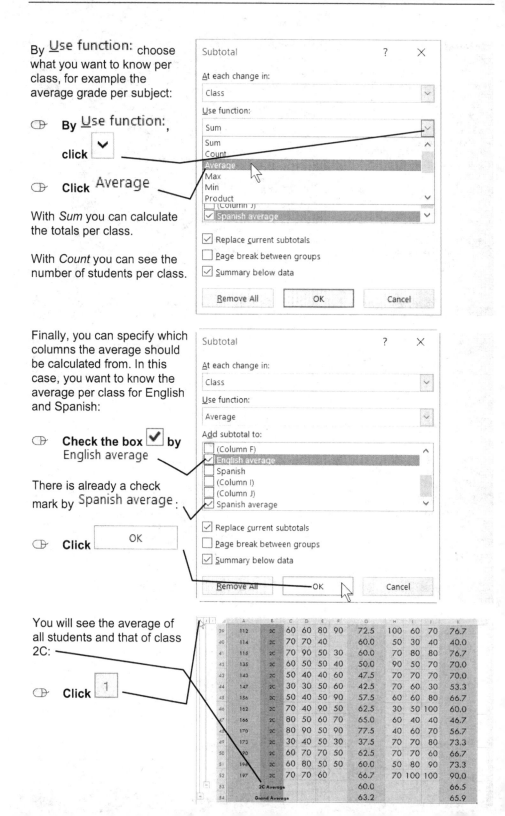

Finally, you can specify which columns the average should be calculated from. In this case, you want to know the average per class for English and Spanish:

⊕ **Check the box** ✔ **by** English average

There is already a check mark by Spanish average :

⊕ **Click** OK

You will see the average of all students and that of class 2C:

⊕ **Click** 1

In order to see the column headers:

☞ **Drag the scroll bar upwards**

You only see the average of all students together:

☞ **Click** 2

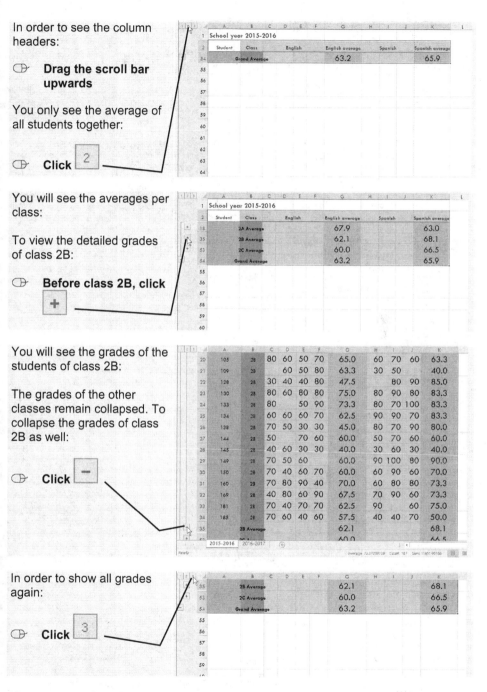

You will see the averages per class:

To view the detailed grades of class 2B:

☞ **Before class 2B, click** +

You will see the grades of the students of class 2B:

The grades of the other classes remain collapsed. To collapse the grades of class 2B as well:

☞ **Click** −

In order to show all grades again:

☞ **Click** 3

You can use subtotals to quickly see the sum, numbers or averages of large amounts of data. It is important that you first sort the data (A-Z) in the column for which you would like to have the subtotals.

Once you have viewed the subtotals, you can disable them again:

☞ **Click** ⊞ Subtotal

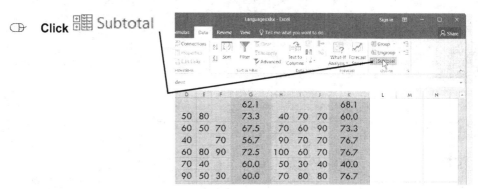

Confirm that the first row contains the column headers:

☞ **Click** OK

☞ **Click** Remove All

Only the subtotals are
removed, not the data.

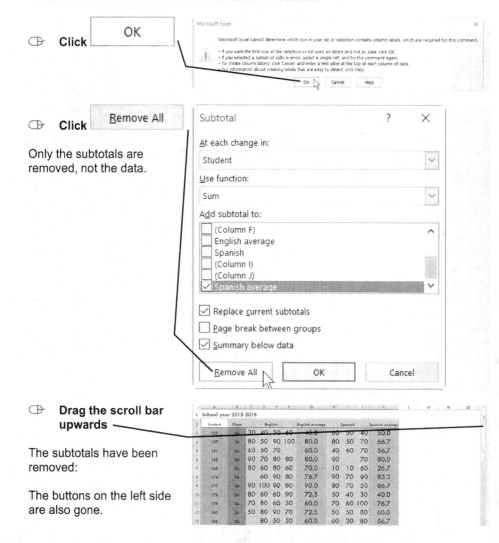

☞ **Drag the scroll bar
upwards**

The subtotals have been
removed:

The buttons on the left side
are also gone.

6.12 Grouping

Even without subtotals, you can hide rows or columns in long worksheets by grouping them together. By doing so, you can quickly focus on the information you need. You simply open the group that you want to view when needed.

➥ Please note:

When grouping, the column which is grouped has to be sorted, too.

☞ **Select the rows with the grades of class 2B**
122

↪ **Click** ⊞ Group ▾

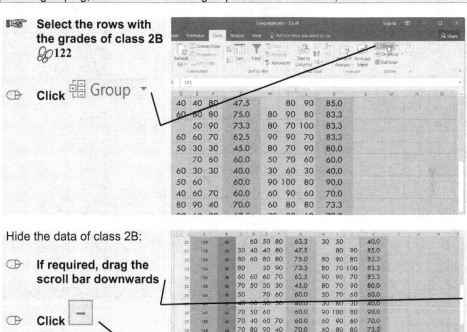

Hide the data of class 2B:

↪ **If required, drag the scroll bar downwards**

↪ **Click** ⊟

Class 2B is hidden:

Open it again:

↪ **Click** ⊞

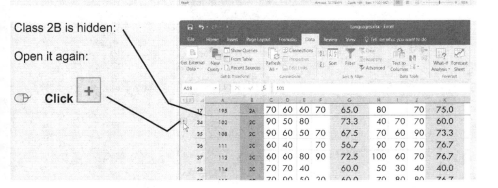

The class is visible again:

To disable grouping:

☞ **Click** 🗇 Ungroup

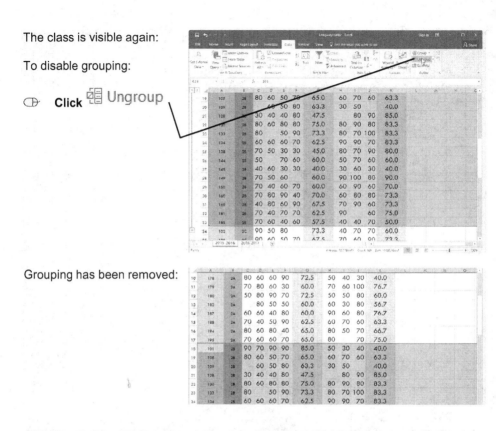

Grouping has been removed:

6.13 Formulas with Names

In extensive worksheets, formulas are often difficult to understand, especially when they refer to cells that are not visible on the screen. By naming a cell and using this name in a formula, they become more understandable. In addition, you can also name a range of cells. In that case, you need to select them first:

☞ **Select cells G3:G50**
    ✂124

☞ **Click the name box**

⌨ **Type:** English

⌨ **Press** Enter ⏎

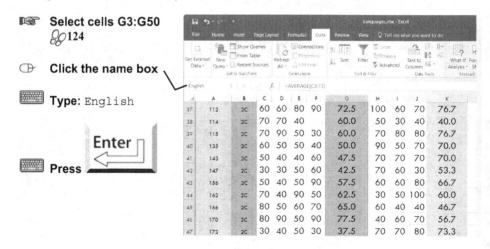

👉 **Select cells K3:K50**
🐾124

☞ **Click the name box**

⌨ **Type:** Spanish

Enter

⌨ **Press**

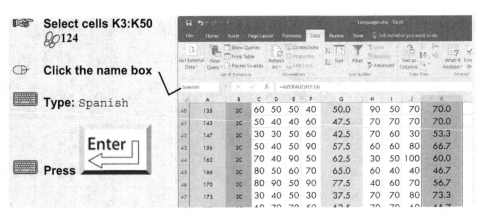

You can also fill in formulas with the names in the name box:

☞ **Click cell L3**

⌨ **Type:** =english
+spanish

Enter

⌨ **Press**

The averages have been
added together:

☞ **Click in cell L3**

The formula bar displays the
formula with names:

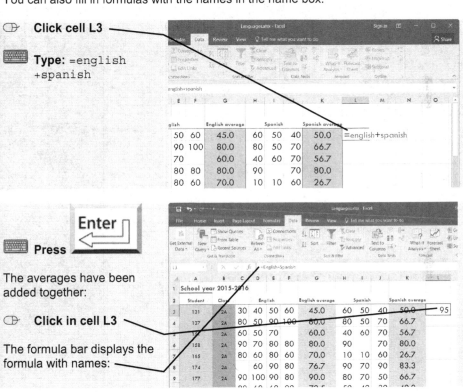

6.14 Showing Formulas

Instead of the result of formulas, you can also display the formula itself in the cells. This will also make it is easier to check and verify a formula.

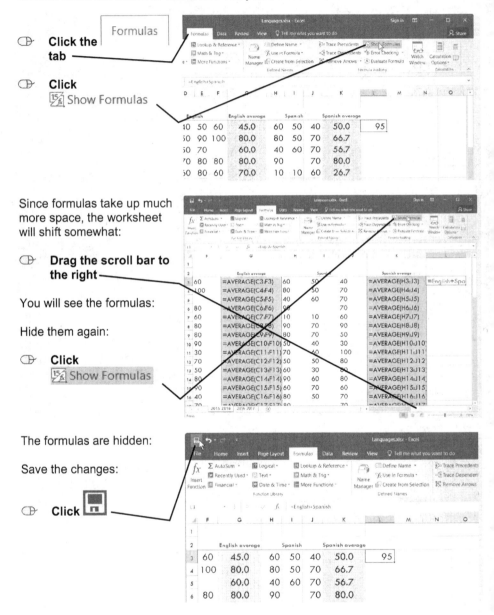

☞ **Click the** Formulas **tab**

☞ **Click** Show Formulas

Since formulas take up much more space, the worksheet will shift somewhat:

☞ **Drag the scroll bar to the right**

You will see the formulas:

Hide them again:

☞ **Click** Show Formulas

The formulas are hidden:

Save the changes:

☞ **Click**

💡 Tip

Copying formulas with names
You can copy formulas with names the same as regular formulas. Since you have named both columns with averages, you can copy the formula downwards:

☞ **Use the fill handle to calculate the total average grade for the other students, too** ✂️**25**

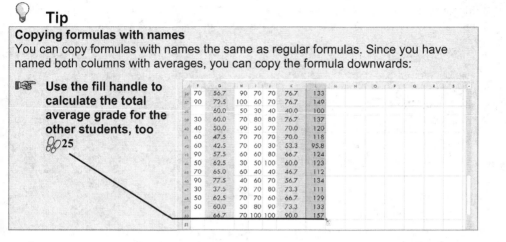

6.15 Recording a Macro

Macros are small programs with which you can easily have a number of actions performed automatically. They are particularly useful for tasks that you perform on a regular basis and for which you have to carry out a number of actions in succession. In this exercise, you will create a macro to hide the columns with separate grades for English and Spanish, so that both columns with averages are shown next to each other. The steps needed to do this are covered in *section 6.4 Hiding Rows, Columns and Worksheets.*

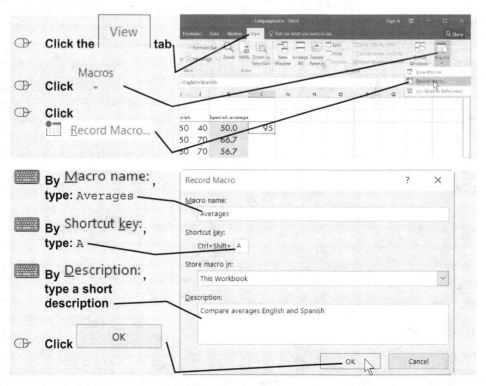

☞ **Click the** View **tab**

☞ **Click** Macros ▾

☞ **Click** 📋 Record Macro...

⌨ **By** Macro name:, **type:** Averages

⌨ **By** Shortcut key:, **type:** A

⌨ **By** Description:, **type a short description**

☞ **Click** OK

In this case, the letter A from "Averages" is chosen, but you may choose a different letter for the macro. The macro can be started with this shortcut key combination.

➥ Please note:

All actions that you carry out from now on will be recorded in the macro.

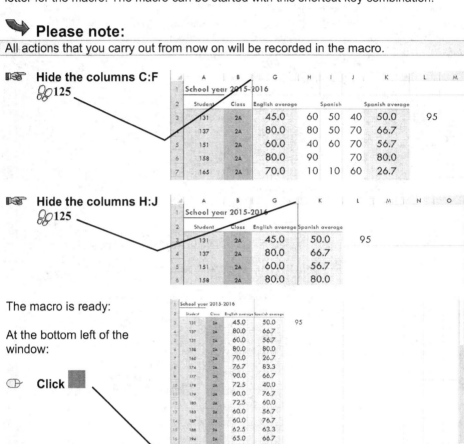

☞ Hide the columns C:F
$\mathcal{QP}$125

☞ Hide the columns H:J
$\mathcal{QP}$125

The macro is ready:

At the bottom left of the window:

☞ Click ▇

☞ Unhide all columns again $\mathcal{QP}$126

☞ Click an empty cell

You can now let the macro run by entering the following key combination:

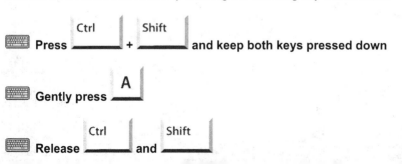

⌨ Press **Ctrl** + **Shift** and keep both keys pressed down

⌨ Gently press **A**

⌨ Release **Ctrl** and **Shift**

The columns are hidden:

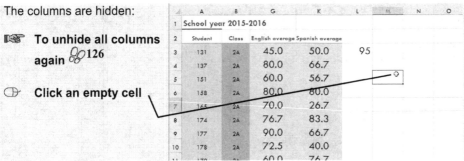

📖 **To unhide all columns again** ✂126

👉 **Click an empty cell**

🩹 HELP! The macro is not working properly.

Recording a macro is meticulous work. If the macro is not working properly, then delete it and record it again:

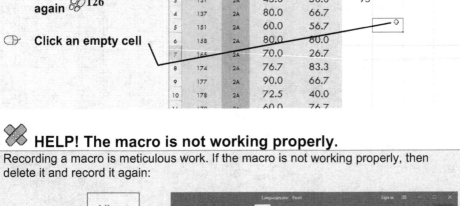

👉 **Click the** View **tab**

Macros

👉 **Click** ▾

👉 **Click** 🗔 View Macros

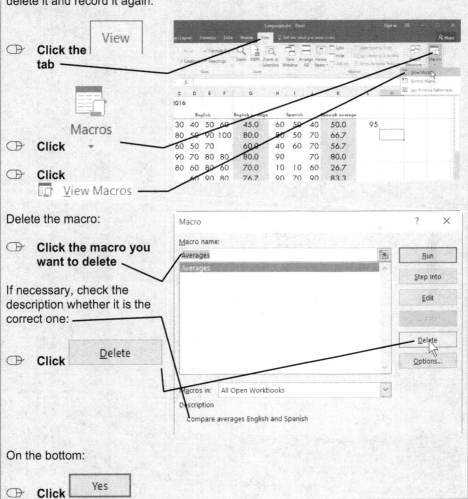

Delete the macro:

👉 **Click the macro you want to delete**

If necessary, check the description whether it is the correct one:

👉 **Click** Delete

On the bottom:

👉 **Click** Yes

6.16 Macro Security

To prevent the spread of macros with unsafe content, macros in worksheets have to be saved with the XLSM file type, instead of XLSX. *Excel* will warn you when you save the workbook:

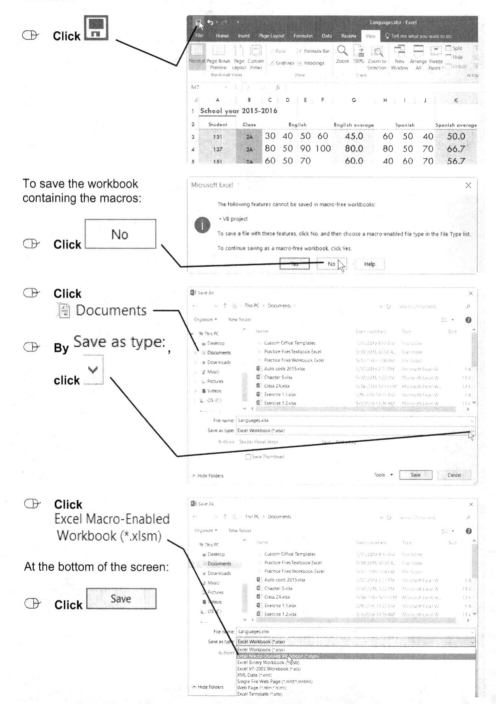

⊕ **Click** 🖫

To save the workbook containing the macros:

⊕ **Click** | No |

⊕ **Click** 📄 Documents

⊕ **By** Save as type:, click ⌄

⊕ **Click** Excel Macro-Enabled Workbook (*.xlsm)

At the bottom of the screen:

⊕ **Click** | Save |

You can see the file type `Languages.xlsm` in the title bar:

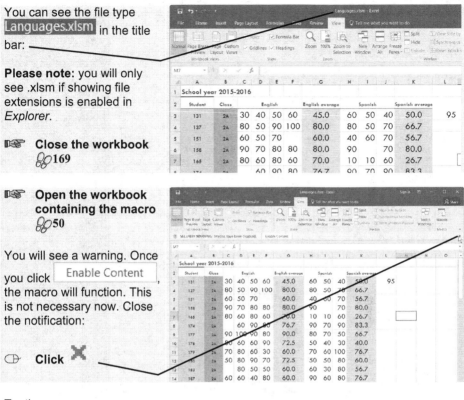

Please note: you will only see .xlsm if showing file extensions is enabled in *Explorer*.

☞ **Close the workbook**
&169

☞ **Open the workbook containing the macro**
&50

You will see a warning. Once you click [Enable Content], the macro will function. This is not necessary now. Close the notification:

⊕ **Click** ✖

Try the macro:

⌨ **Press** [Ctrl] + [Shift] **and hold both down**

⌨ **Gently press** [A]

⌨ **Release** [Ctrl] **and** [Shift]

Nothing happens, because the macro is disabled.

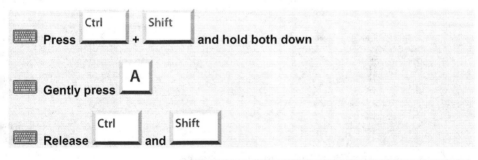

If you want to enable the macro:

☞ **Click** File

☞ **Click** Enable Content ▾

☞ **Click**
Enable All Content

💡 **Tip**

Trust Center
In the Trust Center, you can view how *Excel* handles macros:

☞ **Click**
Trust Center Settings

☞ **If necessary, click**
Macro Settings

You will see the macro
settings in the Trust Center:

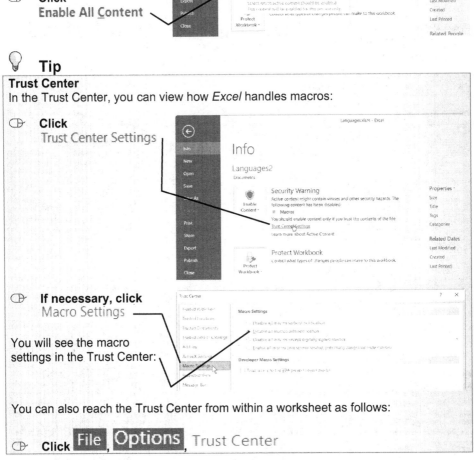

You can also reach the Trust Center from within a worksheet as follows:

☞ **Click** File , Options , Trust Center

Try the macro again:

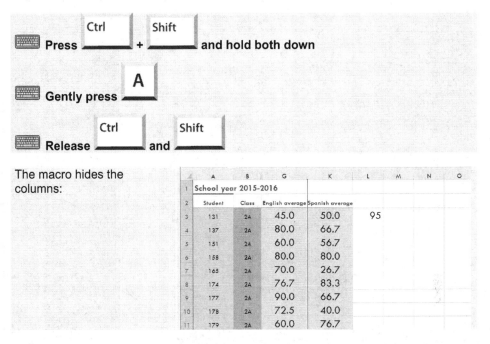

The macro hides the columns:

6.17 Saving for Older Excel Versions

New versions of *Excel* contain more features than older versions. To make a worksheet accessible to users with *Excel* versions prior to *Excel 2007*, you can use the compatibility mode.

⊕ **Click** 🗒 Documents

⊕ **By** Save as type:,

   click ∨

⊕ **Click**
   Excel 97-2003 Workbook
   (*.xls)

⊕ **Click** | Save |

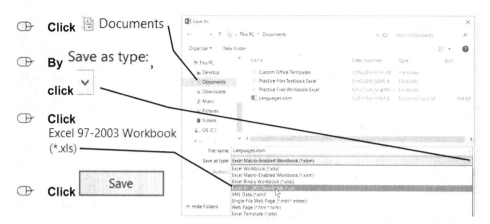

Features which were not yet present in previous versions of *Excel* will be lost. You will be notified by a warning:

⊕ **Click** | Continue |

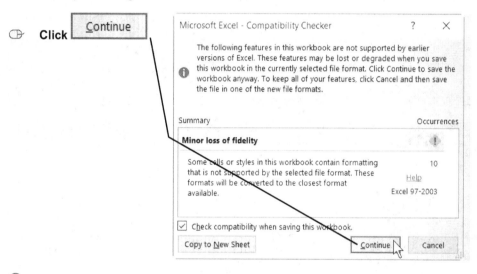

 Tip

First save in the current version
Always save a workbook in your current version of *Excel* first before you save it in an older version. In case important features are lost, you can then open the original saved version of the workbook again.

☞ **If necessary, follow the instructions in the next few windows**

☞ **If necessary, change the file name**

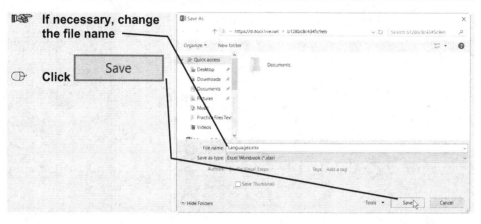

👆 **Click** Save

The file is being uploaded to *OneDrive*. For large files or if you have a slow internet connection this can take some time. Once the file is uploaded, you will be returned to the worksheet.

☞ **Close the workbook without saving the changes** ℰℰ115

Open the file from *OneDrive*:

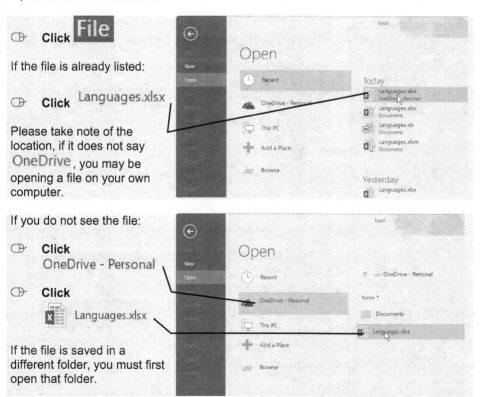

👆 **Click** File

If the file is already listed:

👆 **Click** Languages.xlsx

Please take note of the location, if it does not say OneDrive, you may be opening a file on your own computer.

If you do not see the file:

👆 **Click** OneDrive - Personal

👆 **Click** ⬚ Languages.xlsx

If the file is saved in a different folder, you must first open that folder.

The file is downloaded and opened on your computer.

☞ **Close the workbook without saving the changes** ✂115

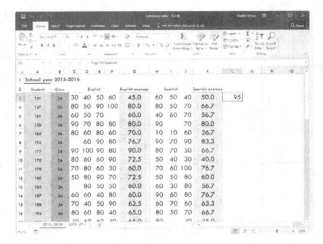

You will remain logged on to *OneDrive* until you log off, even if you have quit *Excel*. If you are not working on your own computer, other people who use the computer may be able to view and change your files. Therefore, log off when you are not working on your own computer. This is how to log off:

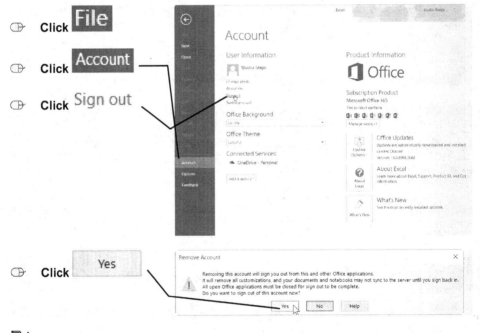

⊕ **Click** File

⊕ **Click** Account

⊕ **Click** Sign out

⊕ **Click** Yes

🐾 **Please note:**

Pay close attention to this note in this window:
All open Office applications must be closed for sign out to be complete.
You need to close *Excel*, *Word*, *PowerPoint*, *Outlook* and any other *Office* programs to be actually logged off.

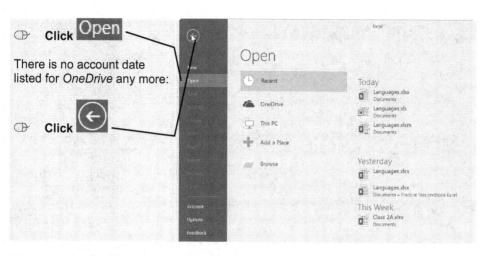

☞ **Click** Open

There is no account date
listed for *OneDrive* any more:

☞ **Click** ←

🖙 **Close** *Excel* ✀16

You are now fully logged off from *OneDrive*.

In this chapter you have learned how to view larger worksheets in a clearer way by grouping data or creating subtotals. You have also learned to automate common tasks with a macro and to save an *Excel* file in various file formats.

6.20 Exercise

To practice a little more with what you have just learned, you can do the following review exercise. If you have forgotten how to do something, use the number beside the footsteps to look it up in the appendix *How Do I Do That Again?* $\mathcal{C}\!\mathcal{C}^1$ at the end of the book.

Exercise: Viewing and Saving

In this exercise you will practice using several viewing options and saving an *Excel* file.

☞ Open *Excel*. $\mathcal{C}\!\mathcal{C}^1$

☞ Open the file *Wholesale.xlsx*. $\mathcal{C}\!\mathcal{C}^{50}$

☞ Select cells C3:C61. $\mathcal{C}\!\mathcal{C}^{124}$

☞ Name the cells `pieces` $\mathcal{C}\!\mathcal{C}^{127}$

☞ Select cells D3:D61. $\mathcal{C}\!\mathcal{C}^{124}$

☞ Name the cells `price` $\mathcal{C}\!\mathcal{C}^{127}$

☞ Use cell names in cell E3 to calculate the total of that day. $\mathcal{C}\!\mathcal{C}^{128}$

☞ Change the view so that the cell names are displayed. $\mathcal{C}\!\mathcal{C}^{129}$

☞ Copy the formula in cell E3 up to E61. $\mathcal{C}\!\mathcal{C}^{25}$

☞ Hide the cell names. $\mathcal{C}\!\mathcal{C}^{130}$

☞ Sort the summary in ascending order by product. $\mathcal{C}\!\mathcal{C}^{131}$

☞ Create a summary with the subtotal of each product. $\mathcal{C}\!\mathcal{C}^{132}$

☞ Show only the totals per product and the grand total. $\mathcal{C}\!\mathcal{C}^{133}$

☞ Widen the total column if you see # # # # #. $\mathcal{C}\!\mathcal{C}^{18}$

☞ Show the details of the vases. $\mathcal{C}\!\mathcal{C}^{134}$

☞ Remove the subtotals. $\mathcal{C}\!\mathcal{C}^{135}$

☞ Set the theme *Circuit*. $\mathcal{C}\!\mathcal{C}^{136}$

☞ Freeze the titles in the top two rows. ✂️**137**

☞ Go to the last line of the summary using the scroll bar. The titles should still be visible.

☞ Set the necessary options to show the whole summary on a single page. ✂️**138**

☞ Return to the worksheet. ✂️**139**

☞ Start recording a macro with the name Columns and add the shortcut key C for it. ✂️**140**

☞ Hide the columns C and D. ✂️**125**

☞ Stop the macro. ✂️**141**

☞ Select the entire worksheet. ✂️**142**

☞ Unhide all columns. ✂️**126**

☞ Run macro C. ✂️**143**

☞ Save the worksheet as a PDF document with the name Wholesale in the *(My) Documents* folder. ✂️**144**

☞ Close the PDF document. ✂️**145**

☞ Close the workbook and save the changes. ✂️**16**

6.21 Tips

💡 Tip

Managing cell names
To delete cell names or adjust the range, use the *Name Manager* window:

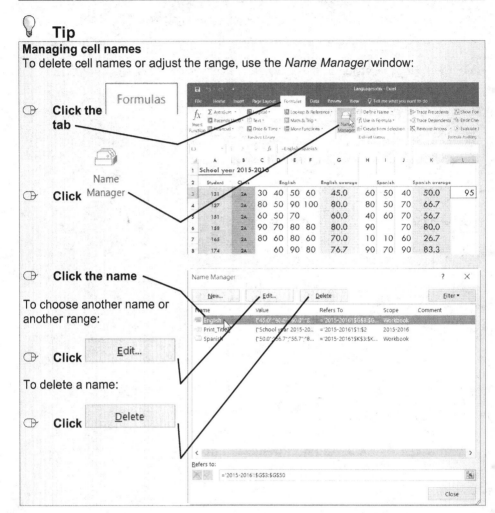

☞ **Click the** Formulas **tab**

☞ **Click** Name Manager

☞ **Click the name**

To choose another name or another range:

☞ **Click** Edit...

To delete a name:

☞ **Click** Delete

Extra exercises

Foreword

This workbook is essential in preparing for the Microsoft Office Specialist® exam (MOS).

Once you have worked through the first chapters of this book, you will know how to perform the necessary actions in *Excel*. However, this does not mean that all actions have been mastered. The many exercises in this book allow you to practice even further with various types of assignments or tasks.

This additional training will ensure that you have the best possible preparation for the exam!

We wish you a lot of success with the exercises in this book and with the exam.

Studio Visual Steps

How to Use This Book

This book contains exercises to prepare you for the MOS exam *Excel*. The exercises are subdivided into footsteps exercises, do-it-yourself exercises and MOS exam exercises.

Footsteps Exercise

In this type of exercise all actions are marked by a footstep icon $\mathcal{O}\!\mathcal{O}^1$. This means the actions have already been handled earlier in the textbook. If you do not know how to perform an action, you can learn how to do so by looking for the corresponding number written next to the footstep icon in the appendix *How Do I Do That Again?* at the end of the book.
At the end of each exercise, reference is made to a file to compare the result with the program window, so you will see if you have done the exercise correctly. The final result files can be found in the practice files folder.

Do-It-Yourself Exercise

In this type of exercise, the required actions are not accompanied by the footstep icons. It is now expected that you can perform the necessary actions without the need of the footsteps. At the end of each exercise, reference is made to a file to compare the result with the program window. This will help you to see if you have done the exercise correctly.

MOS Exam Exercise

This exercise trains you through a simulation that is set on your PC. In this way, you get acquainted with how a MOS test will look like and be prepared for the test environment. At the end of the exercise, reference is made to a file to compare the result with the program window. You will be able to see right away if you have done the exercise correctly. On page 262 you can read how to do these exercises step by step.

The Website and Supplementary Materials

This book is accompanied by the website
www.visualstepsmosbooks.com/excel2016.php. The website features practice files
and supplementary materials that you can download. Check the website often to see if
there are any additions or errata published for this book.

Practice files
The practice files used in this book can be downloaded from
www.visualstepsmosbooks.com/excel2016-practicefiles.php. If these practice
files are not yet on your computer, you will need to copy them first to your *(My)
Documents* folder. A PDF file on the website explains how to do this. Carefully follow
the instructions in the PDF file! If you do not do this, the practice files may end up in
the wrong folder.
If you are working through this book at a school or other educational facility, then
kindly ask your instructor where the practice files are located on the computer you are
working on.

Results
The exercises in this books are accompanied by result files. You can use these files
to check if you have done the exercises correctly. The result files are located in the
practice files folder which can be downloaded from the web page listed above.

The MOS Exam Exercises

You can open the MOS exam exercises on the website for this book as follows:

☞ **Open the browser *Edge* or *Internet Explorer* on your desktop**

☞ **Open the web page www.visualstepsmosbooks.com/excel2016-mos-
examexercises.php**

You will need to fill in the access code in order to open the MOS exam exercises:

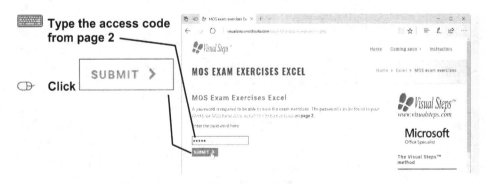

⌨ **Type the access code from page 2**

☞ **Click** SUBMIT >

You see the web page with the MOS exam exercises. Open an exercise:

☞ **Click**
  MOS exam exercise 1:
  Setting Up Excel and Basic F

A new web page opens. This page contains links to the source files:

- ⓘ **Instructions**: opens a web page with instructions for the exercise.

- 🖼 **Final result**: Opens a web page with an image of the final result of the exercise. You can compare the picture on this page with your own result at the end of the exercise.

- 📊 **Climate_Rome.xlsx**: This will open the *Excel* file needed for the exercise. You may also see links to additional files such as images and text files.

We recommend that you open each of these pages in a new window. Then you can place them on your computer screen in the following way:

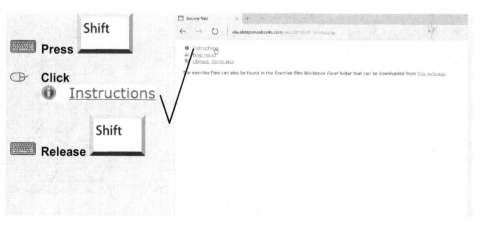

⌨ **Press** **Shift**

☞ **Click**
  ⓘ **Instructions**

⌨ **Release** **Shift**

The new window with the instructions for the exercise opens on top of the current window. Drag this window down to the left corner of your screen:

⊕ **Drag the window
down to the left
corner of your screen**

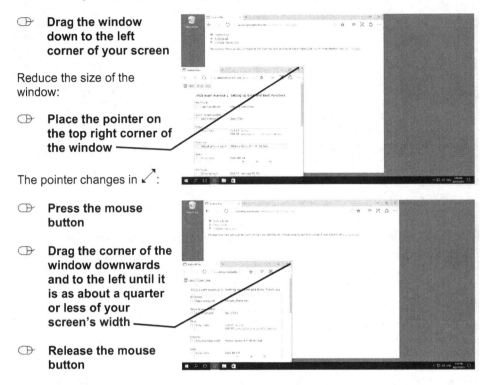

Reduce the size of the window:

⊕ **Place the pointer on
the top right corner of
the window**

The pointer changes in ↙ :

⊕ **Press the mouse
button**

⊕ **Drag the corner of the
window downwards
and to the left until it
is as about a quarter
or less of your
screen's width**

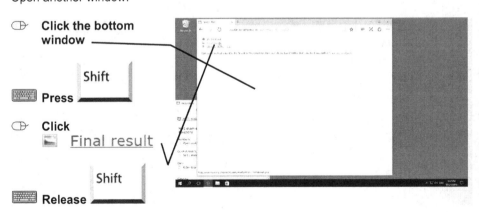

⊕ **Release the mouse
button**

Open another window:

⊕ **Click the bottom
window**

⌨ **Press** Shift

⊕ **Click**
🖼 Final result

⌨ **Release** Shift

You see the window with a picture of the final result of the exercise. Place this window at the bottom center of your screen:

☞ **Reduce this window**

☞ **Place the window at the bottom center of your screen**

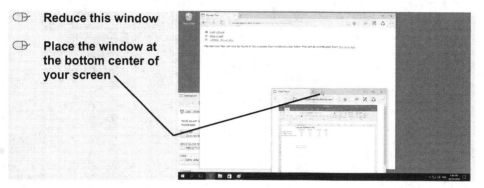

Now you can open the exercise file:

☞ **Click the large window**

☞ **Click**
    Climate_Rome.xl;

The file is downloaded from the Internet. This may take a while. At the bottom of the window a bar appears:

☞ **Click**

    Open

You may first see a button with save. If so, click

    Save
    .

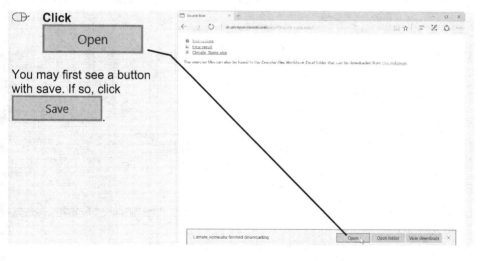

The *Excel* window opens. The file appears in Protected View because you have downloaded it from the Internet. You can turn the protected view off:

⊕ **Click**

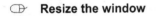

Enable Editing

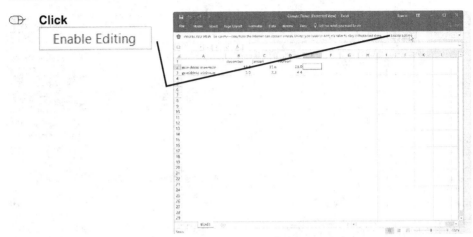

Allow the *Excel* window to fill the entire width of the top of your screen:

⊕ **Resize the window**

⊕ **Move the window to the top of the screen**

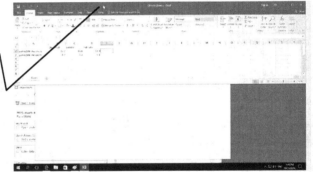

Place the window with the source files at the bottom right of your screen:

⊕ **Click the window**

⊕ **Reduce the size of the window**

⊕ **Move the window to the bottom right of the screen**

Now your screen looks almost the same as during the MOS exam. During the exam you will be expected to do the following:

1. Perform the actions described in the window at the bottom left side of the screen in the *Excel* window at the top.

2. If you have finished the exercise, you can compare your *Excel* window with the final results shown in the small window in the center of your screen.

3. When you are completely done you can close all windows by clicking the ████ in the top right corner of each window.

 HELP! I have a small screen.

If you have a small screen, the setup as described above is not very convenient. In that case, it is better to place the *Excel* window on the left side of the screen and the instructions window on the right or vice versa. The windows will then be displayed larger.

You can minimalize the windows with the final result and the source files. They will still remain open and you just need to click the taskbar button to view them again. You can set up your screen as follows:

☞ **Click ⎯ in the center window**

Do the same for the window on the right:

☞ **Click ⎯ in the right window**

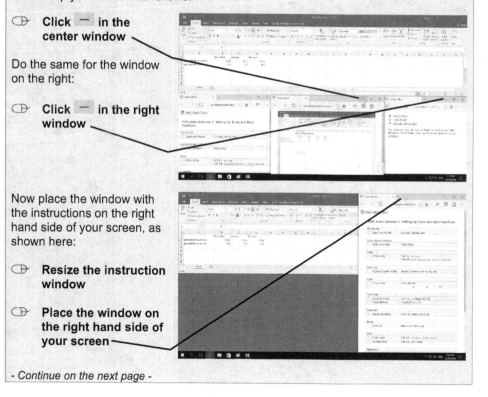

Now place the window with the instructions on the right hand side of your screen, as shown here:

☞ **Resize the instruction window**

☞ **Place the window on the right hand side of your screen**

- Continue on the next page -

Place the *Excel* window on the left hand side of your screen, as shown here:

- ☞ **Click the *Excel* window**

- ☞ **Resize the window**

- ☞ **Place the window on the left side of your screen**

You can now carry out the instructions from the window on the right into the *Excel* window on the left. When you have finished the exercise, click on the taskbar and then on the window with the result. Compare the result window with your own *Excel* window.

When you are completely done you can close all windows by clicking the ⊠ in the top right corner of each window.

➥ Please note:

You can open the necessary *Excel* files by clicking the hyperlink on the web page with the source files, such as Climate_Rome.xlsx. But you can also find these files in the practice files folder which can be downloaded from the website **www.visualstepsmosbook.com/excel2016-practicefiles.php**. It will save you some time performing the exercises, if you have these files already downloaded to your computer. For example, some exercises require insertion of an image or the retrieval of data from a text(.csv) file. It also takes a little more time to download an *Excel* file from the Internet than to open one from your computer.

1. Setting Up Excel and Basic Functions

In Chapter 1 of the textbook you have read how to set up *Excel* by yourself. A number of basic functions in *Excel* has been discussed. You can continue practicing these skills in this chapter.

Footsteps Exercise 1: Setting Up Excel and Basic Functions

🕐 10 minutes

☞ Open *Excel* 👣[1] and open a blank workbook. 👣[2]

☞ Add the *Save As* command to the *Quick Access* toolbar. 👣[9]

☞ Click the | Insert | tab. 👣[3]

☞ Add a new group to this tab. 👣[4]

☞ Change the name of the new group to *Columns*. 👣[34]

☞ Add the *Insert Sheet Columns* command to the new group. 👣[5]

☞ Enter the following data: 👣[17]

◢	A	B	C	D	E
1		June	July	August	
2	average maximum				
3	average minimum				
4					

☞ Automatically adjust the width of the first column to the widest data. 👣[18]

☞ Enter the following data: 👣[17]

◢	A	B	C	D	E
1		June	July	August	
2	average maximum	27	29	27	
3	average minimum	16	20	17	
4					

☞ Format the first row in bold text. 👣[28]

☞ In cell E1, type: Summer 👣[17]

☞ Click cell E2 and calculate the average of the cells B2:D2. 👣^{35}

☞ Copy the formula from cell E2 to cell E3. 👣^{24}

☞ Change the number of decimals of the cells E2 and E3 to one decimal. 👣^{21}

☞ Center the cells B1:E3. 👣^{28}

☞ Change the name of worksheet *Sheet1* to *Summer.* 👣^{12}

☞ Change the color of the tab to red. 👣^{13}

☞ Create a new worksheet. 👣^{11}

☞ Change the name of the new worksheet to *Winter.* 👣^{12}

☞ Change the color of the tab to blue. 👣^{13}

☞ Place the *Summer* worksheet before the *Winter* worksheet. 👣^{15}

☞ Click the tab of the *Summer* worksheet.

☞ Open the *Result Footsteps Exercise 1* workbook 👣^{36} and compare this to your own workbook.

☞ Close the *Result Footsteps Exercise 1* workbook and do not save any changes. 👣^{16}

☞ Save the workbook with the name *Climate Rome 1* in the *(My) Documents* folder. 👣^{26}

☞ Remove the *Save As* command from the *Quick Access* toolbar. 👣^{10}

☞ Revert to the default settings for the [Insert] tab. 👣^{8}

☞ Close *Excel.* 👣^{16}

Do-It-Yourself Exercise 1: Setting Up Excel and Basic Functions

🕐 10 minutes

☞ Open *Excel* and open a new blank workbook.

☞ Add a new group to the [Home] tab.

☞ Add the *Open* command to the new group.

☞ Add the *Center* command to the *Quick Access* toolbar.

☞ Create a new worksheet.

☞ Change the name of Sheet 1 to *January*.

☞ Change the name of Sheet 2 to *February*.

☞ If necessary, place the *January* worksheet before the *February* worksheet.

☞ Click the *January* worksheet tab.

☞ Enter the following data:

	A	B	C	D
1		Retail price		
2	BLT sandwich			
3	Cheese sandwich			
4	Club sandwich			
5				

☞ Widen columns A and B until the text fits exactly.

☞ Enter the following data:

	A	B	C	D
1		Retail price		
2	BLT sandwich	5.5		
3	Cheese sandwich	4		
4	Club sandwich	6		
5				

☞ Insert two columns between columns A and B.

☞ Remove one of the two new columns.

☞ Enter the following data:

	A	B	C	D
1		Expenses	Retail price	Profit
2	BLT sandwich	1.65	5.5	
3	Cheese sandwich	1.2	4	
4	Club sandwich	1.8	6	
5				

☞ Click cell D2 and enter a formula to subtract the amount in cell B2 from the amount in cell C2.

☞ Copy the formula to the cells D3 and D4 by using the fill handle.

☞ In the cells B2:D4, place a $ sign before the amounts and ensure that all amounts get two decimals.

☞ Change the formatting of the first row to italic.

☞ Change the amount in cell B4 to: 1.25 and ensure that the formula in cell D4 is recalculated.

☞ Open the *Result Do-It-Yourself Exercise 1* workbook and compare this to your own workbook.

☞ Close the *Result Do-It-Yourself Exercise 1* workbook and do not save any changes.

☞ Save the workbook with the name *Bread Rolls Cantine 1* in the *(My) Documents* folder.

☞ Remove the *Center* command from the *Quick Access* toolbar.

☞ Revert to the default settings for the | Home | tab.

☞ Close *Excel*.

Do-It-Yourself Exercise 2: More about Setting Up Excel and Basic Functions

🕐 15 minutes

☞ Open *Excel* and open a new blank workbook.

☞ Add a new group to the | Page Layout | tab and name it *Print*.

☞ Add the *Print Preview and Print* command to the new group.

☞ Enter the following data:

◢	A	B	C	D	E
1		January	February	March	
2	number of customers				
3	total turnover				
4					
5					

☞ Automatically adjust the width of the first column to the widest data.

☞ Enter the following data:

◢	A	B	C	D	E
1		January	February	March	
2	number of customers	612	562	568	
3	total turnover	22567.65	17987.65	19876.54	
4					

☞ Change the formatting of cells B3:D3 so that there is a comma between the thousands.

☞ In cell E1, type: 1St quarter and enable text wrapping for this cell.

☞ In cell E2, add up all customers using the *SUM* function.

☞ Copy the formula to cell E3 by using the fill handle.

☞ In cell A4, type: `turnover per customer`.

☞ Widen column A until the text fits exactly.

☞ Click cell B4 and enter a formula to divide the amount in cell B3 by the amount in cell B2.

☞ Copy the division formula to cells C4:E4.

☞ Change the number of decimals of the cells B4:E4 to two decimals.

☞ Insert an empty row on top of row one.

☞ In cell A1, type: `Turnover Visual Games`.

☞ Merge the cells A1:E1 and change the font size to 14.

☞ Change the name of worksheet *Sheet1* to *2016* and change the color of the tab to blue.

☞ Create a new worksheet and change the name of the new worksheet to *2015*.

☞ Change the color of the new worksheet to green.

☞ Place the *2016* worksheet before the *2015* worksheet and click the *2016* worksheet tab.

☞ Open the *Result Do-It-Yourself Exercise 2* workbook and compare this to your own workbook.

☞ Close the *Result Do-It-Yourself Exercise 2* workbook and do not save any changes.

☞ Save the workbook with the name *Visual Games 1* in the *(My) Documents* folder.

☞ Revert to the default settings for the | Page Layout | tab.

☞ Close *Excel*.

MOS Exam Exercise 1: Setting Up Excel and Basic Functions

🕐 10 minutes

☞ Open the web page **www.visualstepsmosbooks.com/excel2016-mos-examexercises.php** and enter the access code from the bottom of page 2 in order to access the web page.

☞ Open the source window by clicking
MOS exam exercise 1: Setting Up Excel and Basic Functions
by **Chapter 1**.

☞ Press **Shift** and hold it down, then click ⓘ <u>Instructions</u>.

☞ Press **Shift** and hold it down, then click ▣ <u>Final result</u>.

☞ Position the instruction window, end result window and source window next to each other in the bottom of the screen.

☞ Open the *Climate_Rome.xlsx* practice file and position the *Excel* window in the top of the screen.

☞ Carry out the actions shown in the instruction window.

MOS Exam Exercise 2: More about Setting Up Excel and Basic Functions

🕐 10 minutes

☞ Open the web page **www.visualstepsmosbooks.com/excel2016-mos-examexercises.php** and enter the access code from the bottom of page 2 in order to access the web page.

☞ Open the source window by clicking by **Chapter 1**
   MOS exam exercise 2: More Setting Up Excel and Basic Functions.

☞ Press **Shift** and hold it down, then click ⓘ <u>Instructions</u>.

☞ Press **Shift** and hold it down, then click ▣ <u>Final result</u>.

☞ Position the instruction window, end result window and source window next to each other in the bottom of the screen.

☞ Open the *Visual_Games.xlsx* practice file and position the *Excel* window in the top of the screen.

☞ Carry out the actions shown in the instruction window.

2. Formulas and Series

In chapter 2 of the textbook, you learned how to work with slightly more complicated formulas and how to add series automatically. You can continue practicing these skills in this chapter.

Footsteps Exercise 2: Formulas and Series

🕐 15 minutes

☞ Open *Excel* &1 and open a new blank workbook. &2

☞ Enter the following data: &17

	A	B	C
1	fixed costs:		
2	rent		
3	gas, water, light		
4	insurance		
5	total		
6			
7	variable costs:		
8	groceries		
9	clothing		
10	other		
11	total		
12			
13	Costs per month		

☞ Change the formatting of the cells A1 and A7 to font size 14. &28

☞ Automatically adjust the width of the first column to the widest data. &18

☞ Enter the following data: &17

	A	B	C
1	fixed costs:		
2	rent	550	
3	gas, water, light	180	
4	insurance	200	
5	total		
6			

☞ In cell B5 add up the data from the cells B2:B4. &22

☞ Insert an empty row between row 6 and 7. &30

☞ In cell B7, type: `January` $\%^{17}$

☞ Automatically fill the cells C7:M7 with the other months. $\%^{42}$

☞ If necessary, widen the columns until the data fits exactly. $\%^{18}$

You will only fill in the data from the first three months.

☞ Enter the following data: $\%^{17}$

7		January	February	March	April
8	variable costs:				
9	groceries	140	150	160	
10	clothing	30	60	90	
11	other	80	100	120	
12	total				

☞ In cell B12 add up the data from the cells B9:B11. $\%^{22}$

☞ Copy the formula from cell B12 to the cells C12 and D12. $\%^{24}$

Now add up the fixed and variable costs for the month of January.

☞ In cell B14 add up the data from the cells B5 and B12. $\%^{22}$

☞ Copy the formula from cell B14 to the cells C14 and D14. $\%^{24}$

Notice that the results are incorrect.

☞ Change the reference to cell B5 in the formula in cell B14 to an absolute one. $\%^{38}$

☞ Copy the formula from cell B14 to the cells C14:D14. $\%^{25}$

The results are now correct.

☞ In cell A15, type: `percentage fixed` $\%^{17}$

Now, you can calculate the percentage of fixed costs per month.

☞ In cell B15, enter a formula to divide cell B5 by cell B14 $\%^{22}$, where the reference to cell B5 is an absolute one. $\%^{38}$

☞ Convert the result in cell B15 to a percentage. $\%^{43}$

☞ Copy the formula from cell B15 to the cells C15 and D15. $\%^{25}$

☞ In cell A18, type: `total costs` $\%^{17}$

☞ In cell B18 add up the data from the cells B14:D14. $\%^{22}$

☞ Enter the following data: 🐾¹⁷

20		March	June
21	per quarter		
22			

☞ Select the cells B20:E20 and automatically fill the series using the ribbon with *September* and *December*. 🐾⁴⁹

☞ If necessary, widen the columns until the data fits exactly. 🐾¹⁸

☞ Change the name of the *Sheet1* worksheet to *2015*. 🐾¹²

☞ Create a new worksheet 🐾¹¹ and change the name of this worksheet to *Annual costs*. 🐾¹²

☞ Place the *2015* worksheet before the *Annual costs* worksheet. 🐾¹⁵

☞ On the *Annual costs* worksheet, in cell A1 type: 2015 🐾¹⁷

☞ In cell B1, create a reference to cell B18 on the *2015* worksheet. 🐾⁴⁴

☞ Convert cell A1 to a hyperlink to the *2015* worksheet. 🐾⁴⁵

☞ Click the hyperlink to test whether it works.

☞ Protect the *2015* worksheet. 🐾⁴⁶

☞ Open the *Result Footsteps Exercise 2* workbook 🐾³⁶ and compare this to your own workbook.

☞ Close the *Result Footsteps Exercise 2* workbook and do not save any changes. 🐾¹⁶

☞ Save the workbook with the name *Household Costs 1* in the *(My) Documents* folder. 🐾²⁶

☞ Remove the hyperlink in cell A1 on the *Annual costs* worksheet. 🐾⁴⁷

☞ Cancel the protection of the worksheet *2015*. 🐾⁴⁸

☞ Save the changes. 🐾⁴⁰

☞ Close *Excel*. 🐾¹⁶

Do-It-Yourself Exercise 3: Formulas and Series

🕐 12 minutes

☞ Open *Excel* and open the *Costs_cell_phone.xlsx* workbook from the *Practice Files Workbook Excel* folder.

☞ Automatically fill the cells A10:A20 with the other months.

☞ Enter a nested formula in cell C9, in which you first subtract cell C4 from cell B9 and then multiply the result by cell D4.

☞ Change the references to cells C4:D4 in the formula in cell C9 to absolute ones.

☞ Copy the formula from cell C9 to the cells C10:C20.

☞ Enter a nested formula in cell E9, in which you first subtract cell C5 from cell D9 and then multiply the result by cell D5.

☞ Change the references to cells C5:D5 in the formula in cell E9 to absolute ones.

☞ Copy the formula from cell E9 to the cells E10:E20.

☞ In cell F9 add up the data from the cells B4, B5, C9 and E9.

☞ Change the references to cells B4 and B5 in the formula in cell F9 to absolute ones.

☞ Copy the formula from cell F9 to the cells F10:F20.

☞ In cell A21, type: total

☞ In cell F21 add up the data from the cells F9:F20.

☞ Change the name of the *Sheet1* worksheet to *2014*.

☞ Create a new worksheet and change the name of this worksheet to *Annual summary*.

☞ Place the *2014* worksheet before the *Annual summary* worksheet.

☞ On the *Annual summary* worksheet, in cell A1 type: 2014

☞ In cell B1, create a reference to cell F21 on the *2014* worksheet.

☞ Convert cell A1 to a hyperlink to the *2014* worksheet.

☞ Click the hyperlink to test whether it works.

☞ Open the *Result Do-It-Yourself Exercise 3* workbook and compare this to your own workbook.

☞ Close the *Result Do-It-Yourself Exercise 3* workbook and do not save any changes.

☞ Save the workbook with the name *Cell Phone Costs 1* in the *(My) Documents* folder.

☞ Close *Excel*.

Do-It-Yourself Exercise 4: More about Formulas and Series

⊕ 10 minutes

☞ Open *Excel* and open a new blank workbook.

☞ Enter the following data, ensuring the columns have the correct width:

	A	B	C
1	fixed labor costs		
2		per month	
3	Knight	1800	
4	Parker	2300	
5	Jackson	1700	
6	total		
7			
8	variable labor costs		
9			
10	Brown		
11	Rogers		
12	total		
13			

☞ Change the formatting of cells A1 and A8 to bold.

☞ In cell B9, type: January

☞ Automatically fill the cells C9:M9 with the other months.

☞ Enter the following data:

9		January	February	March	April
10	Brown	2200	1800	800	
11	Rogers	1200	900	1100	
12	total				

☞ In cell B6 add up the data from the cells B3:B5.

☞ In cell B12 add up the data from the cells B10 and B11.

☞ Copy the formula from cell B12 to the cells C12 and D12.

☞ In cell A14, type: labor costs per month

☞ Change the formatting of cell A14 to bold.

☞ In cell B14, enter a formula to add up the data from the cells B6 and B12.

☞ Change the reference to cell B6 in the formula in cell B14 to an absolute one.

☞ Copy the formula from cell B14 to the cells C14 and D14.

☞ In cell A15, type: variable percentage

☞ In cell B15, enter a formula to divide cell B12 by cell B14.

☞ Convert the result in cell B15 to a percentage.

☞ Copy the formula from cell B15 to the cells C15 and D15.

☞ In cell A17, type: 4-1-2016

☞ Select the cells A17:A28 and automatically fill the series using the ribbon with only the weekdays.

☞ Open the *Result Do-It-Yourself Exercise 4* workbook and compare this to your own workbook.

☞ Close the *Result-Do-It Yourself Exercise 4* workbook and do not save any changes.

☞ Save the workbook with the name *Labor Costs 1* in the *(My) Documents* folder.

☞ Close *Excel*.

MOS Exam Exercise 3: Formulas and Series

🕐 10 minutes

☞ Open the web page **www.visualstepsmosbooks.com/excel2016-mos-examexercises.php** and enter the access code from the bottom of page 2 in order to access the web page.

☞ Open the source window by clicking MOS exam exercise 3: Formulas by **Chapter 2**.

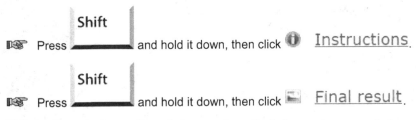

☞ Press **Shift** and hold it down, then click 🛈 Instructions.

☞ Press **Shift** and hold it down, then click 🖼 Final result.

☞ Position the instruction window, end result window and source window next to each other in the bottom of the screen.

☞ Open *Excel* and position the *Excel* window in the top of the screen.

☞ Carry out the actions shown in the instruction window.

MOS Exam Exercise 4: More about Formulas and Series

🕐 15 minutes

☞ Open the web page **www.visualstepsmosbooks.com/excel2016-mos-examexercises.php** and enter the access code from the bottom of page 2 in order to access the web page.

☞ Open the source window by clicking

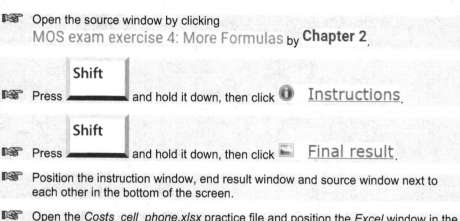

MOS exam exercise 4: More Formulas by **Chapter 2**.

☞ Press **Shift** and hold it down, then click ⓘ Instructions.

☞ Press **Shift** and hold it down, then click 🖳 Final result.

☞ Position the instruction window, end result window and source window next to each other in the bottom of the screen.

☞ Open the *Costs_cell_phone.xlsx* practice file and position the *Excel* window in the top of the screen.

☞ Carry out the actions shown in the instruction window.

Notes

Write your notes down here.

3. Tables

In Chapter 3 of the textbook you have learned how to create tables in *Excel*. You have also seen how these tables can be adjusted separately from the rest of the worksheet. You can continue practicing these skills in this chapter.

Footsteps Exercise 3: Tables

🕐 7 minutes

☞ Open *Excel*. 𝒢𝒫[1] Download the *Movie list* template. It can be found under the *Personal* category in *Suggested searches* at the top of the *Start Screen*. 𝒢𝒫[68]

☞ Close the template without saving it 𝒢𝒫[16] and open a new blank workbook. 𝒢𝒫[2]

☞ In cell A1, type: Temperature and precipitation Rome 𝒢𝒫[17]

☞ Automatically adjust the width of the first column to the widest data. 𝒢𝒫[18]

☞ Change the formatting of cell A1 to bold. 𝒢𝒫[28]

☞ Click cell A3 and import the *Climate_Rome.csv* file. 𝒢𝒫[53]

☞ Save the workbook with the name Climate Rome 2 𝒢𝒫[33]

☞ Convert the imported data to a table. 𝒢𝒫[55]

☞ Adjust the table style to *Table Style Medium 21*. 𝒢𝒫[56]

☞ Use the *Replace* function to replace *Max.* by *Maximum*. 𝒢𝒫[65]

☞ In the same way, replace *Min.* by *Minimum*. 𝒢𝒫[65]

☞ Automatically adjust columns B and C to the correct width. 𝒢𝒫[18]

☞ Add a column on the right side of the table by increasing the table manually. 𝒢𝒫[70]

☞ In the table, add a column between the *Minimum* column and the *Precipitation* column. 𝒢𝒫[71]

☞ Undo the last two actions. 𝒢𝒫[69]

☞ Use combined sorting to sort the table descending by maximum temperature and then descending by minimum temperature and finally ascending by precipitation. 𝒢𝒫[72]

☞ Filter the months with a maximum temperature above 20 degrees. 🐾**59**

☞ Disable the filter buttons so that all data is visible again. 🐾**73**

☞ Add a row to the table using the ⬅Tab➡ key. 🐾**58**

☞ In cell A16, type: average 🐾**17**

☞ Click cell B16 and calculate the average of the cells B4:B15. 🐾**35**

☞ Change the number of decimals of cell B16 to one decimal. 🐾**21**

☞ Copy the formula from cell B16 to the cells C16 and D16. 🐾**24**

☞ Name cell B4 Warmest 🐾**74**

☞ Click cell A1 and then use *Go To* to move to cell B4. 🐾**64**

☞ Open the *Result Footsteps Exercise 3* workbook 🐾**36** and compare this to your own workbook.

☞ Close the *Result Footsteps Exercise 3* workbook and do not save any changes. 🐾**16**

☞ Save the workbook and close *Excel*. 🐾**16**

Do-It-Yourself Exercise 5: Tables

🕐 5 minutes

☞ Open *Excel* and open a new blank workbook.

☞ Import the *Visual_games.csv* file.

☞ Save the workbook in the (*My*) *Documents* folder with the name Visual Games 2

☞ Convert the summary to a table.

☞ Remove the duplicates from the table.

☞ Sort the data by ascending date.

☞ Add a row to the table using the ⬅Tab➡ key.

☞ In the new row, type the following data:
   B. Wilson   12/9/2015 $ 29.99

☞ Filter the data on the basis of the top 5 sales.

☞ Clear the filter.

☞ Enable a row with totals to calculate the total turnover.

☞ Adjust the width of column C so that the value fits the column.

☞ Name the table `ActionGames`

☞ Click cell K1 and then use *Go To* to move to the table.

☞ Use the *Replace* function to replace *James* by *Jameson*.

☞ Convert the table to a range.

☞ Open the *Result Do-It-Yourself Exercise 5* workbook and compare this to your own workbook.

☞ Close the *Result Do-It-Yourself Exercise 5* workbook and do not save any changes.

☞ Save the workbook and close *Excel*.

Do-It-Yourself Exercise 6: More about Tables

🕐 5 minutes

☞ Open *Excel* and open the *Costs_cell_phone_2.xlsx* workbook from the *Practice Files Workbook Excel* folder.

☞ Remove row 8 to row 20.

☞ Click cell A8 and import the *Costs_telephone_January.csv* file.

☞ Save the workbook in the *(My) Documents* folder with the name `Costs Cell Phone 2`

☞ Convert the imported data into a table.

☞ Select the cells B9:C39 and center the selected cells.

☞ Adjust the table style to *Table Style Medium 4*.

☞ Add a column on the right side of the table by increasing the table manually.

☞ Undo the last action.

☞ Add a dollar sign to the cells D9:D39 and ensure all amounts have two decimals.

☞ Use combined sorting to sort the table descending by the variable costs and then ascending by number of MB.

☞ Filter the data so that only the data from 1 to 7 January is visible.

☞ Disable the filter buttons so that all data is visible again.

☞ Select the cells A9:D13 and name this group of cells `MostExpensive`

☞ Click cell A1 and then use *Go To* to move to the group of cells with the name *Most expensive*.

☞ Open the *Result Do-It-Yourself Exercise 6* workbook and compare this to your own workbook.

☞ Close the *Result Do-It-Yourself Exercise 6* workbook and do not save any changes.

☞ Save the workbook and close *Excel*.

MOS Exam Exercise 5: Tables

🕐 5 minutes

☞ Open the web page **www.visualstepsmosbooks.com/excel2016-mos-examexercises.php** and enter the access code from the bottom of page 2 in order to access the web page.

☞ Open the source window by clicking MOS exam exercise 5: Tables by **Chapter 3**.

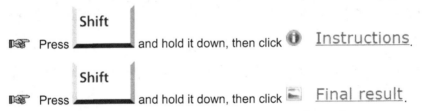

☞ Press **Shift** and hold it down, then click ⓘ Instructions.

☞ Press **Shift** and hold it down, then click ▤ Final result.

☞ Position the instruction window, end result window and source window next to each other in the bottom of the screen.

☞ Open *Excel* and position the *Excel* window in the top of the screen.

☞ Carry out the actions shown in the instruction window.

MOS Exam Exercise 6: More about Tables

🕐 5 minutes

☞ Open the web page **www.visualstepsmosbooks.com/excel2016-mos-examexercises.php** and enter the access code from the bottom of page 2 in order to access the web page.

☞ Open the sources window by clicking MOS exam exercise 6: More Tables by **Chapter 3**.

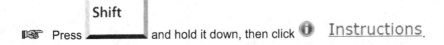

☞ Press **Shift** and hold it down, then click ⓘ Instructions.

☞ Press **Shift** and hold it down, then click 🖃 Final result.

☞ Position the instruction window, end result window and source window next to each other in the bottom of the screen.

☞ Open the *Costs_cell_phone_2.xlsx* practice file and position the *Excel* window in the top of the screen.

☞ Carry out the actions shown in the instruction window.

Notes

Write your notes down here.

4. Analyzing Data

In Chapter 4 of the textbook you were shown how to analyze data by using the *Quick Analysis* function and how this same function can also be used to create a chart. Furthermore, you learned how to make information visually more attractive and easier to comprehend by adding graphical objects such as images. You can continue practicing these skills in this chapter.

Footsteps Exercise 4: Analyzing Data

⏱ 7 minutes

☞ Open *Excel* 😊¹ and open the *Labor_costs.xlsx* workbook from the *Practice Files Workbook Excel* folder. 😊⁵⁰

☞ Select cells A1:B13. 😊¹⁹

☞ Add up the amounts using *Quick Analysis*. 😊⁹³

☞ Use data bars to show the amounts. 😊⁹⁴

☞ Create a *Line* chart. 😊⁷⁹

☞ Change the chart style to *Style 14*. 😊⁹⁵

☞ Switch the rows and columns of the chart. 😊⁹⁶

☞ Undo the last action. 😊⁶⁹

☞ Filter the data in the chart so that only the first three months are visible. 😊⁹⁷

☞ Make all data in the chart visible again. 😊⁹⁷

☞ Place the chart on a separate worksheet with the name Labor costs chart 😊⁸³

☞ To the right of the table on the *Sheet1* worksheet, insert a text box of approximately 3 cells wide and 3.5 cells high with the following text: 😊⁸⁵
Labor costs 2015
Visual Counseling

☞ Change the font size to 16 and center the text. 😊 ²⁸

☞ Change the shape style of the text box to *Colored Fill - Blue, Accent 5*. 😊⁸⁷

☞ Add the *Bevel, Round Convex* shape effect to the text box. 😊⁹⁸

☞ Insert the *Counseling.jpg* image next to the text box. &⁹⁹

☞ Change the color of the image to *Blue, Accent Color 5, Light*. &¹⁰⁰

☞ Insert the *Segmented Cycle* SmartArt illustration. &⁹¹

☞ In the lower shape, type Idea, in the left shape Plan and in the right shape Action. &¹⁰¹

☞ Change the SmartArt style to *Intense Effect*. &¹⁰²

☞ Make the SmartArt illustration approximately a third smaller. &⁷⁶

☞ Place the SmartArt illustration below the text box. &⁷⁵

☞ Open the *Result Footsteps Exercise 4* workbook &³⁶ and compare this to your own workbook.

☞ Close the *Result Footsteps Exercise 4* workbook and do not save any changes. &¹⁶

☞ Save the workbook with the name *Labor Costs 2* in the *(My) Documents* folder. &³³

☞ Close *Excel*. &¹⁶

Do-It-Yourself Exercise 7: Analyzing Data

🕐 7 minutes

☞ Open *Excel* and open the *Sandwiches_cafeteria.xlsx* workbook from the *Practice Files Workbook Excel* folder.

☞ Select cells A1:M4.

☞ Show *Line* type sparklines.

☞ Select cells A1:M4.

☞ Create a *Stacked Column* type chart.

☞ Add data labels to the chart.

☞ Change the chart title to Sales 2015

☞ Change the font size of the chart title to 11 and change the text to italic.

☞ Change the color scheme of the chart to *Monochromatic Palette 4*.

☞ In cells A5:M5, type the following data consecutively:
Ham sandwich 389 246 289 248 268 215 156 98 196 320 369 389

☞ Add row 5 to the chart.

☞ Change the chart type to *3-D Stacked Column*.

☞ Enlarge the chart by about 50% from the bottom left.

☞ To the right of the table, insert a text box of approximately 4 cells wide and 3 cells high with the following text: Brad Baker College

☞ Change the font size to 20, the text color to Blue and center the text.

☞ If necessary, enlarge the text box larger so that the text just fits in.

☞ Place the text box at the top right of the chart so it slightly overlaps a piece of the chart area.

☞ Rotate the text box slightly clockwise.

☞ Create a new worksheet.

☞ On the new worksheet, insert the SmartArt *Basic Block List* illustration.

☞ Click one of the shapes and press ⌷ Delete ⌷ to delete the shape.

☞ In the other shapes, type: BLT sandwich, Cheese sandwich, Club sandwich and Ham sandwich.

☞ Change the color scheme of the SmartArt illustration to *Colored Fill - Accent 4*.

☞ Change the SmartArt style to *Bird's Eye Scene*.

☞ Open the *Result Do-It-Yourself Exercise 7* workbook and compare this to your own workbook.

☞ Close the *Result Do-It-Yourself Exercise 7* workbook and do not save any changes.

☞ Save the workbook with the name *Bread Rolls Cantine 2* in the *(My) Documents* folder.

☞ Close *Excel*.

Do-It-Yourself Exercise 8: Analyzing More Data

🕐 5 minutes

☞ Start *Excel* and open the *Household_costs.xlsx* workbook from the *Practice Files Workbook Excel* folder.

☞ Select cells B2:C6.

☞ Use *Quick Analysis* to calculate the averages.

☞ Let the color scale show on the amounts.

☞ Select cells A1:C6.

☞ Create a *Clustered Column* type chart.

☞ Switch the rows and columns of the chart.

☞ Change the color scheme of the chart to *Colorful Palette 3*.

☞ Change the chart style to *Style 7*.

☞ Filter the data in the chart so that only the fixed costs are visible.

☞ Change the chart title to `Fixed Costs`

☞ Place the chart on a separate worksheet with the name `Chart`

☞ Make all data in the chart visible again.

☞ Change the text of the horizontal and vertical axis to bold and font size 11.

☞ Go to *Sheet1* worksheet and insert the *Dollars.jpg* image underneath the data.

☞ Change the image style to *Bevel Rectangle*.

☞ Apply the artistic effect *Pencil Greyscale* to the image.

☞ Open the *Result Do-It-Yourself Exercise 8* workbook and compare this to your own workbook.

☞ Close the *Result Do-It-Yourself Exercise 8* workbook and do not save any changes.

☞ Save the workbook with the name *Household Costs 2* in the *(My) Documents* folder.

☞ Close *Excel*.

MOS Exam Exercise 7: Analyzing Data

🕐 5 minutes

☞ Open the web page **www.visualstepsmosbooks.com/excel2016-mos-examexercises.php** and enter the access code from the bottom of page 2 in order to access the web page.

☞ Open the source window by clicking
MOS exam exercise 7: Analyzing Data by **Chapter 4**.

☞ Press **Shift** and hold it down, then click ⓘ Instructions.

☞ Press **Shift** and hold it down, then click 🖼 Final result.

☞ Position the instruction window, end result window and source window next to each other in the bottom of the screen.

☞ Open the *Labor_costs.xlsx* practice file and position the *Excel* window at the top of the screen.

☞ Carry out the actions shown in the instruction window.

MOS Exam Exercise 8: Analyzing More Data

🕐 5 minutes

☞ Open the web page **www.visualstepsmosbooks.com/excel2016-mos-examexercises.php** and enter the access code from the bottom of page 2 in order to access the web page.

☞ Open the source window by clicking
MOS exam exercise 8: More Analyzing Data by **Chapter 4**.

☞ Press **Shift** and hold it down, then click ⓘ Instructions.

☞ Press **Shift** and hold it down, then click 🖼 Final result.

☞ Position the instruction window, end result window and source window next to each other in the bottom of the screen.

☞ Open the *Household_costs.xlsx* practice file and position the *Excel* window in the top of the screen.

☞ Carry out the actions shown in the instruction window.

Notes

Write your notes down here.

5. Functions

In Chapter 5 of the textbook you have learned to work with some of *Excel*'s basic and most frequently used functions. Both arithmetic functions and text functions have been discussed. You can continue practicing with these functions in this chapter.

Footsteps Exercise 5: Functions

🕐 7 minutes

☞ Open *Excel* 🦶[1] and open the *Visual_Games_2.xlsx* workbook from the *Practice Files Workbook Excel* folder. 🦶[50]

☞ Save the workbook with the name *Visual Games 3* in the *(My) Documents* folder. 🦶[33]

☞ Click cell E2.

☞ Open the *SUM* function. 🦶[104]

☞ In cell E2, calculate the total number of customers for October through December. 🦶[23]

☞ Copy the formula to the cells E3 and E5. 🦶[25]

☞ In the cells E3 and E5, place a $ sign before the amounts and ensure that all amounts get two decimals. 🦶[116]

☞ In cell E4, calculate the average turnover per customer. 🦶[108]

☞ In cell J18, calculate the number of customers on the basis of the customer numbers. 🦶[105]

☞ Click cell A18.

☞ Open the *COUNTA* function. 🦶[103]

☞ In cell A18, calculate the number of customers on the basis of the names of the customers. 🦶[117]

☞ Place the highest turnover in cell F3. 🦶[107] Please note: Do not select the cell with the total turnover!

☞ Place the lowest costs in cell F5. 🦶[106] Please note: Do not select the cell with the total costs!

☞ Click cell F4.

☞ Open the *AVERAGEIF* function. 🦶[103]

☞ In cell F4, calculate the average turnover per customer, but only for the months in which the average turnover exceeds $35.00. ✂118

☞ In the cell F4, place a $ sign and ensure that the amount gets two decimals.

☞ Mark the cells with average costs per month (B5:D5) of more than $20,000.00 with a red color. ✂111

☞ Use the *TRIM* function to place the name G. Vargas (cell A10) in cell A20 without the extra spaces. ✂121

☞ Copy the formula to the cells A21:A27. ✂25

☞ Use *DATA VALIDATION* to allow a minimum age of 18 years in the cells G10:G17 and have the following error message show if the age is lower:
Minimum age is 18 years old! ✂114

☞ In cell G12, type: 17 and press 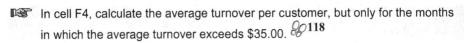 . ✂17

☞ Click *Cancel*.

☞ Use the *UPPER* function to change the street names in cell H10 to upper case. ✂119

☞ Copy the formula to the cells H11:H17. ✂25

☞ Use the *CONCAT* function to place the zip code next to the city name and state abbreviation in cell I10, with a space in between. ✂112

☞ Copy the formula to the cells I11:I17 ✂25 and automatically adjust the column to the widest data. ✂18

☞ Use the *RIGHT* function to place the five numbers of the zip code and the state abbreviation in cell K10. ✂120

☞ Copy the formula to the cells K11:K17. ✂25

☞ Open the *Result Footsteps Exercise 5* workbook ✂36 and compare this to your own workbook.

☞ Close the *Result Footsteps Exercise 5* workbook and do not save any changes. ✂16

☞ Save the workbook and close *Excel*. ✂16

Do-It-Yourself Exercise 9: Functions

⏱ 10 minutes

☞ Open *Excel* and open the *Labor_costs_2.xlsx* workbook from the *Practice Files Workbook Excel* folder.

☞ Save the workbook with the name *Labor Costs 3* in the *(My) Documents* folder.

☞ Click cell B14.

☞ Open the *SUM* function.

☞ In cell B14, calculate the total labor costs.

☞ In cell B15, calculate the average labor costs.

☞ Place the highest labor costs in cell B16.

☞ Mark the cells with labor costs of less than $10,000.00 with a green color.

☞ Click cell C24.

☞ Open the *COUNTIF* function.

☞ In cell C24, calculate the number of women.

☞ Click cell D19.

☞ Open the *IF* function.

☞ In cell D19, place *Mr* if there is an *M* in column C and have *Ms* placed when there is no M. Please note: because this is a string of text, you need to put the *M* between double quotes!

☞ Copy the formula to the cells D20:D23.

☞ Use the *LOWER* function to change the last name in cell E19 to lower case.

☞ Copy the formula to the cells E20:E23.

☞ Use the *CONCAT* function to place initials and last name (in upper case) in cell F19 with a space in between.

☞ Copy the formula to the cells F20:F23 and adjust the column to the widest data.

☞ Open the *Result Do-It-Yourself Exercise 9* workbook and compare this to your own workbook.

☞ Close the *Result Do-It-Yourself Exercise 9* workbook and do not save any changes.

☞ Save the workbook and close *Excel*.

Do-It-Yourself Exercise 10: More Functions

🕐 10 minutes

☞ Open *Excel* and open the *Grades_Math.xlsx* workbook from the *Practice Files Workbook Excel* folder.

☞ Save the workbook with the name *Grades Mathematics* in the *(My) Documents* folder.

☞ In cell H2, calculate the average grade of the first student.

☞ If necessary, change the number of decimals of cell H2 to one decimal.

☞ Copy the formula to the cells H3:H8.

☞ In cell H9, calculate the number of students.

☞ Remove the decimal in cell H9.

☞ In cell I2, place the lowest grade of the first student.

☞ Copy the formula to the cells I3:I8.

☞ Click cell J2.

☞ Open the *AVERAGEIF* function.

☞ In cell J2, calculate the average of the satisfactory grades (higher than 54) of the first student.

☞ If necessary, remove the decimals of cell J2.

☞ Copy the formula to the cells J3:J8.

☞ Click cell K2.

☞ Open the *SUMIF* function.

☞ In cell K2, calculate the total of all unsatisfactory grades (lower than 54) of the first student.

☞ Copy the formula to the cells K3:K8.

☞ Click cell L2.

☞ Open the *SUMIF* function.

☞ In cell L2, calculate the total of all satisfactory grades of the first student.

☞ Copy the formula to the cells L3:L8.

☞ In cell M2, calculate the total number of points of the first student.

☞ Copy the formula to the cells M3:M8.

☞ Mark all cells with an unsatisfactory grade in a red color.

☞ Use *DATA VALIDATION* to allow only grades from 20 or above in the cells B2:G8 and have the following error message show if the grade is lower:
Title: `Please note!`
Error message: `A grade less than 20 may not be awarded!`

☞ In cell B5, try to type the following: `15` and then click *Cancel*.

☞ Use the *TRIM* function to place the name Luke Vargas in cell A11 without the extra spaces.

☞ Copy the formula to the cells A12:A17.

☞ Use the *MID* function to place the phone number without the area code (that is without the first 3 digits and the space) in cell B11.

☞ Copy the formula to the cells B12:B17.

☞ Open the *Result Do-It-Yourself Exercise 10* workbook and compare this to your own workbook.

☞ Close the *Result Do-It-Yourself Exercise 10* workbook and do not save any changes.

☞ Save the workbook and close *Excel*.

MOS Exam Exercise 9: Functions

🕑 10 minutes

☞ Open the web page **www.visualstepsmosbooks.com/excel2016-mos-examexercises.php** and enter the access code from the bottom of page 2 in order to access the web page.

☞ Open the source window by clicking MOS exam exercise 9: Functions by **Chapter 5**

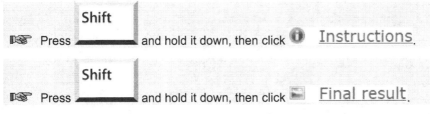

☞ Press **Shift** and hold it down, then click 🛈 Instructions.

☞ Press **Shift** and hold it down, then click ▣ Final result.

☞ Position the instruction window, end result window and source window next to each other in the bottom of the screen.

☞ Open the *Visual_Games_2.xlsx* practice file and position the *Excel* window in the top of the screen.

☞ Carry out the actions shown in the instruction window.

MOS Exam Exercise 10: More Functions

🕐 5 minutes

☞ Open the web page **www.visualstepsmosbooks.com/excel2016-mos-examexercises.php** and enter the access code from the bottom of page 2 in order to access the web page.

☞ Open the source window by clicking
MOS exam exercise 10: More Functions by **Chapter 5**.

☞ Press ▭ Shift ▭ and hold it down, then click . 🛈 Instructions

☞ Press ▭ Shift ▭ and hold it down, then click 🖻 Final result.

☞ Position the instruction window, end result window and source window next to each other in the bottom of the screen.

☞ Open the *Grades_Math_2.xlsx* practice file and position the *Excel* window in the top of the screen.

☞ Carry out the actions shown in the instruction window.

6. Viewing and Saving

In Chapter 6 of the textbook you learned various ways to view large amounts of data in *Excel* more easily and how to print all or part of a workbook. You can continue practicing these skills in this chapter.

Please note:

The following exercises contain tasks to be printed. If necessary, consult your teacher whether printing is allowed.

Footsteps Exercise 6: Viewing and Saving

🕐 15 minutes

☞ Start *Excel* ✆¹ and open the workbook *Household_costs_2.xlsx* file from the folder *Practice Files Workbook Excel*. ✆⁵⁰

☞ Zoom out until you see all the data. ✆¹⁴⁶

☞ Zoom in to 100%. ✆¹⁴⁷

☞ Freeze the titles in the first column. ✆¹⁴⁸

☞ Unfreeze the titles. ✆¹⁴⁹

☞ Click cell O1 and split the window. ✆¹⁵⁰

☞ Undo the splitting. ✆¹⁵¹

☞ Select row 1 and apply cell style *Heading 1*. ✆¹⁵²

☞ Adjust the background color of cell A2 to *Yellow* ✆¹⁵³ and change the font color to *Blue*. ✆²⁸

☞ Copy the formatting from cell A2 to cell A10. ✆¹⁵⁴

☞ Change the print orientation to *Landscape*. ✆¹⁵⁵

☞ Make sure that the titles are printed on each page. ✆¹⁵⁶

☞ Change the left and right margin to 0.5 cm. ✆¹⁵⁷

☞ In the upper right corner of the page, insert a header with the page number and return to the normal view. ✆¹⁵⁸

☞ Set only the data for 2015 as the print range. ✆¹⁵⁹

☞ Open the print preview. 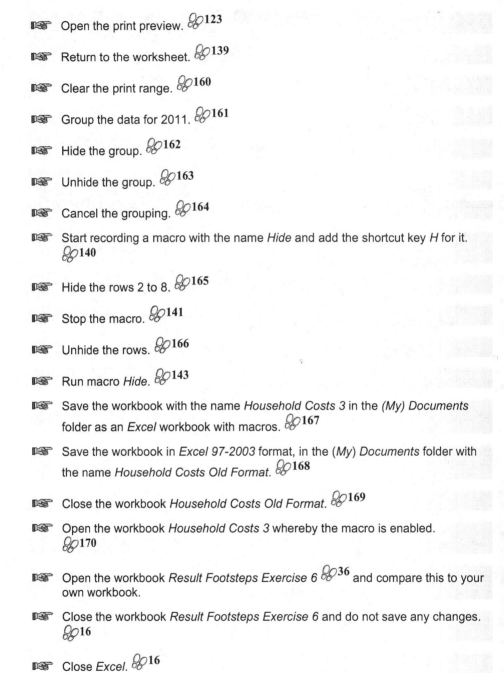**123**

☞ Return to the worksheet. **139**

☞ Clear the print range. **160**

☞ Group the data for 2011. **161**

☞ Hide the group. **162**

☞ Unhide the group. **163**

☞ Cancel the grouping. **164**

☞ Start recording a macro with the name *Hide* and add the shortcut key *H* for it. **140**

☞ Hide the rows 2 to 8. **165**

☞ Stop the macro. **141**

☞ Unhide the rows. **166**

☞ Run macro *Hide*. **143**

☞ Save the workbook with the name *Household Costs 3* in the *(My) Documents* folder as an *Excel* workbook with macros. **167**

☞ Save the workbook in *Excel 97-2003* format, in the *(My) Documents* folder with the name *Household Costs Old Format*. **168**

☞ Close the workbook *Household Costs Old Format*. **169**

☞ Open the workbook *Household Costs 3* whereby the macro is enabled. **170**

☞ Open the workbook *Result Footsteps Exercise 6* **36** and compare this to your own workbook.

☞ Close the workbook *Result Footsteps Exercise 6* and do not save any changes. **16**

☞ Close *Excel*. **16**

Do-It-Yourself Exercise 11: Viewing and Saving

🕐 10 minutes

☞ Start *Excel* and open the workbook *Grades_Math_3.xlsx* file from the folder *Practice Files Workbook Excel*.

☞ Freeze the titles in the first row.

☞ Make sure that the titles are printed on each page.

☞ Hide the worksheet *2014-2015*.

☞ Unhide the worksheet again and return to worksheet *2015-2016*.

☞ Select cells A1:H104.

☞ In column B (*Student*), add the subtotals of the number of students per class (function: *COUNT*).

☞ Widen column A until the text fits in the column.

☞ Show only the numbers per class.

☞ Show only the grades of class 1A.

☞ Show all data.

☞ Apply the background color *Blue, Accent 1, Lighter 80%* to the cells A1:H1.

☞ Apply the background color *Green, Accent 6, Lighter 80%* to the cells A2:H110.

☞ Set the theme *Ion*.

☞ Change the color scheme of the theme to *Red*.

☞ Change the left and right margin to 1 cm.

☞ Open the print preview.

☞ Print the whole summary on a single page.

☞ Select the cells C2:C21 and name these cells *Test1*.

☞ Select the cells D2:D21 and name these cells *Test2*.

☞ Use the cell names to calculate the total of the two grades in cell I2.

☞ Copy the formula from cell I2 to the cells I3:I21.

☞ Have the formulas show instead of the result.

☞ Hide the formulas again.

☞ Open the workbook *Result Do-It-Yourself Exercise 11* and compare this to your own workbook.

☞ Close the workbook *Result Do-It-Yourself Exercise 11* and do not save any changes.

- Save the workbook with the name *Grades Mathematics 2* in the *(My) Documents* folder.
- Save the worksheet as a PDF document in the *(My) Documents* folder with the name *Grades Mathematics.*
- Close the PDF document.
- Close *Excel.*

Do-It-Yourself Exercise 12: More Viewing and Saving

🕐 8 minutes

- Start *Excel* and open the workbook *Sandwiches_cafeteria_2.xlsx* file from the folder *Practice Files Workbook Excel.*
- Zoom out until you see all the data.
- Zoom in to 100%.
- Hide the rows 3 to 33.
- Unhide the rows.
- Apply the cell style *Title* to cell A1.
- Apply the cell style *Accent1* to cells A2:D2.
- In the center at the bottom of the page, insert the following footer: Sales 2015.
- Return to the normal view.
- Make sure that the titles in the first two rows are printed on each page.
- Set only the data for December as the print range.
- Open the print preview and print the print range.
- Clear the print range.
- Group the data for October.
- Hide the group.
- Unhide the group.
- Start recording a macro with the name *Split* and add the shortcut key S for it.
- Click cell A23 and split the window.
- Stop the macro.
- Undo the splitting.
- Run macro *Split*.
- Undo the splitting.

☞ Save the workbook with the name *Sandwiches Cafeteria 3* in the *(My) Documents* folder as an *Excel* workbook with macros.

☞ Close the workbook.

☞ Open the workbook *Sandwiches Cafeteria 3* whereby the macro is <u>not</u> enabled.

☞ Open the workbook *Result Do-It-Yourself Exercise 12* and compare this to your own workbook.

☞ Close the workbook *Result Do-It-Yourself Exercise 12* and do not save any changes.

☞ Close *Excel*.

MOS Exam Exercise 11: Viewing and Saving

🕐 8 minutes

☞ Open the web page **www.visualstepsmosbooks.com/excel2016-mos-examexercises.php** and enter the access code from the bottom of page 2 in order to access the web page.

☞ Open the source window by clicking
MOS exam exercise 11: Viewing and Saving by **Chapter 6**.

☞ Press and hold **Shift** and click ⓘ Instructions.

☞ Press and hold **Shift** and click 🖼 Final result.

☞ Position the instruction window, end result window and source window next to each other in the bottom of the screen.

☞ Open the practice file *Household_costs_2.xlsx* and position the *Excel* window in the top of the screen.

☞ Carry out the actions shown in the instruction window.

MOS Exam Exercise 12: More Viewing and Saving

🕐 8 minutes

☞ Open the web page **www.visualstepsmosbooks.com/excel2016-mos-examinexercises.php** and enter the access code from the bottom of page 2 in order to access the web page.

☞ Open the source window by clicking
MOS exam exercise 12: More Viewing and Saving by **Chapter 6**.

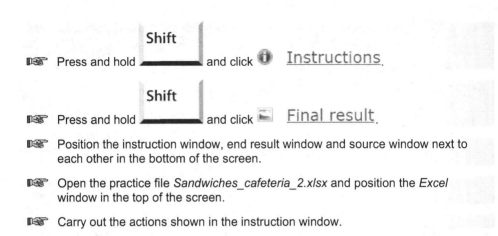

☞ Press and hold **Shift** and click 🛈 <u>Instructions</u>.

☞ Press and hold **Shift** and click 🖼 <u>Final result</u>.

☞ Position the instruction window, end result window and source window next to each other in the bottom of the screen.

☞ Open the practice file *Sandwiches_cafeteria_2.xlsx* and position the *Excel* window in the top of the screen.

☞ Carry out the actions shown in the instruction window.

7. Exercises Chapter 1 to 3

This chapter features additional exercises relating to Chapters 1 to 3 in the textbook.

Do-It-Yourself Exercise 13: Visual Games

🕐 15 minutes

☞ Open *Excel* and open a new blank workbook.

☞ Import the *Visual_Games.csv* text file (this file contains headers and data separated by a semicolon).

☞ Save the workbook with the name Visual Games 4

☞ Collapse the ribbon and then show the ribbon again.

☞ Add the *Sum* command to the *Quick Access* toolbar.

☞ Add a blank row above the first row and in cell A1 type: Turnover Visual Games 2015

☞ Merge cells A1:C1, change the font size to 16 and center the data.

☞ Place a $ sign before the amounts in column C.

☞ In cell A18, type: total

☞ In cell C18, add up all turnover using the *SUM* function.

☞ Change the amount in cell C17 to: 89.50 and ensure that the formula in cell C18 is recalculated.

☞ Remove the *Sum* command from the *Quick Access* toolbar.

☞ Create a new worksheet.

☞ Change the name of the first worksheet to *2015* and that of the second worksheet to *2016*.

☞ Make sure worksheet *2015* is positioned before the *2016* worksheet.

☞ Change the tab color of the 2015 worksheet to green and that of the 2016 worksheet to red.

☞ Click the tab for the *2016* worksheet.

☞ In cell A1, type: 1/4/2016.

☞ Automatically fill the cells A2:A28 with the other dates from January.

☞ Widen column A until the text fits the column.

☞ Select the cells A2:A28 and replace the series by data with only the days of the week (it will then continue until 2/10/2016).

☞ In cell C1, type: `2015` and change this text into a hyperlink to the *2015* worksheet.

☞ Click the hyperlink to test whether it works.

☞ Remove the hyperlink.

☞ Undo the last action.

☞ Protect the *2015* worksheet.

☞ Try to change data in the *2015* worksheet.

☞ Cancel the protection of the *2015* worksheet.

☞ Change cells A2:C18 on the *2015* worksheet to a table.

☞ Remove duplicate copies from the table and sort the data by ascending date.

☞ Adjust the table style to *Table Style Medium 21*.

☞ After the last row of the table, insert a new row.

☞ In cell A18, type: `average/customer`

☞ Enter a formula in cell C18 for the calculation of the average of the cells C3:C16.

☞ Filter the data so that only customers with a turnover of more than 50 dollars are visible.

☞ Name the table: `Turnover2015`

☞ Open the *2016* worksheet and then use *Go To* to return to the table.

☞ Open the *Result Do-It-Yourself Exercise 13* workbook and compare this to your own workbook.

☞ Close the *Result Do-It-Yourself Exercise 13* workbook and do not save any changes.

☞ Save the workbook and close *Excel*.

Do-It-Yourself Exercise 14: Cell Phone Costs

🕑 15 minutes

☞ Open *Excel*. Download the *Annual financial report* template. It can be found under the *financial management* category in *Suggested searches* at the top of the *Start Screen*.

☞ Close the template without saving it and open the *Costs_cell_phone.xlsx* workbook from the *Practice Files Workbook Excel* folder.

☞ Add a new group to the | Home | tab and name it *Tables*.

☞ Add the *Insert table* command to the new group.

☞ Automatically fill the cells A10:A20 with the other months.

☞ Make column A slightly wider than the text.

☞ Set text wrapping for cells B3 and D3.

☞ Enter a nested formula in cell C9, in which you first subtract cell C4 from cell B9 and then multiply the result by cell D4.

☞ In the formula in cell C9, change the references to the cells C4 and D4 to absolute ones and copy the formula of cell C9 to the cells C10:C20.

☞ Enter a nested formula in cell E9, in which you first subtract cell C5 from cell D9 and then multiply the result by cell D5.

☞ In the formula in cell E9, change the references to the cells C5 and D5 to absolute ones and copy the formula of cell E9 to the cells E10:E20.

☞ In cell F9 add up the data from the cells B4, B5, C9 and E9 and change the references to the cells B4 and B5 into absolute ones.

☞ Copy the formula from cell F9 to the cells F10:F20.

☞ Change the cells A8:F20 into a table and allow the table to contain headers.

☞ Adjust the table style to *Table Style Medium 8*.

☞ Enable a row with totals to calculate the total costs.

☞ Add a column on the right side of the table by increasing the table manually.

☞ Replace the text *Column4* in cell G8 by: `fixed costs`.

☞ Automatically adjust column G to the correct width.

☞ In cell G9 add up the data from the cells B4 and B5 and change the references to the cells into absolute ones.

☞ Copy the formula from cell G9 to the cells G10:G20.

☞ Filter the data in the table on the basis of the top 5 expenses.

☞ Disable the filter buttons so that all data is visible again.

☞ Create a new worksheet.

☞ Click the tab of *Sheet1* worksheet.

☞ Convert the table into a range again.

☞ Remove the new worksheet.

☞ Use the *Replace* function to replace *min.* by *minutes*.

☞ Revert to the default settings for the | Home | tab.

☞ Open the *Result Do-It-Yourself Exercise 14* workbook and compare this to your own workbook.

☞ Close the *Result Do-It-Yourself Exercise 14* workbook and do not save any changes.

☞ Save the workbook with the name *Cell Phone Costs 3* in the *(My) Documents* folder.

☞ Close *Excel*.

MOS Exam Exercise 13: Climate Rome

🕐 12 minutes

☞ Open the web page **www.visualstepsmosbooks.com/excel2016-mos-examexercises.php** and enter the access code from the bottom of page 2 in order to access the web page.

☞ Open the source window by clicking
MOS exam exercise 13: Climate Rome by **Chapter 1 to 3**.

☞ Press **Shift** and hold it down, then click ⓘ Instructions.

☞ Press **Shift** and hold it down, then click ▭ Final result.

☞ Position the instruction window, end result window and source window next to each other in the bottom of the screen.

☞ Open *Excel* and position the *Excel* window in the top of the screen.

☞ Carry out the actions shown in the instruction window.

MOS Exam Exercise 14: Labor Costs

🕐 12 minutes

☞ Open the web page **www.visualstepsmosbooks.com/excel2016-mos-examexercises.php** and enter the access code from the bottom of page 2 in order to access the web page.

☞ Open the source window by clicking
MOS exam exercise 14: Labor costs by **Chapter 1 to 3**.

☞ Press **Shift** and hold it down, then click ⓘ Instructions.

☞ Press **Shift** and hold it down, then click ▭ Final result.

☞ Position the instruction window, end result window and source window next to each other in the bottom of the screen.

☞ Open the *Labor_costs.xlsx* practice file and position the *Excel* window at the top of the screen.

☞ Carry out the actions shown in the instruction window.

Notes

Write your notes down here.

8. Exercises Chapter 4 to 6

This chapter features additional exercises relating to Chapter 4 to 6 in the textbook.

🍂 Please note:

The following exercises contain tasks to be printed. If necessary, consult your teacher whether printing is allowed.

Do-It-Yourself Exercise 15: Mathematics Grades

🕐 20 minutes

🖝 Open *Excel* and open the *Grades_Math_4.xlsx* workbook from the *Practice Files Workbook Excel* folder.

🖝 Select the cells C2:H21 and use *Quick Analysis* to show icons with the grades.

🖝 Select the cells B1:H21 and create a chart of the *Scatter* type.

🖝 Change the chart type to *Clustered Column*.

🖝 Enlarge the chart by about 50% from the top right.

🖝 Place the chart next to the completed cells.

🖝 Change the color scheme of the chart to *Colorful Palette 3*.

🖝 Add axis titles to the chart.

🖝 Change the vertical axis title to Grades and the horizontal axis title to Students.

🖝 Change the vertical and horizontal axis titles to bold.

🖝 Undo the last two actions.

🖝 Filter the data in the chart so that only the grades from column *1st* are visible.

🖝 Add the data of class 1B to the chart by dragging the corner point of the selected cells to the desired location.

🖝 Change the chart title to 1A and 1B.

🖝 Below the chart, insert a text box of approximately 4 cells wide and 1.5 cells high with the following text: Test Pythagorean theorem.

🖝 Change the font size to 14 and center the text.

🖝 Place the text box in the middle below the chart.

🖝 Change the shape style of the text box to *Gradient Fill - Orange, Accent 2, no outline*. If you do not see this option, choose a different option. For example *Subtle Effect - Orange, Accent 2*.

☞ Go to the *Sheet2* worksheet and in cell H2, calculate the average grade of Luke Vargas.

☞ Copy the formula to the cells H3:H8.

☞ In cell I2, calculate the highest grade of Luke Vargas.

☞ Remove the decimal.

☞ Copy the formula to the cells I3:I8.

☞ In cell A9, calculate the number of students on the basis of the names of the students using the *COUNTA* function.

☞ In cell J2, calculate the average of the satisfactory grades (higher than 54) of Luke Vargas using the *AVERAGEIF* function.

☞ Copy the formula to the cells J3:J8.

☞ In cell K2, calculate the total of all satisfactory grades of Luke Vargas using the *SUMIF* function.

☞ Remove the decimal.

☞ Copy the formula to the cells K3:K8.

☞ Use the *TRIM* function to place the students name from cell A2 in cell M2 without the extra spaces.

☞ Copy the formula to the cells M3:M8.

☞ Use the *LEFT* function to place the first 3 digits of the phone number of Luke Vargas in cell N2.

☞ Align the numbers to the right and copy the formula to the cells N3:N8.

☞ Use the *Right* function to place the phone number without the first 3 digits in cell O2.

☞ Copy the formula to the cells O3:O8.

☞ Go to *Sheet1* worksheet and zoom out until see you all data.

☞ Zoom in to 100%.

☞ Freeze the titles in the first row.

☞ Hide the *Sheet1* worksheet.

☞ Unhide the *Sheet1* worksheet.

☞ Change the background color of cell A1 to *Yellow* and copy the formatting to the cells B1:H1.

☞ Make sure that the titles are printed on each page.

☞ View the print preview and reduce the chart, if necessary, to fit it on the page.

☞ Set the data from Class 1A and Class 1B and the chart as the print range.

☞ Open the print preview and print the print range.

☞ Select the cells A1:H104 and add subtotals of the number of students per class in the column *Student*.

☞ Widen column A until the text fits in the column and show only the numbers per class.

☞ Show only the grades of class 1B see and then show all data again.

☞ Name cell B22 to *Class1A* and name cell B47 to *Class1B*.

☞ Use the cell names to calculate the total number of students in class 1A and 1B in cell I47.

☞ Show the formulas instead of the result.

☞ Save the workbook in the *(My) Documents* folder with the name *Mathematics Grades 3*.

☞ Save the workbook in *Excel 97-2003* format, in the (My) documents folder with the name *Mathematics Grades Old Format*.

☞ Close the *Mathematics Grades Old Format* workbook and open the *Mathematics Grades 3* workbook.

☞ Open the *Result Do-It-Yourself Exercise 15* workbook and compare this to your own workbook.

☞ Close the *Result Do-It-Yourself Exercise 15* workbook and do not save any changes.

☞ Close *Excel*.

Do-It-Yourself Exercise 16: Household Costs

🕐 15 minutes

☞ Open *Excel* and open the *Household_costs_2.xlsx* workbook from the *Practice Files Workbook Excel* folder.

☞ Select the cells B3:B5 and add up the amounts with *Quick analysis*, thereby replacing the current data.

☞ Click in cell D2, insert the *Dollars.jpg* image and change the picture style to *Soft Edge Oval*.

☞ Change the color of the image to *Grayscale*.

☞ Insert the SmartArt illustration *Relationship - Equation* and in the three shapes, type successively: Fixed costs, Variable costs and Total costs.

☞ Change the color scheme of the SmartArt illustration to *Colored Fill - Accent 5*.

☞ Drag the SmartArt illustration downwards so you can click in the cells M16 and M17.

☞ Open the *SUM* function and calculate the total variable costs for 2011 in cell M16.

☞ Use the *MIN* function to place the lowest variable costs for 2011 in cell M17.

☞ Select the cells B14:BI14 and show the amounts that exceed $299.00 in red.

☞ Use the *IF* function to show "correct" in cell AX16 if the value in cell AX14 is less than $300.00 and have it show "too high" if that is not the case.

☞ Copy the formula to the cells AY16:BI16.

☞ Use the *UPPER* function to place the content of cell A11 in cell A16 in upper case.

☞ Copy the formula to the cells A17:A19.

☞ Click cell N1 and split the window.

☞ Undo the splitting.

☞ Change the cell style of column A to *40% - Accent3* and then change the cell style of row 1 to *Accent3*.

☞ Set the theme *Depth* and change the color scheme of the theme to *Violet*.

☞ In the lower right corner of the page, insert a footer with the page number and return to the normal view.

☞ Make sure that the titles in the first column are printed on each page.

☞ Change the print orientation to *Landscape* and change the left and right margin to 2.3 cm.

☞ View the print preview and move the SmartArt illustration, if necessary, so that it fits on the first page.

☞ Start recording a macro with the name *Hide* and add the shortcut key *H* for it.

☞ Hide the columns B to M, stop the macro and unhide the columns again.

☞ Save the workbook with the name *Household Costs 4* in the *(My) Documents* folder as an *Excel* workbook with macros.

☞ Close the workbook and then open the workbook thereby enabling the macro.

☞ Open the *Result Do-It-Yourself Exercise 16* workbook and compare this to your own workbook.

☞ Close the *Result Do-It-Yourself Exercise 16* workbook and do not save any changes.

☞ Save the worksheet as a PDF document in the *(My) Documents* folder with the name *Household Costs*.

☞ Close the PDF document.

☞ Close *Excel*.

MOS Exam Exercise 15: Labor Costs

🕐 10 minutes

☞ Open the web page **www.visualstepsmosbooks.com/excel2016-mos-examexercises.php** and enter the access code from the bottom of page 2 in order to access the web page.

☞ Open the source window by clicking
MOS exam exercise 15: Labor costs by **Chapter 4 to 6**.

Shift

☞ Press ▬▬▬▬ and hold it down, then click ⓘ Instructions.

Shift

☞ Press ▬▬▬▬ and hold it down, then click 🖼 Final result.

☞ Position the instruction window, end result window and source window next to each other in the bottom of the screen.

☞ Open the *Labor_costs_2.xlsx* practice file and position the *Excel* window in the top of the screen.

☞ Carry out the actions shown in the instruction window.

MOS Exam Exercise 16: Sandwiches Cafeteria

🕐 10 minutes

☞ Open the web page **www.visualstepsmosbooks.com/excel2016-mos-examexercises.php** and enter the access code from the bottom of page 2 in order to access the web page.

☞ Open the source window by clicking
MOS exam exercise 16: Sandwiches Cafeteria by **Chapter 4 to 6**.

Shift

☞ Press ▬▬▬▬ and hold it down, then click ⓘ Instructions.

Shift

☞ Press ▬▬▬▬ and hold it down, then click 🖼 Final result.

☞ Position the instruction window, end result window and source window next to each other in the bottom of the screen.

☞ Open the *Sandwiches_cafeteria_2.xlsx* practice file and position the *Excel* window at the top of the screen.

☞ Carry out the actions shown in the instruction window.

Notes

Write your notes down here.

9. Exercises Chapter 1 to 6

This chapter features additional exercises relating to Chapter 1 to 6 in the textbook.

↘ Please note:

The following exercises contain tasks to be printed. If necessary, consult your teacher whether printing is allowed.

Do-It-Yourself Exercise 17: Labor Costs

🕐 12 minutes

📖 Open *Excel* and open the *Labor_costs_2.xlsx* workbook from the *Practice Files Workbook Excel* folder.

📖 Collapse the ribbon and then show the ribbon again.

📖 Change the name of the worksheet to Labor Costs 2015 and change the color of the tab to *Blue*.

📖 Create a new worksheet and change the name of the new worksheet to Labor Costs 2016 and change the color of the tab to *Red*.

📖 Make sure the *Labor Costs 2015* worksheet is positioned before the *Labor Costs 2016* worksheet.

📖 Go to the *Labor Costs 2015* worksheet an in cell B14, add up all labor costs using the *SUM* function.

📖 In cell B15, calculate the average labor costs and use the *MAX* function to place the highest labor costs in cell B16.

📖 Go to the *Labor Costs 2016* worksheet and in cell A2 type: January and automatically fill the cells A3:A13 with the other months.

📖 Automatically adjust column A to the correct width.

📖 In cell B1, type: Labor costs, change the text to bold and centered.

📖 Adjust the column to the correct width.

	labor costs
January	30000
February	25000
March	18000
April	17000
May	21000
June	25000

📖 Enter the following data:

📖 In the cells B2:B7, place a $ sign before the amounts and ensure that all amounts get two decimals.

☞ Protect the *Labor costs 2015* worksheet.

☞ Cancel the protection of the *Labor Costs 2015* worksheet.

☞ Convert the cells A1:B16 to a table (on *Labor Costs 2015* worksheet) and set the table style to *Table style Medium 18*.

☞ Insert a new row between row 17 and 18 and then add a row to the table using the ⇆ **Tab** key.

☞ In cell A17, type: Minimum and, if necessary, change the text to bold.

☞ Use the *MIN* function to place the lowest labor costs in cell B17.

☞ Name the table LaborCosts2015.

☞ Click the tab of the Labor Costs 2016 worksheet and then use *Go To* to move to the table.

☞ Select the cells B2:B13 and use *Quick Analysis* to show a color scale on the amounts.

☞ Select the cells A1:B13 and create a chart of the *Clustered Column* type.

☞ Change the chart style to S*tyle 2* and change the color scheme of the chart to *Monochromatic Palette 7*.

☞ Change the chart type to *3-D Column*.

☞ Insert a SmartArt illustration of the *Basic Process* type.

☞ Place the SmartArt illustration below the data in column A to C and reduce it in size from the bottom right by about a third.

☞ In the three shapes, type successively: Plan, Action and Idea

☞ Change the color scheme of the SmartArt illustration to *Colored Fill - Accent 3*.

☞ Use the *CONCAT* function to place the initials from cell A20 and last name from cell B20 in cell D20 with a space in between.

☞ Copy the formula to the cells D21:D24.

☞ Hide the *Labor Costs 2016* worksheet.

☞ Unhide the worksheet again and return to the *Labor Costs 2015* worksheet.

☞ In the top center of the page, insert a header with the text Labor Costs 2015 and return to the normal view.

☞ Change the print orientation to *Landscape* and view the print preview.

☞ If necessary, place the chart next to the table so that it is printed on the first page.

☞ Save the workbook with the name *Labor Costs 4* in the *(My) Documents* folder.

🖙 Save the workbook in *Excel 97-2003* format, in the *(My) Documents* folder with the name *Labor Costs Old Format*.

🖙 Close the *Labor Costs Old Format* workbook and open the workbook *Labor Costs 4*.

🖙 Open the *Result Do-It-Yourself Exercise 17* workbook and compare this to your own workbook.

🖙 Close the *Result Do-It-Yourself Exercise 17* workbook and do not save any changes.

🖙 Close *Excel*.

Do-It-Yourself Exercise 18: Cell Phone Costs

🕐 15 minutes

🖙 Open *Excel* and open the *Costs_cell_phone.xlsx* workbook from the *Practice Files Workbook Excel* folder.

🖙 Add the *Sort descending* command to the *Quick Access* toolbar.

🖙 Automatically fill the cells A10:A20 with the other months.

🖙 Widen column A until the text fits exactly.

🖙 Change the cells A8:F20 into a table and indicate that the table contains headers.

🖙 Adjust the table style to *Table Style Medium 21*.

🖙 To the left of column 2 and to the left of column 3, insert a new table column.

🖙 Change *Column1* to `Month`, *Column4* to `min-abo`, *Column2* to `call costs`, *Column5* to `MB-abo`, *Column3* to `internet costs`.

🖙 Widen the columns C, D, G and H until the text fits exactly.

🖙 Enter a formula in cell C9, in which you subtract the value in cell C4 from the value in cell B9 and then change the reference to cell C4 to an absolute one.

🖙 Enter a formula in cell D9, in which you multiply the value in cell C9 with the value in cell D4 and then change the reference to cell D4 to an absolute one.

🖙 Enter a formula in cell F9, in which you subtract the value in cell C5 from the value in cell E9 and then change the reference to cell C5 to an absolute one.

🖙 Enter a formula in cell G9, in which you multiply the value in cell F9 with the value in cell D5 and then change the reference to cell D5 to an absolute one.

🖙 Enter a formula in cell H9, in which you add up the values from the cells B4, B5, D9 and G9 and change the references to the cells B4 and B5 into absolute ones.

🖙 Enable a row with totals to calculate the total costs.

☞ Change the value in cell D4 to 0.02 and the value in cell D5 to 0.01 and recalculate the formulas.

☞ From cell G3, insert a text box of approximately 2 cells wide and 3 cells high with the following text: We are proud to be fast and reliable!

☞ Change the font size to 14 and center the text.

☞ Change the shape style of the text box to *Intense effect - Green, Accent 6* and turn the text box slightly clockwise.

☞ Select the cells H9:H20 and let all cells with more than $16.00 show in red.

☞ In cell A23, type: Number of months with more than 700 MB and adjust text wrapping for this cell.

☞ In cell B23, use the function *COUNTIF* to place the number of months in which more than 700 MB is used.

☞ Apply the background color *Green, Accent 6, Lighter 80%* to the cells A3:F5 and set the theme to *Circuit*.

☞ Change the color scheme of the theme to *Slipstream*.

☞ Change the print orientation to *Landscape*.

☞ Change the left margin to 2.3 cm and the top margin to 3.4 cm and print the worksheet.

☞ Start recording a macro with the name *Formulas* and a shortcut key with the letter *F*.

☞ Allow the formulas to show instead of the result and stop recording.

☞ Start recording a macro with the name *Hide* and a shortcut key with the letter *H*.

☞ Hide the formulas and stop recording.

☞ Allow the *Formulas* and *Hide* macros to run successively.

☞ Save the workbook with the name *Costs Cell Phone 4* in the *(My) Documents* folder as an *Excel* workbook with macros.

☞ Close the *Costs Cell Phone 4* workbook.

☞ Open the *Costs Cell Phone 4* workbook whereby the macros are enabled.

☞ Open the *Result Do-It-Yourself Exercise 18* workbook and compare this to your own workbook.

☞ Close the *Result Do-It-Yourself Exercise 18* workbook and do not save any changes.

☞ Remove the *Sort ascending* command from the *Quick Access* toolbar.

☞ Close *Excel*.

Do-It-Yourself Exercise 19: Sandwiches Cafeteria

⏱ 12 minutes

☞ Open *Excel* and download the *Monthly sales report* template. It can be found under the *Small Business* category in *Suggested searches* at the top of the *Start Screen*.

☞ Close the template without saving it and open the *Sandwiches_cafeteria_2.xlsx* workbook from the *Practice Files Textbook Excel* folder.

☞ Create a new worksheet and change the name of the new worksheet to 2016

☞ Change the name of worksheet *Sheet1* to 2015 and remove worksheet *2016*.

☞ Freeze the titles in the first two rows.

☞ Enter a formula in cell B95, in which you count the sandwiches and copy the formula to the cells C95 and D95.

☞ In cell B96, calculate the average number of sandwiches and remove the decimals.

☞ Copy the formula to the cells C96 and D96.

☞ Convert the cells A2:D96 into a table.

☞ Filter the data so that only the month of December is visible.

☞ Clear the filter and convert the table to a range.

☞ Select cells A2:D94.

☞ Use custom sorting to sort the selected data ascending by BLT sandwich, then ascending by Cheese sandwich and finally ascending by Club sandwich.

☞ Select the cells A2:D94 and sort the data by the date again.

☞ Select the cells B3:D94 and use *Quick Analysis* to show spark lines of the *Line* type.

☞ Click cell G5 and insert the *Sandwich.png* image.

☞ Reduce the image until it is about 4 cells wide.

☞ Change the image style to *Reflected Perspective Right* and apply the artistic effect *Pastels Smooth* to the picture.

☞ In cell A97, type Number of Days and widen the column until the text fits exactly.

☞ Open the COUNTA function and in cell B97, calculate the number of days on the basis of the data in column A.

☞ Use the *UPPER* function to place the content of cell B2 in cell H21 in upper case.

☞ Zoom out until you see all the data and then zoom in to 100%.

☞ Unfreeze the titles, click in cell A21 and split the window.

☞ Undo the splitting and hide rows 3 to 63.

☞ Unhide the rows again and group rows 3 to 33.

☞ Hide the group and then unhide it again.

☞ In the lower right corner of the page, insert a footer with the page number and return to the normal view.

☞ Make sure that the titles in the first two rows are printed on each page and view the print preview.

☞ Open the *Result Do-It-Yourself Exercise 19* workbook and compare this to your own workbook.

☞ Close the *Result Do-It-Yourself Exercise 19* workbook and do not save any changes.

☞ Save the workbook with the name *Bread Rolls Cantine 4* workbook in the *(My) Documents* folder.

☞ Save the worksheet as a PDF document with the name *Sandwich cafeteria*.

☞ Close the PDF document.

☞ Close *Excel*.

Do-It-Yourself Exercise 20: Household Costs

🕐 15 minutes

☞ Start *Excel* and open the *Household_costs_2.xlsx* workbook from the *Practice Files Workbook Excel* folder.

☞ Add a new group to the ⎾ Home ⏌ tab and name it *Functions*.

☞ Add the *Insert function* command to the new group.

☞ Insert a new column between column M and N and enter in cell N9: *Average*.

☞ In cell N11, calculate the average shopping of 2011 by first adding up the amounts and then dividing them by 12.

☞ Copy the formula to the cells N12:N14 and change the data in column N to bold.

☞ Insert two new rows above the upper row and type in cell A1: Household expenses Fam. Anderson.

☞ Change the font size of cell A1 to 16 and merge the cells A1:D1.

☞ Undo the merging of the cells and set text wrapping for cell A1.

☞ Widen Column A until the word *Household expenses* fits exactly.

☞ Copy worksheet *2015* and change the name of the new worksheet to *2016*.

☞ Change the name of the *2015* worksheet to `2011-2015` and place the *2011-2015* worksheet before the *2016* worksheet.

☞ Go to the *2016* worksheet and remove the data in the cells B3:BJ16 by selecting them and pressing [Delete].

☞ In cell B3, type `2016`, in cell B11, type `January` and fill the cells C11:M11 automatically with the other months.

☞ Go to the *2011-2015* worksheet and type in cell A19 `Fixed and Variable:`

☞ Change the font size of cell A19 to 14.

☞ In cell B19, add up the value of cell B8 to the value of cell B16 and change the reference to cell B8 to an absolute one.

☞ Copy the formula to the cells C19:M19.

☞ In cell C8, divide the value of cell B8 by the value of cell B19 and change the result into a percentage.

☞ Go to the *2016* worksheet and replace the text in cell A1 by a reference to cell A1 on the *2011-2015* worksheet.

☞ Go to the *2011-2015* worksheet and change *Fam. Anderson* to `Fam. Perry`.

☞ Go to the *2016* worksheet, type in cell A19 `Previous years` and create a hyperlink to the *2011-2015* worksheet.

☞ Click the hyperlink to test whether it works and then remove the hyperlink.

☞ Undo the last action.

☞ On the *2011-2015* worksheet, change the cells AY11:BJ16 into a table and indicate that the table contains headers.

☞ Add a column on the right side of the table by increasing the table manually.

☞ Change the text in cell BK11 to `Max`.

☞ Use the *MAX* function to place the highest value of the cells AY13:BJ13 in cell BK13.

☞ Remove the data in cell BK12 by selecting the cell and then pressing [Delete].

☞ Select the cells O3:Z16 and name this group of cells `Year2012`.

☞ Click cell A1 and then use *Go To* to move to the group of cells with the name *Year2012*.

☞ Select the cells AY13:BK16 and add up the data using *Quick analysis*, whereby you calculate the totals per row and place the results in a new column.

☞ Change the text *Column1* to `Total`

☞ Select the cells AY11:BJ15, create a chart of the *Line* type and place the chart below the table.

☞ Invert the rows and columns of the chart.

☞ Undo the last action.

☞ Change the chart title to `2015` and add axis titles.

☞ Change the vertical axis title to `Variable costs` and remove the horizontal axis title.

☞ Change the value of the vertical axis to 25.

☞ Undo the last action.

☞ Change the color scheme of the chart to *Colorful Palette 2*.

☞ Filter the data in the chart, so that only the data from July to December is visible.

☞ Open the *IF* function to show "good" in cell AY17 if the value in cell AY16 is less than $350.00 and have it show "not good" if that is not the case.

☞ Copy the formula to the cells AZ17:BK17.

☞ Use the *RIGHT* function to place the name from cell A1 in cell A22 (that is without the word *Household expenses* and the space).

☞ In cell N19, calculate the sum of the cells B19:M19, widen the column and name the cell `variable2011`

☞ Enter a formula in cell B9 in which you multiply the value of cell B8 by 12 and name the cell `fixed2011`

☞ Use the cell names to add up the values of the cells B9 and N19 in cell B22.

☞ In cell B22, place a $ sign before the amount and ensure that the amount gets two decimals.

☞ Set only the data of 2015 as the print area and make sure that the titles in the first column are printed on each page.

☞ Change the print orientation to *Landscape* and print the print area on a single page.

☞ Clear the print range.

☞ Open the *Result Do-It-Yourself Exercise 20* workbook and compare this to your own workbook.

☞ Close the *Result Do-It-Yourself Exercise 20* workbook and do not save any changes.

☞ Revert to the default settings for the | Home | tab.

☞ Save the workbook with the name *Household Costs 5* in the *(My) Documents* folder.

☞ Close *Excel*.

Do-It-Yourself Exercise 21: Mathematics Grades

🕐 12 minutes

☞ Open *Excel* and open the *Grades_Math_3.xlsx* workbook from the *Practice Files Workbook Excel* folder.

☞ Go to the *2014-2015* worksheet, click cell A1 and import the *Grades_Math.csv* file (with headers, data separated by semicolons).

☞ Place the *2014-2015* worksheet before the *2015-2016* worksheet.

☞ Remove the duplicates and change the data in the first row to bold.

☞ In cell H2, calculate the average of the grades of Luke Vargas and have the grade rounded to one decimal.

☞ Copy the formula to the cells H3:H8.

☞ Change the names in column A to a series which continues to cell A15.

☞ Use the *Replace* function to replace *Luke* by *Lucas*.

☞ In cell A19, type: *2/11/2015*

☞ Select the cells A19:A39 and use the ribbon to automatically fill the series with only the weekdays.

☞ Go to the *2015-2016* worksheet and select cells B1:H21.

☞ Create a *Clustered Column* type chart.

☞ Insert a row in between rows 21 and 22 and fill in the following data:

1A	1100	42	57	62	71	55	69

☞ Add row 22 to the chart and move the chart to a new worksheet with the name Class 1A.

☞ Place the new worksheet after the *2015-2016* worksheet.

☞ Open worksheet *2015-2016*.

☞ In cell A107, type: Number and in cell B107, calculate the number of students on the basis of the student numbers.

☞ Go to the *2014-2015* tab and use the *MIN* function to place the lowest grade of Lucas Vargas in cell I2.

☞ Copy the formula to the cells I3:I8.

☞ Use the *AVERAGEIF* function to calculate in cell J2 the average of the sufficient grades (higher than 54) of Lucas Vargas.

☞ Reduce the number of decimals to one decimal and copy the formula to the cells J3:J8.

☞ Use the *SUMIF* function to add up the total of all sufficient grades of Lucas Vargas in cell K2.

☞ Copy the formula to the cells K3:K8.

☞ Insert two blank rows between rows 8 and 9 and type in cell B10: Age and change the text to bold.

☞ Use *DATA VALIDATION* to allow a minimum age of 10 years in the cells B11:B17 and a maximum age of 20 years and have the following error message appear if that is invalid: Between 10 and 20 years!

☞ In cell B11, try to type the following: 21 and then click *Cancel*.

☞ In the cells B11:B13, B15 and B16, type: 12.

☞ In cell B14, type 11 and in cell B17, type 13.

☞ Use the *TRIM* function to place the name from cell A2 in cell A11 without spaces.

☞ Copy the formula to the cells A12:A17.

☞ Go to the *2015-2016* worksheet and apply the cell style *20% - Accent6* to column A.

☞ Copy the formatting from column A to row 1.

☞ Select the cells A1:H105 and in column B (*Student*) add the subtotals of the number of students per class (function: *COUNT*).

☞ Widen column A until the text fits in the column and remove the data in the cells A113 and B113.

☞ Show only the numbers per class, then only the grades of class B and finally, show all data.

☞ Start recording a macro with the name *Hide* and a shortcut key with the letter *H*.

☞ Hide the columns C to F and stop recording.

☞ Start recording a macro with the name *Unhide* and a shortcut key with the letter U.

☞ Unhide the columns C to F and stop recording.

☞ Allow the *Hide* and *Unhide* macros to run successively.

☞ Save the workbook with the name *Mathematics Grades 4* in the *(My) Documents* folder as an *Excel* workbook with macros.

☞ Close the workbook.

☞ Open the *Mathematics Grades 4* workbook whereby the macros are not enabled.

☞ Enable the macros.

☞ Open the *Result Do-It-Yourself Exercise 21* workbook and compare this to your own workbook.

☞ Close the *Result Do-It-Yourself Exercise 21* workbook and do not save any changes.

☞ Close *Excel*.

MOS Exam Exercise 17: Labor Costs

🕐 12 minutes

☞ Open the web page **www.visualstepsmosbooks.coml/excel2016-mos-examexercises.php** and enter the access code from the bottom of page 2 in order to access the web page.

☞ Open the source window by clicking
MOS exam exercise 17: Labor costs by **Chapter 1 to 6**.

☞ Press **Shift** and hold it down, then click ⓘ Instructions.

☞ Press **Shift** and hold it down, then click ▣ Final result.

☞ Position the instruction window, end result window and source window next to each other in the bottom of the screen.

☞ Open the *Labor_costs_2.xlsx* practice file and position the *Excel* window at the top of the screen.

☞ Carry out the actions shown in the instruction window.

MOS Exam Exercise 18: Cell Phone Costs

🕐 12 minutes

☞ Open the web page **www.visualstepsmosbooks.coml/excel2016-mos-examexercises.php** and enter the access code from the bottom of page 2 in order to access the web page.

☞ Open the source window by clicking
MOS exam exercise 18: Costs cell phone _{by} **Chapter 1 to 6**.

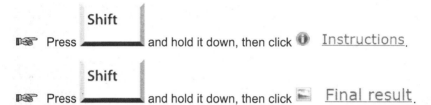

☞ Press **Shift** and hold it down, then click ⓘ Instructions.

☞ Press **Shift** and hold it down, then click 🖼 Final result.

☞ Position the instruction window, end result window and source window next to each other in the bottom of the screen.

☞ Open the *Costs_cell_phone.xlsx* practice file and position the *Excel* window at the top of the screen.

☞ Carry out the actions shown in the instruction window.

MOS Exam Exercise 19: Sandwiches Cafeteria

🕐 12 minutes

☞ Open the web page **www.visualstepsmosbooks.coml/excel2016-mos-examexercises.php** and enter the access code from the bottom of page 2 in order to access the web page.

☞ Open the source window by clicking
MOS exam exercise 19: Sandwiches Cafeteria _{by} **Chapter 1 to 6**.

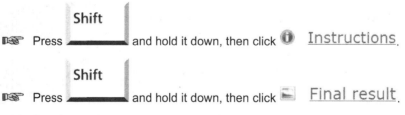

☞ Press **Shift** and hold it down, then click ⓘ Instructions.

☞ Press **Shift** and hold it down, then click 🖼 Final result.

☞ Position the instruction window, end result window and source window next to each other in the bottom of the screen.

☞ Open the *Sandwiches_cafeteria_2.xlsx* practice file and position the *Excel* window at the top of the screen.

☞ Carry out the actions shown in the instruction window.

MOS Exam Exercise 20: Household Costs

🕐 15 minutes

☞ Open the web page **www.visualstepsmosbooks.coml/excel2016-mos-examexercises.php** and enter the access code from the bottom of page 2 in order to access the web page.

☞ Open the source window by clicking

MOS exam exercise 20: Household costs by **Chapter 1 to 6**.

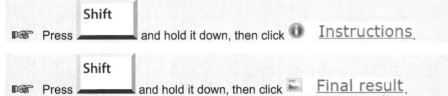

☞ Press **Shift** and hold it down, then click 🛈 Instructions.

☞ Press **Shift** and hold it down, then click 📧 Final result.

☞ Position the instruction window, end result window and source window next to each other in the bottom of the screen.

☞ Open the *Household_costs_2.xlsx* practice file and position the *Excel* window at the top of the screen.

☞ Carry out the actions shown in the instruction window.

MOS Exam Exercise 21: Mathematics Grades

🕐 15 minutes

☞ Open the web page **www.visualstepsmosbooks.coml/excel2016-mos-examexercises.php** and enter the access code from the bottom of page 2 in order to access the web page.

☞ Open the source window by clicking

MOS exam exercise 21: Grades Math by **Chapter 1 to 6**.

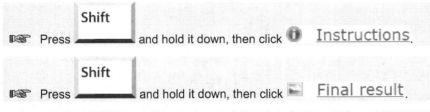

☞ Press **Shift** and hold it down, then click 🛈 Instructions.

☞ Press **Shift** and hold it down, then click 📧 Final result.

☞ Position the instruction window, end result window and source window next to each other in the bottom of the screen.

☞ Open the *Grades_Math_3.xlsx* practice file and position the *Excel* window at the top of the screen.

☞ Carry out the actions shown in the instruction window.

Notes

Write your notes down here.

Appendix

Appendix A. How Do I Do That Again?

The actions and exercises in this book are marked with footsteps: 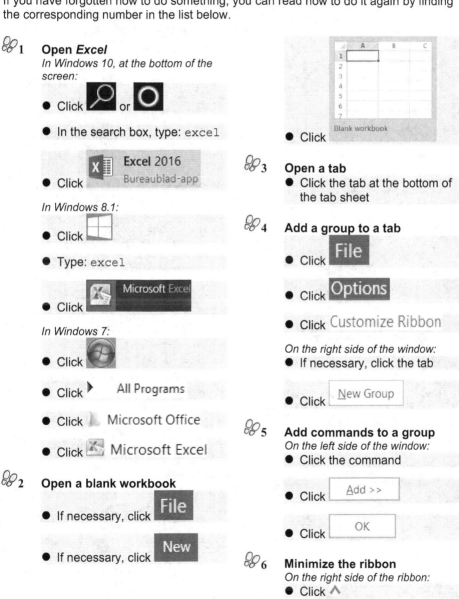1
If you have forgotten how to do something, you can read how to do it again by finding
the corresponding number in the list below.

1   **Open** *Excel*
    In Windows 10, at the bottom of the screen:
    - Click 🔍 or ⭕

    - In the search box, type: `excel`

    - Click **Excel 2016** Bureaublad-app

    In Windows 8.1:
    - Click ⊞

    - Type: `excel`

    - Click **Microsoft Excel**

    In Windows 7:
    - Click ⊛

    - Click ▶ All Programs

    - Click ▮ Microsoft Office

    - Click ✖ Microsoft Excel

2   **Open a blank workbook**
    - If necessary, click **File**

    - If necessary, click **New**

- Click **Blank workbook**

3   **Open a tab**
    - Click the tab at the bottom of the tab sheet

4   **Add a group to a tab**
    - Click **File**

    - Click **Options**

    - Click Customize Ribbon

    On the right side of the window:
    - If necessary, click the tab

    - Click **New Group**

5   **Add commands to a group**
    On the left side of the window:
    - Click the command

    - Click **Add >>**

    - Click **OK**

6   **Minimize the ribbon**
    On the right side of the ribbon:
    - Click ∧

7   **Show the ribbon**
    - Click a tab

On the right side of the ribbon:
- Click ⊞

⚜ 8   Default layout of tabs
- Click File
- Click Options
- Click Customize Ribbon
- Click Reset ▾
- Click Reset only selected Ribbon tab
- Click OK

⚜ 9   Add commands to the Quick Access toolbar
- Click ▾
- Click the command or More Commands...
- Click the command
- Click Add >>
- Click OK

⚜ 10   Remove commands from the Quick Access toolbar
- Click ▾
- Click More Commands...

On the right side of the window:
- Click the command
- Click << Remove
- Click OK

⚜ 11   Add a worksheet
- Click the Home tab

- By ⊞ Insert , click ▾
- Click Insert Sheet

Or:
- Next to the existing tab, click ⊕

⚜ 12   Name a worksheet
On the worksheet:
- Click Format ▾
- Click Rename Sheet
- Type the desired name
- Press  Enter

⚜ 13   Other tab color of worksheet
On the worksheet:
- Click Format ▾
- Click Tab Color
- Click the color

⚜ 14   Remove a worksheet
- If necessary, click the tab of the desired worksheet

On the worksheet:
- By ⊞ Delete , click ▾
- Click Delete Sheet

If another window appears:
- Click Delete

⚜ 15   Move worksheets
At the bottom of the worksheet:
- Drag the tab of the worksheet to the desired place

⚜ 16   Close *Excel*
- Click ✕

If there is data on a worksheet that you do not want to save:
- Click Delete

To save the workbook:
- Click

Don't save the workbook:
- Click [Don't Save]

17 Enter data into cells
- Click the cell

- Type the data

- Press an arrow key,

  [Enter] or [Tab]

18 Change column width or row height
Column width:
- Place the pointer in the column headers on the border between the columns

- Drag the pointer

Row height:
- Place the pointer in the row numbers on the border

  between the rows [3 / 4]

- Drag the pointer

Automatically adjust the correct column width:
- Double-click the column border. This automatically sizes the column to fit the widest data it contains.

  [B + C]

Automatically adjust the correct row height:
- Double-click the row border. This automatically sizes the row to fit the widest data it contains.

  [3 / 4]

19 Select multiple cells
- Drag the pointer across the cells

20 Add a comma between thousands
- If necessary, select the cell(s)

- If necessary, click the

  [Home] tab

- Click 000

21 Change the number of decimals
- If necessary, click the

  [Home] tab

More decimals:
- Click .00

Fewer decimals:
- Click .00

22 Enter a formula
- Click the cell where the result should be

- Type =

Use the mouse:
- Click in the first cell of the formula

- Click +, -, * or /

- Click in the second cell of the formula

- Repeat the last two steps until the formula is complete

- Press

Use the keyboard:
- Type the formula

- Press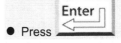

23 Add up with *SUM* function
- Click the cell where the result should be

- Click Σ

- Click

Or:
- Select the cells

- Click Σ

24 Copy a formula
- Click the cell containing the formula

- Click ⧉

- Click the cell where the formula should be copied

- Click 📋

25 Copy with the fill handle
- Point to the fill handle of the cell

  | 825.000 |

  with the formula   ╋

- Drag the fill handle across the cells where the formula should be copied

26 Save new workbook
- Click 💾

- Click 📁 Browse

- Click the desired location

- Type the name of the file by

  File name:

- Click [Save]

27 Select row or column
Select a row:
- Click the row number

Select a column:
- Click the column header

28 Change the cell formatting
- Select the cell(s)

- Adjust the formatting, for example **B**, *I*, U̲ or for centering: ≣.

29 Set text wrapping
- Select the cell(s)

- Click ⊞

On the right side of the ribbon:
- Click ⇥

30 Insert a row or column
- Click to select a row or column. *Excel* inserts a new row *above* the selected row and a new column to the *left* of the selected column.

- By ⊞ Insert, click ▾

Insert a column:
- Click ⇧ Insert Sheet Columns

Insert a row:
- Click ⇥ Insert Sheet Rows

31 Merge cells
- Select the cells

- Click ⬌

32 Change the font size
- Select the cell(s)

- By 11, click ▾

- Click the size

Or:
- Click A˄ to enlarge or A˅ to reduce

33 Save a workbook with a different name
- Click File

- Click Save As

- Click 📁 Browse

- Click the desired location

- By **File name:** , type the new name

- Click [Save]

34 Change the name of a group tab

- Click [Rena**m**e...]

- Type the desired name

- Click [OK]

35 Calculate an average

- By Σ, click ˅

- Click **A**verage

- If necessary, select the desired cell(s)

- Press [Enter]

36 Open a workbook from practice files
If Excel has just been opened:
- Click
  📂 Open Other Workbooks

If a workbook has been previously opened in Excel:
- Click **File**

- Click **Open**

In both situations:
- Click **Browse**

- If necessary, click
  📄 Documents

- Double-click the required folder

- Click the desired file

- Click [OK]

37 Copy a worksheet
- Click 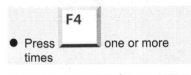 **Format ˅**

- Click **M**ove or Copy Sheet...

- Click to check ☑ by
  Create a copy

If necessary:
- Click **(move to end)**

- Click [OK]

38 Create absolute reference
In the formula bar:
- Click the cell indication

- Press **F4** one or more times

- Press **Enter**

39 Change a formula
- Click the cell containing the formula

- Click the cell formula bar

- Change the formula

- Press **Enter**

40 Temporary saving
In the Quick Access toolbar:
- Click 💾

41 Move to another worksheet
At the bottom of the worksheet:
- Click the tab of the worksheet

42 Supplement a series
- Point to the fill handle

- Drag the fill handle in the desired direction

43 Convert result to percentage
- Click the cell

- Click %

44 Create a reference to another worksheet
- Click the cell

- Type: =

- Click the tab of the other worksheet

- Click the desired cell

- Press **Enter**

45 Create a hyperlink to worksheet
- Click the cell

- Click the | Insert | tab

- Click Hyperlink

- Click Place in This Document

- Click the desired worksheet

- Click | OK |

46 Protect a worksheet
- Click the | Review | tab

- Click Protect Sheet

- Click | OK |

47 Remove a hyperlink to worksheet
- Click the cell

- Click the | Insert | tab

- Click Hyperlink

- Click | Remove Link |

48 Cancel protection of worksheet
- Click the worksheet

- Click the | Review | tab

- Click Unprotect Sheet

49 Supplement series automatically using the ribbon
- Select the cells

- Click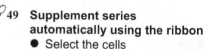

- Click Series...

- Choose the desired option

- Click | OK |

50 Open practice file
- Click File

- Click Open

- Click Browse

- Click the desired folder

- Click the file

- Click | Open |

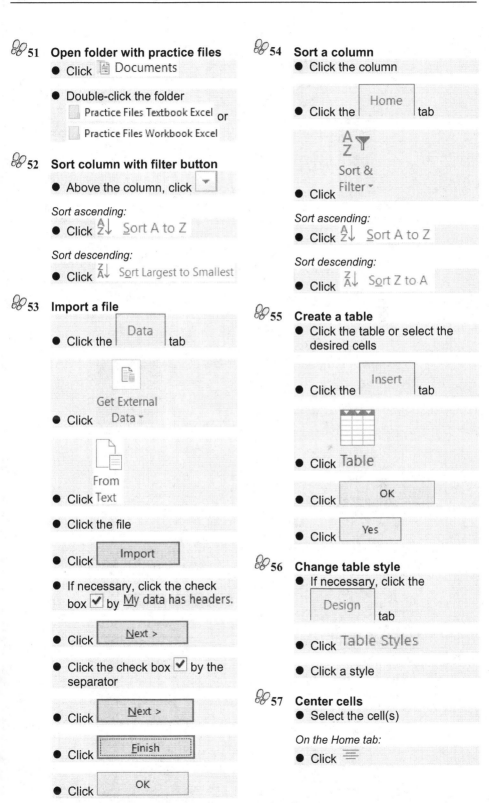

51 Open folder with practice files
- Click 📄 Documents

- Double-click the folder
  🗔 Practice Files Textbook Excel or
  🗔 Practice Files Workbook Excel

52 Sort column with filter button
- Above the column, click ▾

Sort ascending:
- Click ↕ Sort A to Z

Sort descending:
- Click ↕ Sort Largest to Smallest

53 Import a file
- Click the | Data | tab

- Click Get External Data ▾

- Click From Text

- Click the file

- Click | Import |

- If necessary, click the check box ☑ by My data has headers.

- Click | Next > |

- Click the check box ☑ by the separator

- Click | Next > |

- Click | Finish |

- Click | OK |

54 Sort a column
- Click the column

- Click the | Home | tab

- Click Sort & Filter ▾

Sort ascending:
- Click ↕ Sort A to Z

Sort descending:
- Click ↕ Sort Z to A

55 Create a table
- Click the table or select the desired cells

- Click the | Insert | tab

- Click Table

- Click | OK |

- Click | Yes |

56 Change table style
- If necessary, click the | Design | tab

- Click Table Styles

- Click a style

57 Center cells
- Select the cell(s)

On the Home tab:
- Click ≡

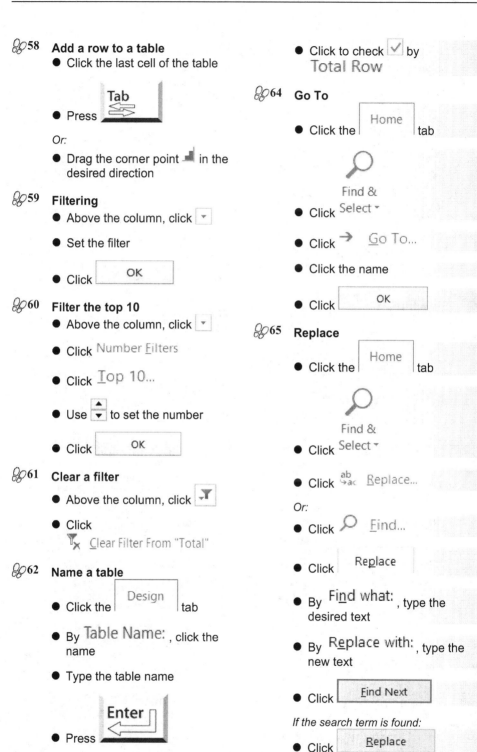

58 Add a row to a table
- Click the last cell of the table
- Press **Tab**

Or:
- Drag the corner point ◢ in the desired direction

59 Filtering
- Above the column, click ▾
- Set the filter
- Click OK

60 Filter the top 10
- Above the column, click ▾
- Click Number Filters
- Click Top 10...
- Use ▲▼ to set the number
- Click OK

61 Clear a filter
- Above the column, click ▾▼
- Click ▼✗ Clear Filter From "Total"

62 Name a table
- Click the **Design** tab
- By Table Name:, click the name
- Type the table name
- Press **Enter**

63 Totals row below table
- Click the **Design** tab

- Click to check ✓ by **Total Row**

64 Go To
- Click the **Home** tab
- Click 🔍 Find & Select ▾
- Click → Go To...
- Click the name
- Click OK

65 Replace
- Click the **Home** tab
- Click 🔍 Find & Select ▾
- Click ᵃᵇ⁄ₐc Replace...

Or:
- Click 🔍 Find...
- Click Replace
- By Find what:, type the desired text
- By Replace with:, type the new text
- Click Find Next

If the search term is found:
- Click Replace

Repeat this until the search term is no longer found. Then:

- Click OK

- Click Close

66 Convert a table into a range
- Click the table

- Click the Design tab

- Click 🔄 Convert to Range

- Click Yes

67 Insert a table row
- Click the row where the new row will be inserted above

- By 📑 Insert , click ▼

- Click 📑 Insert Cells...

68 Download a template
To search a template:
- Click on a proposed search

Or:
- Type a query in
  Search for online templates 🔍

- Click 🔍

To open a template:
- Click a template

- Click Create

69 Undo an action
- Click ↩

70 Manually enlarge a table
- Drag the corner point ◢ to the right or downwards to the desired number of columns or rows

71 Insert a column in a table
- In the table, click the desired column

- By 📑 Insert , click ▼

- Click 📑 Insert Table Columns to the Left

72 Multiple sorting in a table
- If necessary, click the table

- Click the Home tab

- Click $\begin{smallmatrix}A\\Z\end{smallmatrix}$▽ Sort & Filter ▼

- Click 🔢 Custom Sort...

- By Sort by , click ▼

- Click the desired column

- If desired, choose other sorting settings

- Click ⁺🔢 Add Level

- By Then by , click ▼

- Click the desired column

- If desired, choose other sorting options

- If desired, insert multiple levels in the same way

- Click OK

73 Disable filter buttons
- Click the Data tab

- Click **Filter**

74   Name a cell
- If necessary, click the cell

- Click in the name box to select the current name

- Type the new name

- Press

75   Move an object
- Click the object

- Make sure the pointer is inside the surrounding border of the object

- Drag the object to the desired place

76   Resize an object
- Click the object

- Place the pointer on the sizing handle

- Drag the sizing handle in the desired direction

77   Calculate averages
With Quick Analysis:
- Select the cells

- Click

- Click T**o**tals

- Click Average

78   Show icons
With Quick Analysis:
- Select the cells

- Click

- Click Icon Set

79   Create a chart
With Quick Analysis:
- Select the cells

- Click

- Click **C**harts

- Click the chart

80   Adjust the chart area
- Click the chart

- Click

- Click Select Data...

- Click **Add**

- By Series **n**ame: , click

- Click the title that needs to be added

- Click

- By Series **v**alues: , click

- Select the cells that need to be added

- Click

- Click OK

- Click OK

81   Adjust the chart title
- Click the chart three times

- Type the new title

82   Change chart type
- Click the chart

- If necessary, click the

  Design tab

  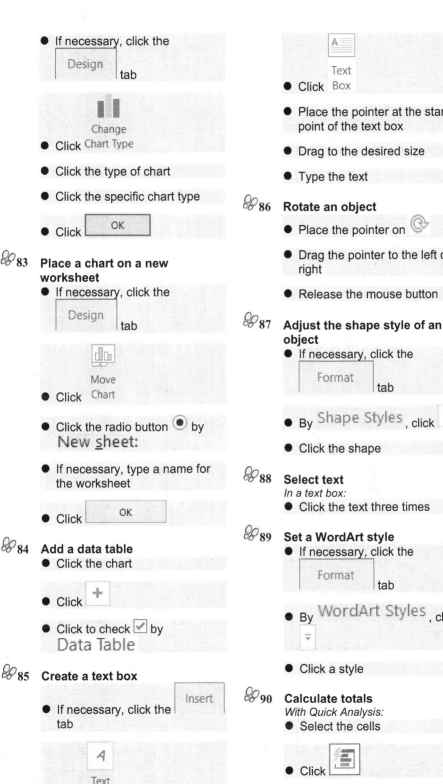

- Click Change Chart Type

- Click the type of chart

- Click the specific chart type

- Click [OK]

83 Place a chart on a new worksheet
- If necessary, click the

  Design tab

- Click Move Chart

- Click the radio button ● by

  New sheet:

- If necessary, type a name for the worksheet

- Click [OK]

84 Add a data table
- Click the chart

- Click [+]

- Click to check ☑ by

  Data Table

85 Create a text box
- If necessary, click the Insert tab

- Click A Text ▾

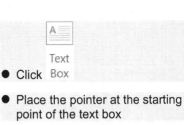
- Click Text Box

- Place the pointer at the starting point of the text box

- Drag to the desired size

- Type the text

86 Rotate an object
- Place the pointer on ↻

- Drag the pointer to the left or right

- Release the mouse button

87 Adjust the shape style of an object
- If necessary, click the

  Format tab

- By Shape Styles , click [▼]

- Click the shape

88 Select text
In a text box:
- Click the text three times

89 Set a WordArt style
- If necessary, click the

  Format tab

- By WordArt Styles , click [▼]

- Click a style

90 Calculate totals
With Quick Analysis:
- Select the cells

- Click [▦]

- Click **T**o**tals**

- Click Sum

To replace the data:

- Click OK

91   Insert a SmartArt shape

- If necessary, click the Insert tab

- Click Illustrations

- Click SmartArt

- Click the shape

- Click OK

92   Add a SmartArt shape
- Click the SmartArt object

- If necessary, click the Design tab

- By ⁺☐ Add Shape, click ˅

- Click where the shape should be placed

93   Calculate sum
With Quick Analysis:
- Select the cells

- Click

- Click the T**o**tals tab

- Click Sum

94   Place data bars
With Quick Analysis:
- Select the cells

- Click

- Click Data Bars

95   Adjust the chart style
- If necessary, click the chart

- Click

- Click a style

Or:

- Click the Design tab

- By Chart Styles, click ˅

- Click the desired style

96   Switch rows and columns
On the Design tab:

- Click Switch Row/ Column

- If necessary, click the chart

97   Set chart filters
- If necessary, click the chart

- Click ▼

- Choose the desired settings

- Click Apply

98   Apply shape effect to object
On the Format tab:
- Click 🔵 Shape Effects ▾

- Choose the desired effect

99   Insert a picture
On the Insert tab:

- Click Illustrations

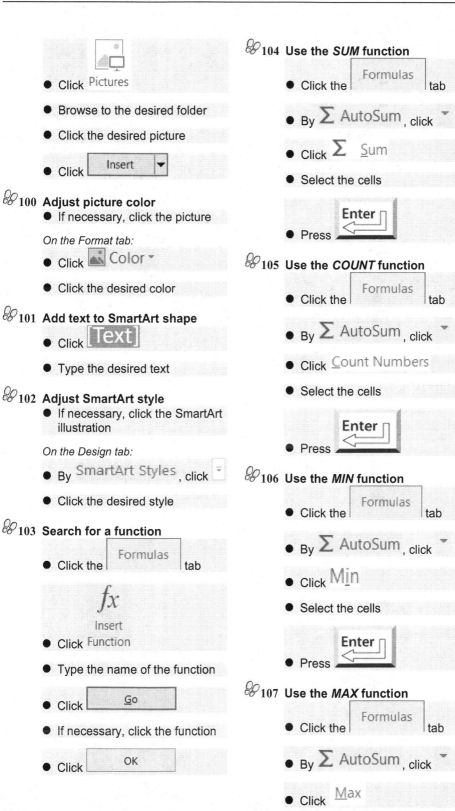

- Click Pictures

- Browse to the desired folder

- Click the desired picture

- Click | Insert | ▼

100 Adjust picture color
- If necessary, click the picture

On the Format tab:

- Click Color ▾

- Click the desired color

101 Add text to SmartArt shape
- Click Text

- Type the desired text

102 Adjust SmartArt style
- If necessary, click the SmartArt illustration

On the Design tab:

- By SmartArt Styles , click ▼

- Click the desired style

103 Search for a function
- Click the | Formulas | tab

- Click *fx* Insert Function

- Type the name of the function

- Click | Go |

- If necessary, click the function

- Click | OK |

104 Use the *SUM* function
- Click the | Formulas | tab

- By Σ AutoSum , click ▼

- Click Σ Sum

- Select the cells

- Press Enter

105 Use the *COUNT* function
- Click the | Formulas | tab

- By Σ AutoSum , click ▼

- Click Count Numbers

- Select the cells

- Press Enter

106 Use the *MIN* function
- Click the | Formulas | tab

- By Σ AutoSum , click ▼

- Click Min

- Select the cells

- Press Enter

107 Use the *MAX* function
- Click the | Formulas | tab

- By Σ AutoSum , click ▼

- Click Max

- Select the cells

- Press

108 Use the *AVERAGE* function

- Click the | Formulas | tab

- By Σ AutoSum ▾, click ▾

- Click Average

- Select the cells

- Press

109 Use the *SUMIF* function

- By **Range**, click

- Select the cells

- Click

- Type the condition by **Criteria**

- Click | OK |

110 Use the *COUNTIF* function

- By **Range**, click

- Select the cells

- Click

- Type the condition by **Criteria**

- Click | OK |

111 Conditional formatting

- Click Conditional Formatting ▾

- Click ⊑ Highlight Cells Rules ›

- Click the condition

- Enter the criteria

- By Light Red Fill with Dark F, click ∨

- Click the desired colors

- Click | OK |

112 Merge text

- Click the | Formulas | tab

- Click 🅰 Text ▾

- Click CONCAT

- Type the text or select the first cell

- Click the next box

- Type the text or select the next cell

If necessary, repeat this for the following cells that are to be merged.

- Click | OK |

113 Use the *IF* function
- Type the condition

- By Value_if_true, type the text or value if the condition is met

- By Value_if_false, type the text or value if the condition is not met

- Click [OK]

114 Data validation
- Select the cell(s)
- Click the [Data] tab
- Click
- If necessary, click the [Settings] tab
- By **Allow:**, click the type of data
- By **Data:**, click the condition
- Enter the values in the next box or following boxes

To enter an input message:
- Click the [Input Message] tab
- By **Title:**, type the header of the message
- By **Input message:** type the message

To enter an error message:
- Click the [Error Alert] tab
- By **Style:**, choose the action
- By **Title:**, type the header of the message
- By **Error message:**, type the error message
- Click [OK]

115 Close a workbook
- Click **File**

- Click **Close**

To save the workbook:
- Click [Save]

Don't save the workbook:
- Click [Don't Save]

116 Place the $ sign before the amount and add two decimals
- Click [icon]

117 Use the *COUNTA* function
- By **Value1**, click [icon]
- Select the cells
- Click [icon]
- Click [OK]

118 Use the *AVERAGEIF* function
- By **Range**, click [icon]
- Select the cells
- Click [icon]
- By **Criteria**, enter the criteria
- Click [OK]

119 Use the *UPPER* function
- Click the [Formulas] tab
- Click **Text ▾**
- Click **UPPER**
- Select the cell
- Click [OK]

120 Use the *LEFT / RIGHT* function

- Click the Formulas tab

- Click Text ▾

- Click LEFT / RIGHT

- Select the cell

- By **Num_chars**, type the desired number of characters

- Click OK

121 Use the *TRIM* function

- Click the Formulas tab

- Click Text ▾

- Click TRIM

- Select the cell

- Click OK

122 Select rows/columns
Select a column:
- Click the column header

Select a row:
- Click the row number

123 View the print preview

- Click File

- Click Print

124 Select continuous cells
- Click the first cell

- Press Shift and it hold down

- Click the last cell

- Release Shift

125 Hide columns

- Click the Home tab

- Select the columns

- Click Format ▾

- Click Hide & Unhide

- Click Hide Columns

126 Unhide columns

- Click the Home tab

- Select the columns before and after or select the entire worksheet

- Click Format ▾

- Click Hide & Unhide

- Click Unhide Columns

127 Name cells
- Select the cells

- Click the name box

- Type the new name

- Press Enter

128 Formulas with names
- Type =

- Type the name of the cell

- Type the action

- Type the name of the cell

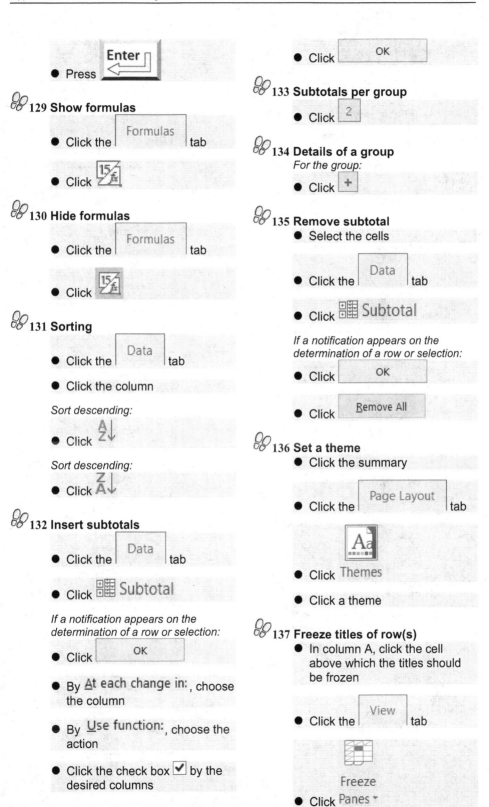

- Press **Enter**

129 Show formulas

- Click the **Formulas** tab
- Click ⌗

130 Hide formulas

- Click the **Formulas** tab
- Click ⌗

131 Sorting

- Click the **Data** tab
- Click the column

Sort descending:

- Click A↓Z

Sort descending:

- Click Z↓A

132 Insert subtotals

- Click the **Data** tab
- Click ⌗ Subtotal

If a notification appears on the determination of a row or selection:

- Click **OK**
- By <u>A</u>t each change in:, choose the column
- By <u>U</u>se function:, choose the action
- Click the check box ☑ by the desired columns

- Click **OK**

133 Subtotals per group

- Click 2

134 Details of a group

For the group:

- Click +

135 Remove subtotal

- Select the cells
- Click the **Data** tab
- Click ⌗ Subtotal

If a notification appears on the determination of a row or selection:

- Click **OK**
- Click **Remove All**

136 Set a theme

- Click the summary
- Click the **Page Layout** tab
- Click Themes
- Click a theme

137 Freeze titles of row(s)

- In column A, click the cell above which the titles should be frozen
- Click the **View** tab
- Click Freeze Panes ▾

- Click <u>F</u>reeze Panes

138 Adjust print scale

- If necessary, click the tab

- Click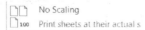

- Click
   No Scaling
  Print sheets at their actual s

- Click the desired scale

139 Return to worksheet

- Click

140 Create a macro

- Click the | View | tab

- Click Macros

- Click <u>R</u>ecord Macro...

- Type the name of the macro

- Type the shortcut key

- If necessary, type a description

- Click | OK |

141 Stop macro recording

- In the status bar, click ▪

142 Select entire worksheet
At the top left of the worksheet:

- Click ◢

143 Run a macro
- Press the key combination for the macro

144 Create a PDF file
- Click the tab

- Click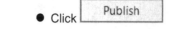

- Click  Create PDF/XPS

- Go to the desired folder

- If necessary, type a name for the file

- Click | Publish |

145 Close (task)window
- Click [x] or ✕

146 Zoom out
- Drag the slider ▮ in the lower right corner of the window to the left

147 Zoom in to 100%
- Click the zoom percentage at the bottom right of the window

- Click the radio button ◉ by <u>1</u>00%

- Click | OK |

148 Freeze titles of column(s)
- Click in row 1 in the cell to the left of which the titles should be frozen

- Click the | View | tab

- Click  Freeze Panes ▾

- Click <u>F</u>reeze Panes

149 Unfreeze titles
- Click the| View |tab

- Click Freeze Panes ▾

- Click Unfreeze Panes

150 Split the window
- Click ▭

151 Undo the splitting
- Click ▭

152 Add cell style to cells
- Select the desired cells

- Click the| Home |tab

- Click Cell Styles ▾

- Click the desired style

153 Add background color to cells
- Select the desired cells

- By 🖐, click ▾

- Click the desired color

154 Copy the formatting
- Click the cell or value of which you want to copy the formatting

- If necessary, click the| Home |tab

- Click 🖌

- Select the cell(s) or value (in chart) to which you want to copy the formatting

155 Adjust print orientation
- Click the| Page Layout |tab

- Click Orientation

- Click the desired print orientation

156 Print titles on each page
- Click the| Page Layout |tab

- Click Print Titles

- Click Rows to repeat at top: or Columns to repeat at left: on 🔳

- Select the desired rows or columns

- Click 🔳

- Click| OK |

157 Adjusting margins
- Click the| Page Layout |tab

- Click Margins

- Click Custom Margins...

- Set the desired margins

- Click| OK |

⅋ 158 Inserting header or footer

- Click the [Insert] tab

- If necessary, click [*A*] Text ▾

- Click [ ] Header & Footer

- Click the desired box

- Type or select the desired header or footer

To return to the normal view:

- Click the [View] tab

- Click an empty cell

- Click [ ] Normal

⅋ 159 Set the print area
- Select the desired cells

- Click the [Page Layout] tab

- Click [ ] Print Area ▾

- Click [ ] Set Print Area

⅋ 160 Clear the print area

- Click the [Page Layout] tab

- Click [ ] Print Area ▾

- Click Clear Print Area

⅋ 161 Group data
- Select the desired rows or columns

- Click the [Data] tab

- If necessary, click [ ] Outline

- Click [ ]

⅋ 162 Hide a group
- Click [−]

⅋ 163 Unhide a group
- Click [+]

⅋ 164 Cancel grouping
- Select the rows or columns for which you want to cancel the grouping

- Click the [Data] tab

- If necessary, click [ ] Outline

- Click [ ]

⅋ 165 Hide rows

- Click the [Home] tab

- Select the columns

- Click 🗔 Format ▾

- Click Hide & Unhide

- Click Hide Rows

166 Unhide rows

- Click the | Home | tab

- Select the columns before and after or select the entire worksheet

- Click 🗔 Format ▾

- Click Hide & Unhide

- Click Unhide Rows

167 Save a workbook with macros

- Click File

- Click Save As

- Click No

- Click 📁 Browse

- Select the desired location

- By File name:, type the new name

- By Save as type:, click ⌄

- Click Excel Macro-Enabled Workbook (*.xlsm)

- Click Save

168 Save a workbook in *Excel 97-2003* format

- Click File

- Click Save As

- Click 📁 Browse

- Select the desired location

- By Save as type:, click ⌄

- Click Excel 97-2003 Workbook (*.xls)

- Click Save

169 Close a workbook

- Click File

- Click Close

170 Open a workbook with macros

- Click File

- Click Open

- Click 📁 Browse

- Select the desired location

- Click the file

- Click Open

- Click Enable Content

171 Change axis formatting

- Click the value of an axis

- Click the | Home | tab

To change a text to bold:

- Click **B**

To adjust the font size:

- Click A˄ or A˅ for the desired size

172 **Adjust the scale**

- Double-click a value along an
  axis

- By , click the value
  three times

- Type the desired value

- Press
  ![Enter key]

Appendix B. Glossary

Glossary

Absolute reference	In a formula, the absolute cell reference is the exact address of a cell, regardless of the position of the cell that contains the formula. An absolute cell reference is often used to calculate with constants and uses the reference style $A$1. The two dollar signs indicate that both the row and the column are absolute. Absolute cell references do not change when a formula is copied or moved.
Aligning (left or right)	Positioning characters to the left or right in a cell.
Alphanumeric data	Text or numbers with which cannot be calculated in *Excel*.
Autofill	One of *Excel's* handy tools that allows you to automatically complete content in a series as long as the first characters typed are part of a series, for example January-February-March.
Backup	Backup copy of a file. *Excel* regularly creates a backup while you are working.
Calculation model	Summary in *Excel* with which calculations can be made. For example: the profit can be calculated using a calculation model.
Cell	Smallest unit in a worksheet.
Cell names	Name given to a cell or selected group of cells. Cell names can be calculated in the same way as default cell reference values and they can be referred to as well.
Cell properties	The way in which the content of a cell is displayed. For example displayed as text, date, number or time, with commas and other separators or currency symbols.
Cell reference	The column letter and row number that intersect at a cell's location. With the cell reference, you can tell *Excel* where to find the values or data that you want to use in a formula. A cell reference can be relative, absolute or mixed.
Centering	Positioning of characters exactly in the middle of a cell.
Chart	A chart or diagram is a visual representation or graphical display (drawn figure) of a series of data.
Circle chart	A circle chart is a chart type in which the contribution of each value to a total is displayed. Also called a pie chart.

Cloud	A storage space for saving and editing files on the Internet, offered by a company such as Microsoft. With the cloud, you can always access your files, even if you are not behind your own computer. The cloud also makes it possible to share certain files easily with others.
Column	Vertical series of cells.
Column chart	A column chart displays columns as vertical bars representing the size of the individual data.
Column header	Cell name above a column of data.
Conditional formatting	*Conditional formatting* changes the appearance of a cell if a condition has been met. If the condition is true, the cell is formatted as you have set. If the condition is false, the format of the cell remains as it was.
Date format	The way dates are displayed. Examples are 25-7-2013 or Tuesday 25 July 2013.
Date series	A group of dates that is organized in a linear way, for example always with a week in between.
Decimals	Numbers that have one or more digits to the right of the decimal point. The decimal point is used to separate the ones place from the tenths place. It is also used to separate dollars from cents in money, for example $10.00.
Diagram	See chart.
Drop-down menu	Menu with an assortment of options to choose from.
Excel	Microsoft's calculation program (also called spreadsheet). It is also a part of the Microsoft Office suite of applications.
Exporting	Saving data in another file type.
Field	Box which can hold a number or word.
Field code	A place holder in a document on the position where information from a data source must be displayed.
Fill handle	The small square at the bottom right of a selected cell with which the cell is copied or may be automatically supplemented in adjacent cells.
Filtering	*Excel* feature that lets you display selected data. As soon as you remove the filter, all data is displayed again.
Font	A font is a collection of numbers, symbols and characters. A font describes a particular typeface together with other features such as font size, spacing and character width. A font is also called a *typeface*.
Footer	Text which is shown at the bottom of a page when printing.

Formula	Always start with an equal sign (=) followed by a cell reference or calculation using numbers, other cell references, names, functions and arithmetical symbols.
Formula bar	Bar at the top of the *Excel* window in which you enter or edit values or formulas in cells or charts.
Freezing panes	Feature in *Excel* with which you can select rows or columns which must remain visible when scrolling through the worksheet. You can, for example, freeze titles to keep row and column labels visible during scrolling.
Function	Functions are predefined formulas that perform calculations using specific values, which are called arguments, in a specific order or structure.
Header	Text which is shown at the top of a page when printing.
Importing	Reading data derived from another program or in a different file type.
Internet browser	Also known as a web browser. Program that allows you to surf the Internet, such as *Edge* or *Internet Explorer*.
Italic	Font style whereby the character is displayed at an angle.
Layout	The design of a document including elements such as font size, font type, formatting of headers, alignment, character spacing and margins. Layout is sometimes called *formatting*.
Legend	List with an explanation of characters in a chart or diagram.
Line chart	Chart in the form of one or more lines. Line charts can be used to display trends over a period of time.
Macro	A sequence of actions that are recorded and can be run with a special key combination or button. The purpose of a macro is to automate common tasks.
Maximum value	The highest possible value in the scale of a diagram.
Microsoft account	An account with which you can use the various services of Microsoft, such as *OneDrive*. This account consists of an email address and a password.
Minimum value	The lowest possible value in the scale of a diagram.
Mixed reference	Formula in which both absolute and relative cell references are used.
Multiple sorting	Two or more consecutive sortings. For example, first by city name and then by zip code.
Name box	Box to the left of the *Formula bar* in which the cell names can be typed.

Nested formulas	Formulas within parentheses are called *nested formulas*. You can place multiple nested formulas within a single formula. *Excel* calculates the deepest, or innermost formula first and then works its way outward.
Nesting	It is sometimes necessary to use a function as one of the arguments of a different function. A function is then included in another function. This is called the *nesting* of functions.
Numeric data	Numbers that can be used for calculations.
OneDrive	One of Microsoft's cloud services whereby you get a specified amount of free storage space. *OneDrive* can be accessed directly from *Office* programs and *Windows 10* and *8.1*.
Page settings	Feature in *Excel* which allows you to adjust the layout and formatting of data on the worksheet as desired before printing.
PDF	Portable Document Format. Default file type for viewing and printing documents. The advantage is that a document looks exactly the same on all screens and printers.
Print area	The selected part of the worksheet that will be printed.
Print preview	Example of the page as it will be printed on paper.
Quick Access toolbar	Special toolbar above or below the ribbon, which is always visible. The user can extend this toolbar by himself with frequently used commands in order to be able to choose faster.
Quick Analysis	Button that automatically appears with a selected area to allow for easy analyzing of the data or to make graphs from it.
Range	Area(s) in a worksheet of associated cells.
Relative reference	Reference to a cell that moves with the location of the formula. If the position of the formula changes, the cell reference also changes.
Result	The value that is reached after a calculation.
Ribbon	The ribbon is the toolbar with commands at the top of the window in *Excel*. The commands are divided into logical groups, sorted by tabs. Each tab has its own set of options.
Rounding	Rounding a number up or down to a multiple of 5 or 10. Numbers ending in a 5 or higher are rounded up to the nearest higher number, numbers lower than 5 are rounded down to the nearest lower number.
Row	Horizontal series of cells.
Scale	The values used in a diagram or chart; regularly divided between a minimum and a maximum value.
Series	Row with ordered, often consecutive content, for example January-February-March, etcetera.

Series name	Name of a series of combined data.
Series of numbers	Consecutive numbers which, according to a certain regularity, decrease or increase.
Sizing handle	A sizing handle can be used to change the size of objects located in a worksheet. There are eight sizing handles per object and are only visible when an object is selected. They are located in the four corners of the border and in the middle of each side. To increase or decrease the size of the object, drag one of the handles with the mouse.
SmartArt	Series of readymade shapes.
Sorting	Arranging data. Ascending sorting yields a sequence from low to high, descending sorting a sequence from high to low.
Sparkline	With sparklines you can create miniature charts in one cell. This allows for an easy way to show a trend.
Splitting	Dividing the worksheet in two or more parts which can each individually display parts of the worksheet.
Spreadsheet	A worksheet with numbered rows and columns for the presentation of various types of data. A calculation program such as *Excel* is also called spreadsheet program.
Style	Combination of lines, colors and fonts, meant to give a cell or group of cells a certain design.
Sum	Function that adds values in selected cells in a row or column.
Tabs	The tabs in the ribbon or horizontal bar at the top of the *Excel* window offer various groups of commands and options in an orderly fashion.
Tab key	Key that allows you to move the cursor to the next cell.
Template	Example document in which parts of the layout and text have already been configured. A template can be filled in with the desired data.
Text wrapping	Dividing text in a column over multiple lines if it does not fit in the cell or if otherwise, the column becomes unnecessarily wide.
Theme	Combination of lines, colors and fonts, meant to give a worksheet an attractive and professional look.
Thousand format	This format is used for the general display of numbers. You can determine how many decimals are displayed, whether you want to use a separator for thousands and how you want to display negative numbers. In the event of a currency, the currency symbol can also be displayed.
Titles	Names of chart parts that specify what information is displayed.
Validating	A check whether entered or selected data meets a condition or appear in a list.

WordArt	A feature that lets you quickly insert decorative text effects in your workbook.
Workbook	The total file, consisting of one or more worksheets.
Worksheet	A single specific sheet within a workbook. A worksheet consists of cells that are arranged in rows and columns. The worksheet is used to calculate, edit and save data and for the design and layout of an attractive presentation of the data, if necessary.
Zoom factor	Percentage which indicates how much the display of a worksheet on the screen is enlarged or reduced.
3-D Effect	3-D stands for three-dimensional. A diagram displayed with height, width and depth information.

Source: Windows Help and Support, Microsoft Office Help, Wikipedia

Appendix C. Index